IMAGES
of America

QUAKER HILL

On the Cover: This image shows Arthur Harmon and the Wilmington Friends School bus. For decades, Harmon drove the primary school children of Wilmington Friends School to and from school, first in a horse-drawn carriage and then in a school bus. (Courtesy of Wilmington Friends School.)

IMAGES
of America

QUAKER HILL

Quaker Hill Historic
Preservation Foundation

ARCADIA
PUBLISHING

ISBN 978-0-7385-8577-2

Published by Arcadia Publishing
Charleston, South Carolina

Printed in the United States of America

Library of Congress Control Number: 2009940080

For all general information contact Arcadia Publishing at:
Telephone 843-853-2070
Fax 843-853-0044
E-mail sales@arcadiapublishing.com
For customer service and orders:
Toll-Free 1-888-313-2665

Visit us on the Internet at www.arcadiapublishing.com

This book is dedicated to the valiant men and women of Quaker Hill of the past and those yet to come.

Contents

ACKNOWLEDGMENTS

We at Quaker Hill Historic Preservation Foundation would like to acknowledge the others whose fine work made this book possible: Wilmington Friends School, Wilmington Friends Meeting, and the Historical Society of Delaware for providing many old photographs; Robert Seeley, a descendent of Thomas Garrett, who provided pictures from his family's collection; Cassandra Marshall and John Kurth, who provided many of the pictures; photographers James Bierbaum, Tim Bayard, Nicole Bright, and Earl White, who provided many of the fine photographs; and James Bierbaum, Thomas C. Davis, and Earl M. White, who provided able technical support.

We could not have completed the book without the help of these volunteers:
Bayard Marin
Mary Starkweather-White

INTRODUCTION

The Quaker Hill Historic Preservation Foundation is a nonprofit organization established in 1992 to aid in the restoration and preservation of the Quaker Hill area. This National Historic Register area is roughly bounded by Second Street, Jefferson Street, Eighth Street, and Tatnall Street in Wilmington, Delaware. The Quaker Hill Historic Preservation Foundation sponsors historical research studies and presentations; creates greater awareness of the area's multicultural history; stimulates research in the history of the Underground Railroad; draws on academic, civic, and community resources; produces educational and promotional materials; sponsors social, cultural, and historical events; and promotes restoration efforts.

The Quaker Hill District dates back to the founding of Wilmington around the Quaker Hill area in 1738. The Swedes had arrived around Wilmington in 1638. Control of the area passed from the Swedes to the Dutch to the English within the next 50 years. Shortly after King Charles II of England granted the province of Pennsylvania to a member of the Religious Society of Friends (called Quakers), William Penn, the "lower three counties" of Delaware were conveyed to Penn. Thomas Willing first laid out the streets of a village he called "Willingtown" in 1731. However, the municipality was not developed until 1738. A Philadelphia Quaker, Elizabeth Shipley, had had a vision of a land surrounded by three rivers and discovered that area was the site of Wilmington about 10 years later. She and her husband brought other Philadelphia Quakers with them to settle the site. The arrival of several Quaker millers and traders really caused a growth spurt for the town. In 1739, the citizens' petition for a charter of the municipality by George II was granted with the stipulation that it be named for his friend, the Earl of Wilmington. In 1738, the first Friends meetinghouse was built. It was replaced by another meetinghouse in 1748. Quakers settled the surrounding community. In 1816, the current meetinghouse was built at Fourth and West Streets. It is a perfect example of Quaker planning and simple Quaker architecture. Since 1748, Friends have worshiped there or at the site across the street, which long after served as the Friends School. The Friends meetinghouse also serves as the focal point for the activities of the Quaker Hill Neighborhood Association and its functions.

Also in 1816, the Cathedral of St. Peter was erected at Fifth and West Streets. It is the seat of the bishop of the Diocese of Wilmington and is a splendid example of the architecture of the period. Some additions to the cathedral have been made since 1816, and Catholic schools for both boys and girls were added. Also, Salesianum School, another Catholic school, was built on Quaker Hill and later became the first school in Delaware to (voluntarily) racially integrate its student body. Several churches of other denominations have sprung up in the area as well. Nearby churches include Tabernacle Full Gospel Baptist Church, an African American church on the site of the former Union United Methodist Church, which was instrumental in the establishment of the Sunday Breakfast Mission; Grace United Methodist Church, a patron to the artistic community with its own large gallery; and the former West Presbyterian Church, which was involved in many cultural and service pursuits.

The area was initially settled by wealthy merchants and their families as well as their employees. Some mansions were intermingled among smaller houses for the workers. This led to an economically well-integrated neighborhood.

Several key events occurred on Quaker Hill. Thomas Garrett, a wealthy Quaker merchant, lived on Quaker Hill and was very involved in the Underground Railroad, the system of safe houses that assisted freedom-seeking slaves to escape to the North and Canada. Thomas Garrett, working in conjunction with Harriet Tubman, the conductor on the Underground Railroad who was called the "Moses of her people," and with William Still of the Philadelphia Vigilance Committee, was responsible for ushering an estimated 3,000 slaves to freedom. Thomas Garrett has been called one of the greatest "stationmasters" on the Underground Railroad. He is buried in the Friends meetinghouse graveyard.

Many 18th- and 19th-century politicians are also buried in the meetinghouse graveyard. One of the greatest of these is John Dickinson, delegate to the independence convention and signer of the U.S. Constitution as well as the author of the Articles of Confederation, the forerunner to the U.S. Constitution. Also it is rumored that Gen. George Washington and the Marquis de Lafayette met in Quaker Hill at Third Street and Washington Street at the time of the Battle of the Brandywine during the American Revolutionary War.

The architecture of Quaker Hill is remarkable for fine examples of Colonial, Federal, Greek revival, and Victorian architecture. During the period of 1830 to 1870, many mansions were built.

In the late 19th century to early 20th century, the arrival of streetcars meant that many people could commute to work, and so they moved out of the city to points farther west. Some Quaker Hill mansions were divided up into smaller homes and apartments. During the 1960s and 1970s, harder times came to Quaker Hill, as many people left the city following the riots of 1968 after the assassination of Martin Luther King and the yearlong siege by the Delaware National Guard. Many properties were neglected and abandoned.

Then, beginning in the late 1970s, a wave of young urban professionals began developing the area and families began to move back and remodel their homes with good, authentic restoration. They discovered that the area was an easy walk to the downtown and riverfront areas. Once again, Quaker Hill became a nice, economically mixed area in which to live.

Small though it is, the Quaker Hill historic area has played an important role in the rich history of Wilmington and of Delaware. Its Quaker beginnings led to the establishment of Wilmington, the largest city in Delaware. Champions of liberty and freedom such as John Dickinson and Thomas Garrett flourished here. Its institutions led the way to integration and social service. Its architecture and cultural pursuits speak to a vibrant community. Clearly, Quaker Hill has something to offer to everyone.

One

Early Settlers

About 1734, Elizabeth Shipley, wife of William Shipley of Ridley, Pennsylvania, undertook a journey to the eastern shore of Maryland. Elizabeth was recognized as a "weighty Friend," a religious leader commanding special respect in Quaker belief, which has no designated ministers or hierarchy of authority.

Elizabeth was ascending a steep hill when her attention was gripped by the scene below her: the fast-moving Brandywine River she had just crossed, flowing into the wider, slow-moving Christina River. She recognized this scene—from a dream. In her dream, she was led by a spiritual "guide," who stated it was God's will that she and her husband should settle there to become "instruments of great benefit to people and place alike." Now she saw that very prospect—in real life.

After completing her journey, she spoke of her vision to her practical husband, William. He realized she was describing a river for milling and another for shipping. Moved by commercial as well as religious considerations, William relocated his family to "Willington," later called Wilmington. Other Quaker merchants followed his lead. In 1738, on the spot of Elizabeth's vision, they built a tiny Meeting for Worship. Later they erected a larger one for their growing numbers and made the little building a school for their own children and those of the poor. Washington headquartered near the meetinghouse in 1777, and later British troops occupied it briefly. A yet larger building was finished in 1817. These events were recounted in 1846 by Benjamin Ferris, a member of Wilmington Monthly Meeting, whose *A History of the Original Settlements on the Delaware: From its Discovery by Hudson to the Colonization under William Penn* was the area's first history.

Meeting members were leaders of Wilmington in the 19th century: bankers, Brandywine mill-owners, merchants, and later owners of heavy industries along the Christina River. The Bancroft, Ferris, Canby, Poole, and Tatnall families, among many others, were important philanthropists for the region. Thomas Garrett became the foremost stationmaster of the Underground Railroad, 2,700 fugitives passing through his home near the Christina River. People of other faiths moved to Quaker Hill and began schools of their own. Elizabeth Shipley's dream was being fulfilled.

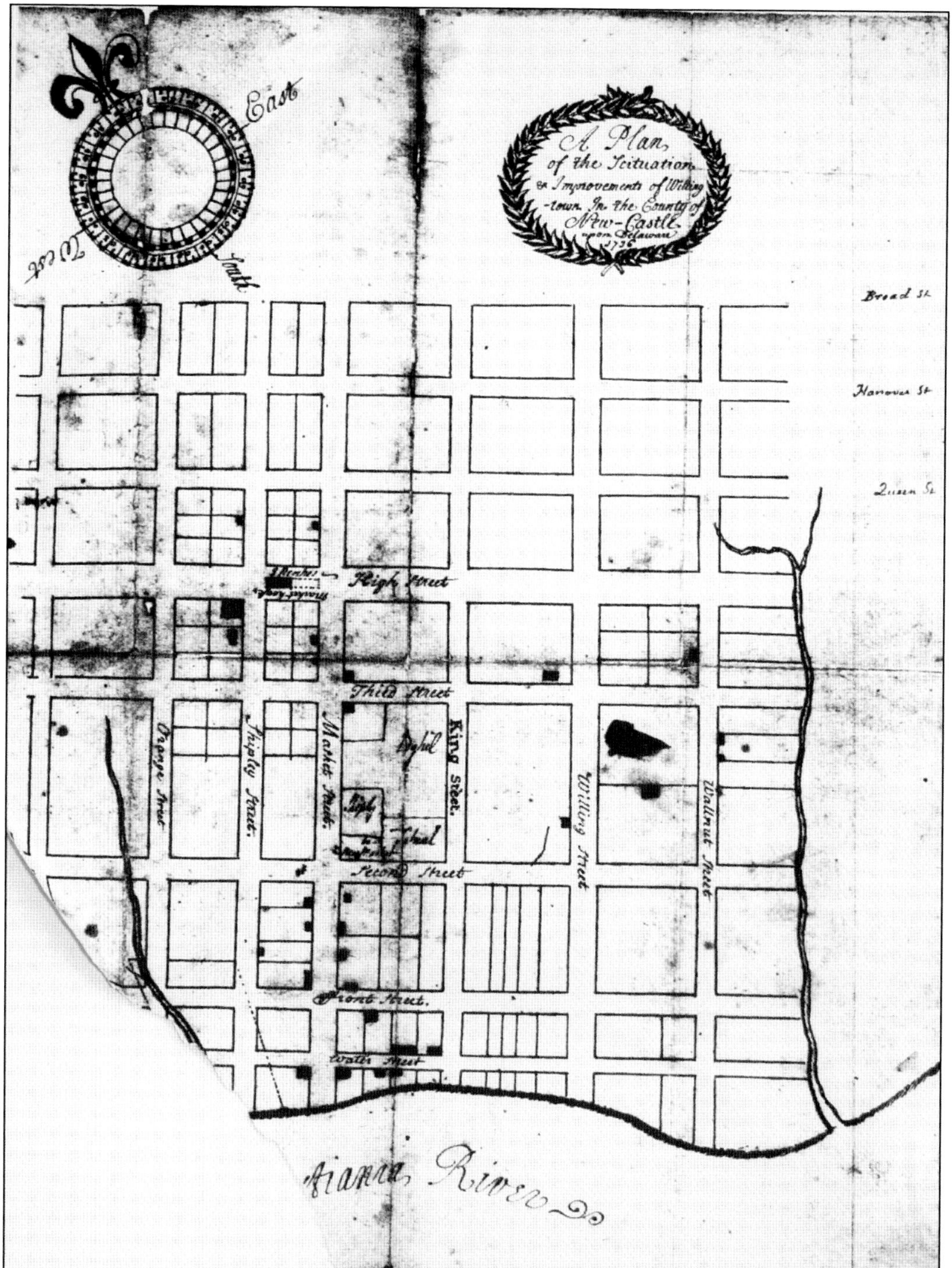

This is a map of early Willington, according to the 1736 plan for the town when William and Elizabeth Shipley arrived. This map comes from the *A History of the Original Settlements on the Delaware: From its Discovery by Hudson to the Colonization under William Penn* by Benjamin Ferris. Note the streets that still exist: Orange Street, Shipley Street, Market Street, and Walnut Street. (Courtesy of Wilmington Friends School.)

George Fox was born in 1624 and died in 1690. He was the founder of the Religious Society of Friends, which holds that everyone is divinely inspired by the Inner Light. Fox visited America in 1674. He was a contemporary of William Penn. (Courtesy of Wilmington Friends School.)

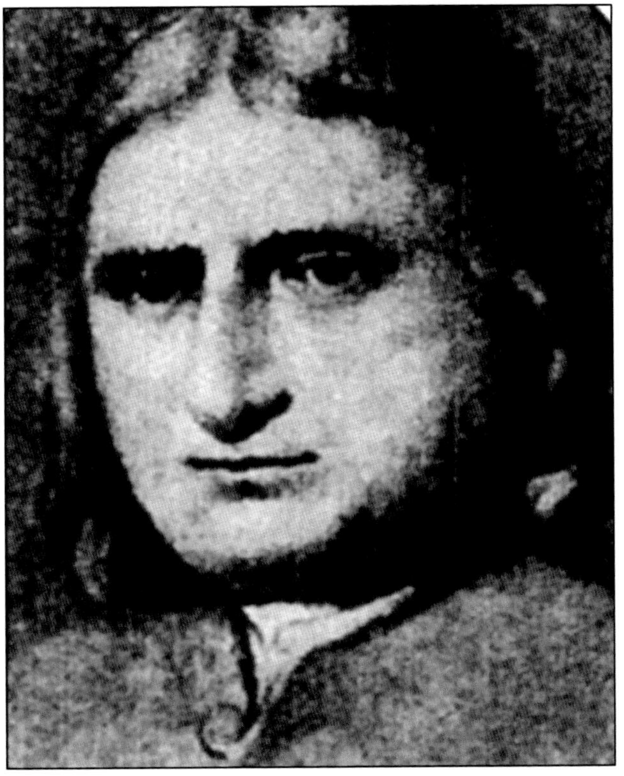

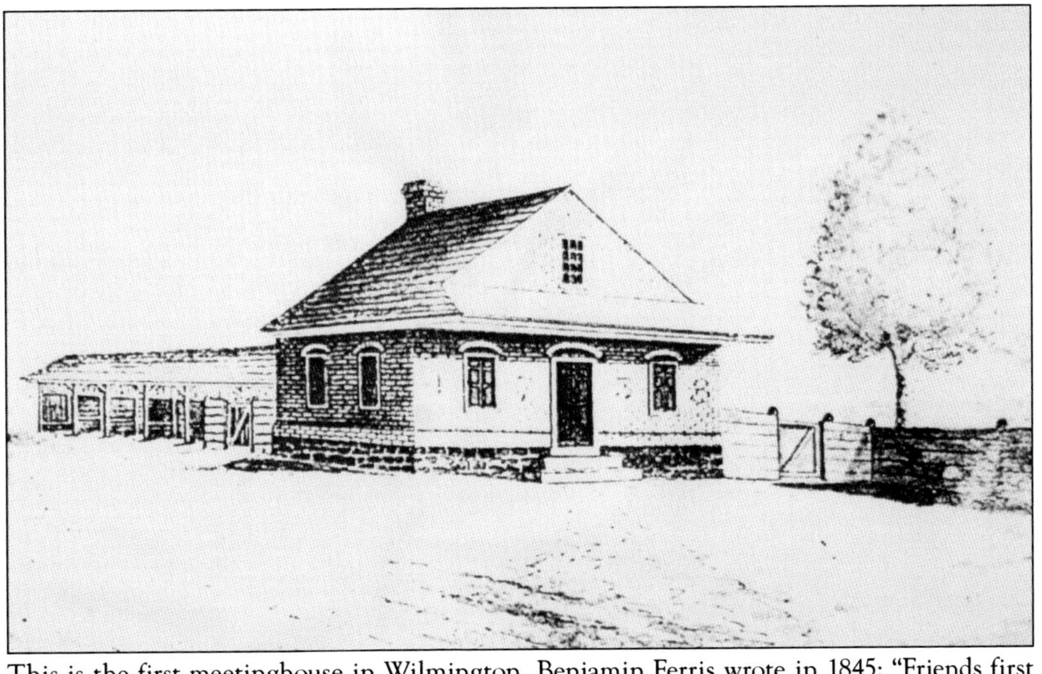

This is the first meetinghouse in Wilmington. Benjamin Ferris wrote in 1845: "Friends first meetinghouse and the first place built for divine worship in the city of Wilmington after it was laid out for a town. This house is yet standing, but the balcony has been removed about sixty years." (Courtesy of Wilmington Friends School.)

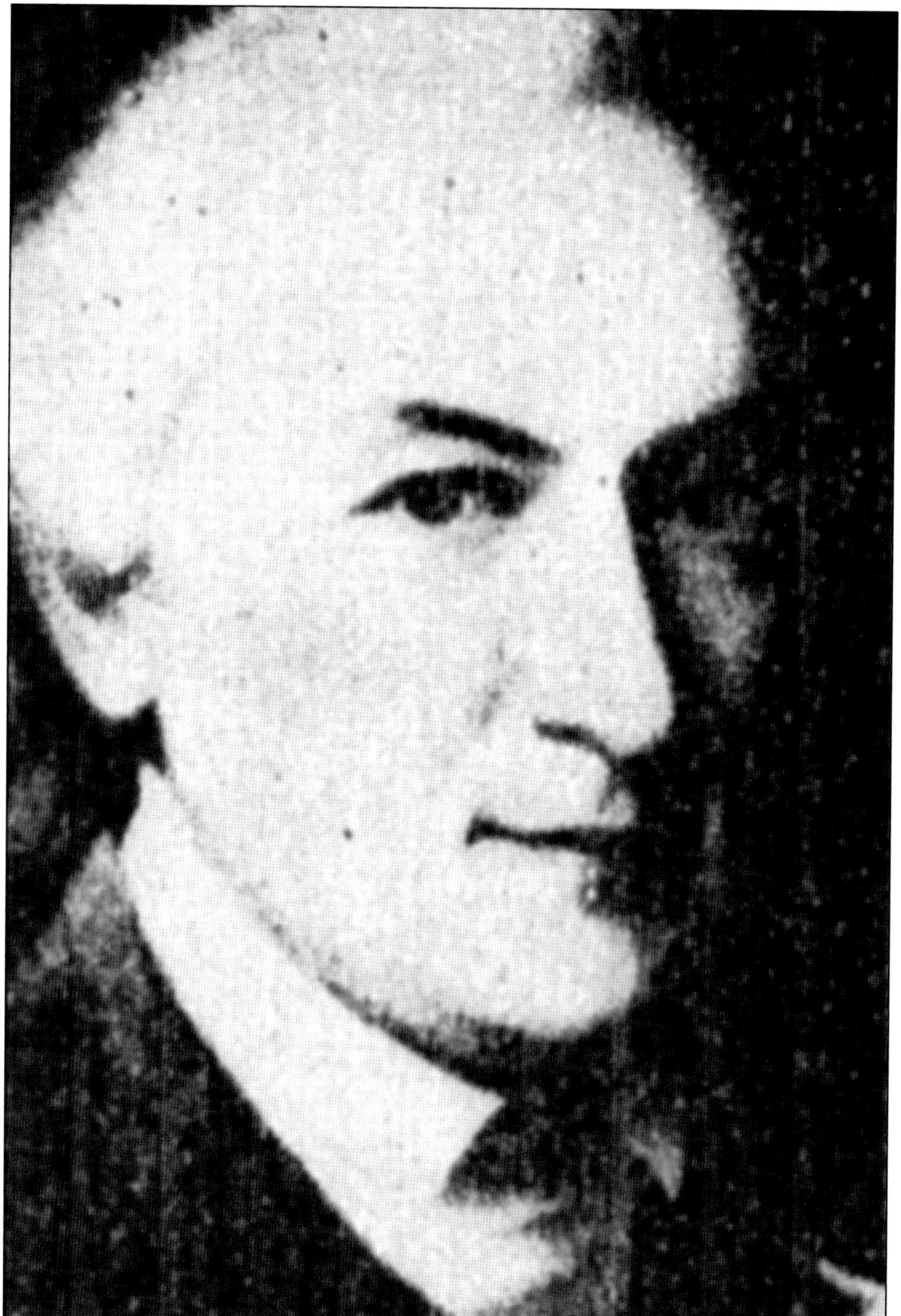

John Dickinson attended the convention on independence and was a signer of the U.S. Constitution, as well as the author of the Articles of Confederation, a precursor of the U.S. Constitution. He is buried in the graveyard of Wilmington Friends Meeting. (Courtesy of Wilmington Friends Meeting.)

John Dickinson not only was an architect of the U.S. Constitution, but also was the president of the Delaware and School Fund. He was a benefactor who left 200 pounds "for the schooling of poor children." (Courtesy of Wilmington Friends School.)

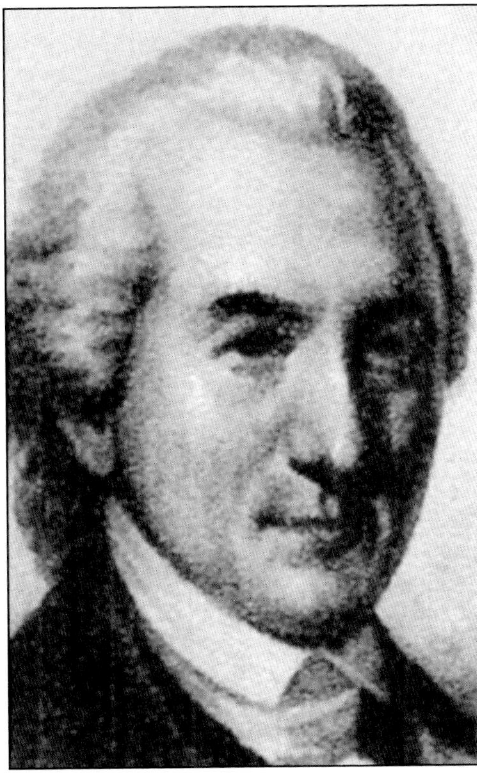

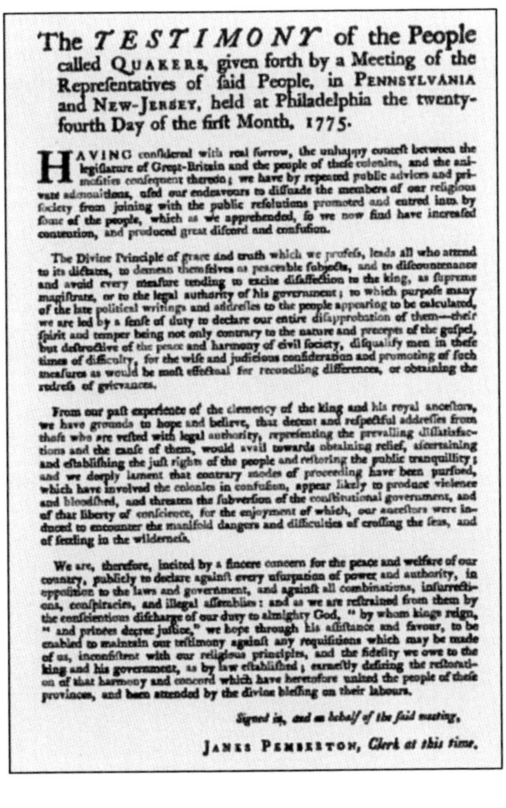

The *TESTIMONY* of the People called QUAKERS, given forth by a Meeting of the Repreſentatives of ſaid People, in PENNSYLVANIA and NEW-JERSEY, held at Philadelphia the twenty-fourth Day of the firſt Month, 1775.

HAVING conſidered with real ſorrow, the unhappy conteſt between the legiſlature of Great-Britain and the people of theſe colonies, and the animoſities conſequent thereon; we have by repeated public advices and private admonitions, uſed our endeavours to diſſuade the members of our religious ſociety from joining with the public reſolutions promoted and entred into by ſome of the people, which as we apprehended, ſo we now find have increaſed contention, and produced great diſcord and confuſion.

The Divine Principle of grace and truth which we profeſs, leads all who attend to its dictates, to demean themſelves as peaceable ſubjects, and to diſcountenance and avoid every meaſure tending to excite diſaffection to the king, as ſupreme magiſtrate, or to the legal authority of his government; to which purpoſe many of the late political writings and addreſſes to the people appearing to be calculated, we are led by a ſenſe of duty to declare our entire diſapprobation of them—their ſpirit and temper being not only contrary to the nature and precepts of the goſpel, but deſtructive of the peace and harmony of civil ſociety, diſqualify men in theſe times of difficulty, for the wiſe and judicious conſideration and promoting of ſuch meaſures as would be moſt effectual for reconciling differences, or obtaining the redreſs of grievances.

From our paſt experience of the clemency of the king and his royal anceſtors, we have grounds to hope and believe, that decent and reſpectful addreſſes from thoſe who are veſted with legal authority, repreſenting the prevailing diſſatisfactions and the cauſe of them, would avail towards obtaining relief, aſcertaining and eſtabliſhing the juſt rights of the people and reſtoring the public tranquillity; and we deeply lament that contrary modes of proceeding have been purſued, which have involved the colonies in confuſion, appear likely to produce violence and bloodſhed, and threaten the ſubverſion of the conſtitutional government, and of that liberty of conſcience, for the enjoyment of which, our anceſtors were induced to encounter the manifold dangers and difficulties of croſſing the ſeas, and of ſettling in the wilderneſs.

We are, therefore, incited by a ſincere concern for the peace and welfare of our country, publicly to declare againſt every uſurpation of power and authority, in oppoſition to the laws and government, and againſt all combinations, inſurrections, conſpiracies, and illegal aſſemblies: and as we are reſtrained from them by the conſcientious diſcharge of our duty to almighty God, "by whom kings reign, "and princes decree juſtice," we hope through his aſſiſtance and favour, to be enabled to maintain our teſtimony againſt any requiſitions which may be made of us, inconſiſtent with our religious principles, and the fidelity we owe to the king and his government, as by law eſtabliſhed; earneſtly deſiring the reſtoration of that harmony and concord which have heretofore united the people of theſe provinces, and been attended by the divine bleſſing on their labours.

Signed in, and on behalf of the ſaid meeting,

JAMES PEMBERTON, *Clerk at this time.*

This is a broadside issued for the guidance of Friends by the Philadelphia Yearly Meeting for Sufferings in 1775, encouraging Quakers, who were pacifists because of their belief in the divinity of all life, to avoid participation in the then emerging American Revolution. (Courtesy of Wilmington Friends School.)

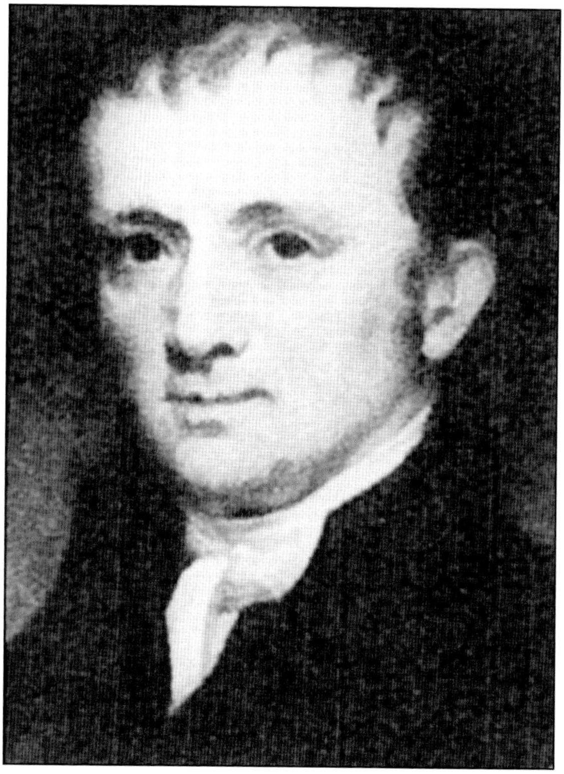

Benjamin Ferris (1780–1867) was born in a house at Third and Shipley Streets in Wilmington, Delaware. Descended from colonists who came to America in 1682 and settled in Wilmington in 1748, he worshiped at Wilmington Friends Meeting and worked on behalf of Native Americans. He wrote a book about Delaware history. (Courtesy of Wilmington Friends School.)

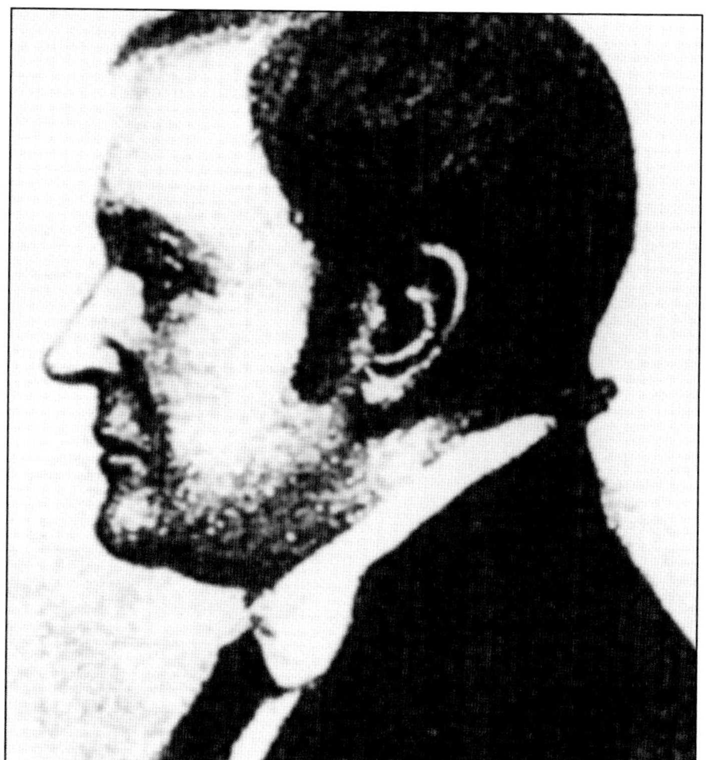

Joseph Tatnall worshiped at Wilmington Friends Meeting at Fourth Street and West Street in Wilmington. He was an early supporter of Quaker education and one of Wilmington's streets is named after him. This picture comes from *The History of Delaware*, published in 1888. (Courtesy of Wilmington Friends School.)

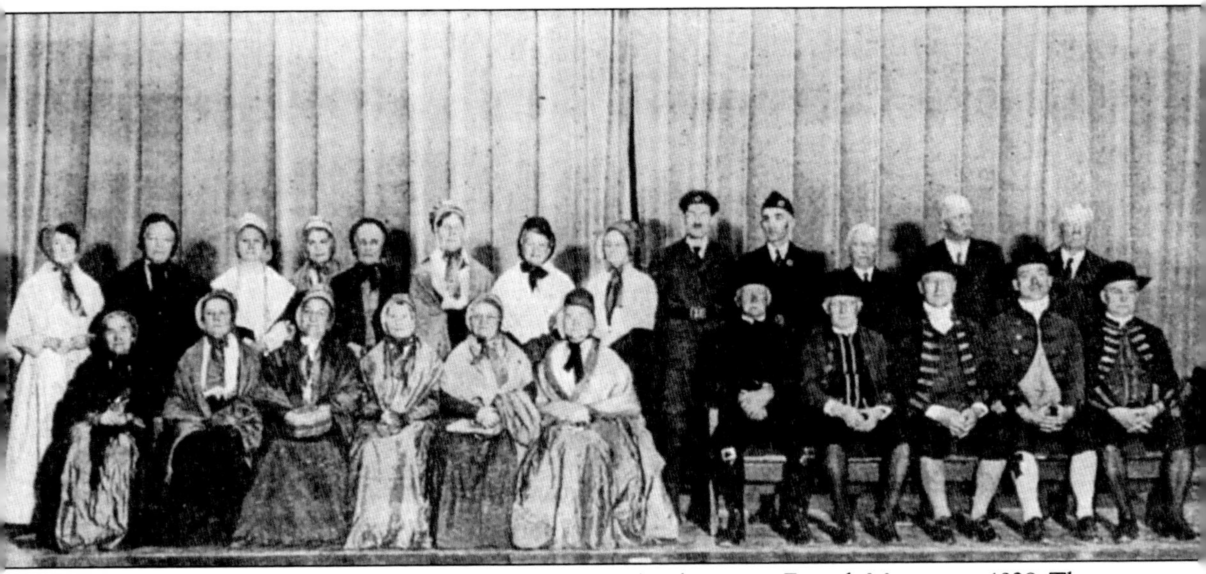

Posing as Quakers of the 19th century are members of Wilmington Friends Meeting in 1938. They include many from old Quaker families, like Edith Rhoads, Frances and William Phillips, May and Malcolm Brosius, John Mendenhall, Frank Garrett, Benjamin Smedley, Edward Bringhurst, and Miriam Webb. (Courtesy of Wilmington Friends Meeting.)

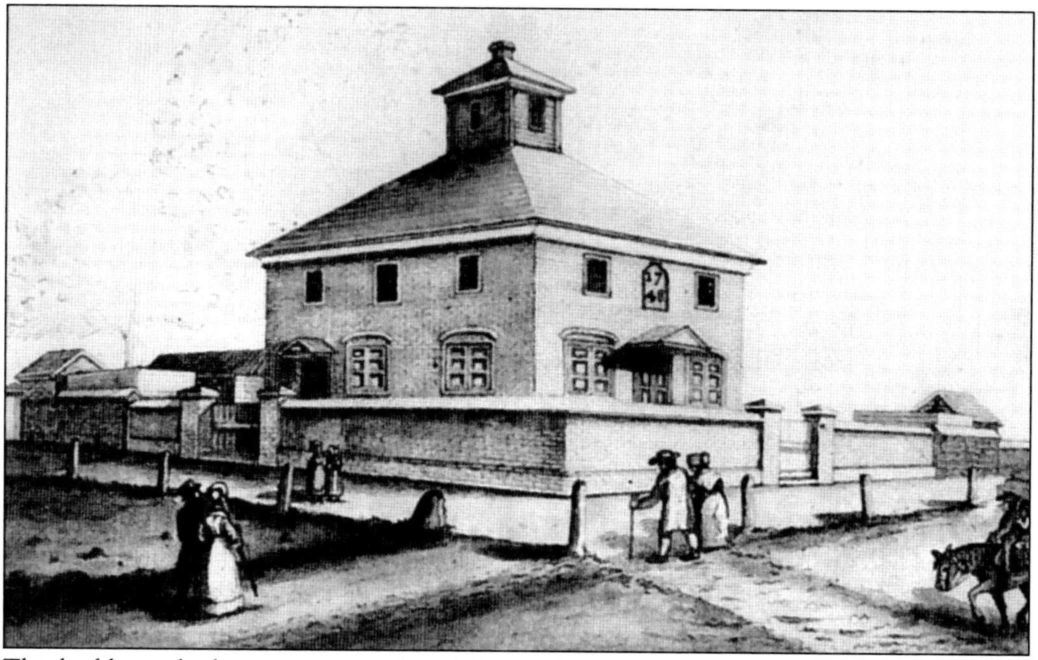

This building, which was constructed in 1748, was the second meetinghouse on Quaker Hill. It replaced the first meetinghouse, built in 1738, and was used by the Wilmington Friends School teachers and students for midweek meeting. The sketch is by Benjamin Ferris. (Courtesy of Wilmington Friends School.)

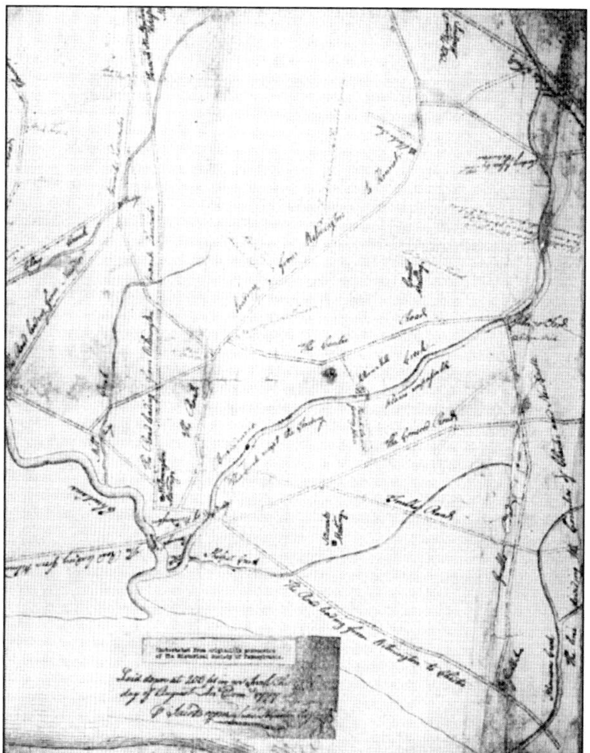

This is a map of Wilmington and the surrounding area of New Castle County drawn in 1772. Note the presence of several neighboring meetinghouses: Newark Friends meetinghouse, Old Kennett Friends meetinghouse, Centre Friends meetinghouse, and New Castle Friends meetinghouse. (Courtesy of Wilmington Friends Meeting.)

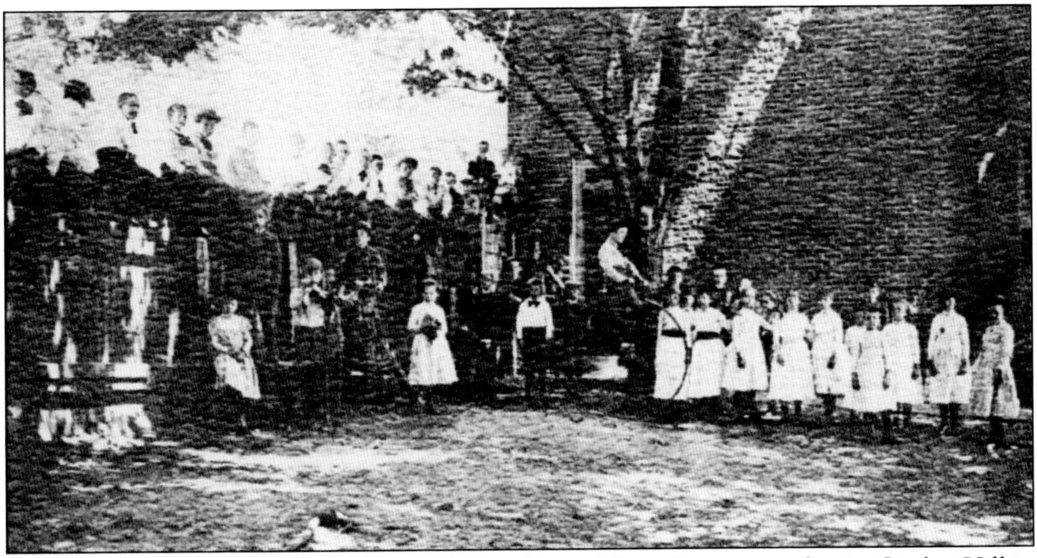

This is a picture of several people formally posed out of doors for a group shot in Quaker Hill in Wilmington sometime around the turn of the 20th century. Note the small boy in the middle of the picture who is riding a bicycle with an extremely large wheel. (Courtesy of Historical Society of Delaware.)

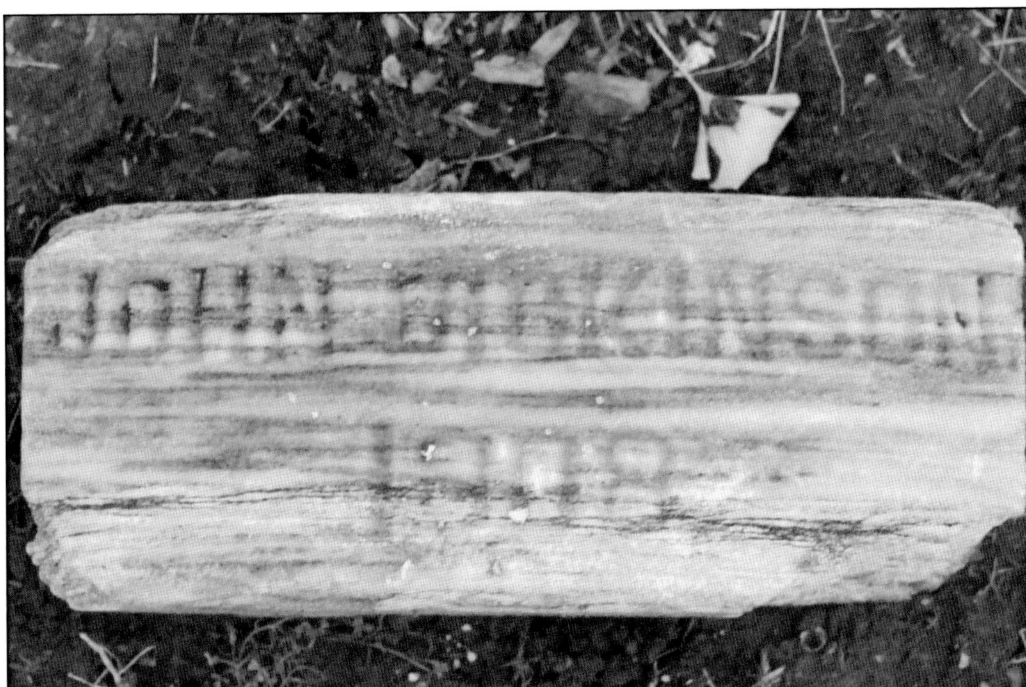

This is the grave of John Dickinson, who lived from 1732 to 1808. He was speaker of the assembly of the Lower Counties (Delaware) and was in the Pennsylvania legislature. He drew up a petition to the king of England in protest of the Stamp Act. (Photograph by James Bierbaum.)

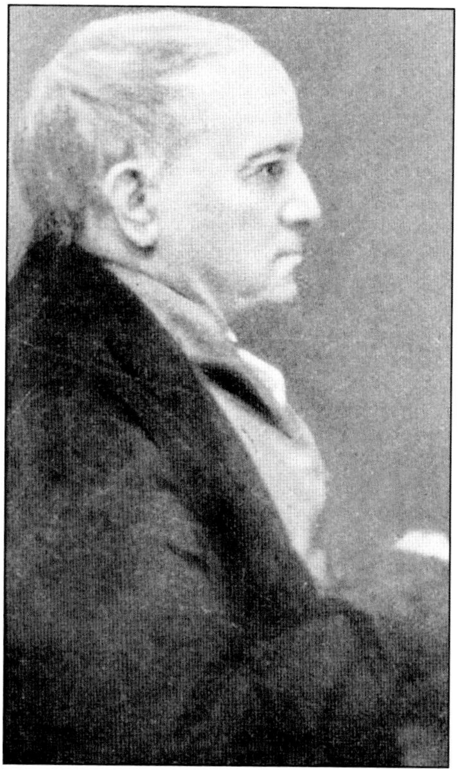

This is a daguerreotype of Benjamin Ferris (1780 to 1867) that is in the family's possession. He was a watchmaker and a historian, as well as a champion of Native Americans. He was appointed the city surveyor for Wilmington. (Courtesy of Historical Society of Delaware.)

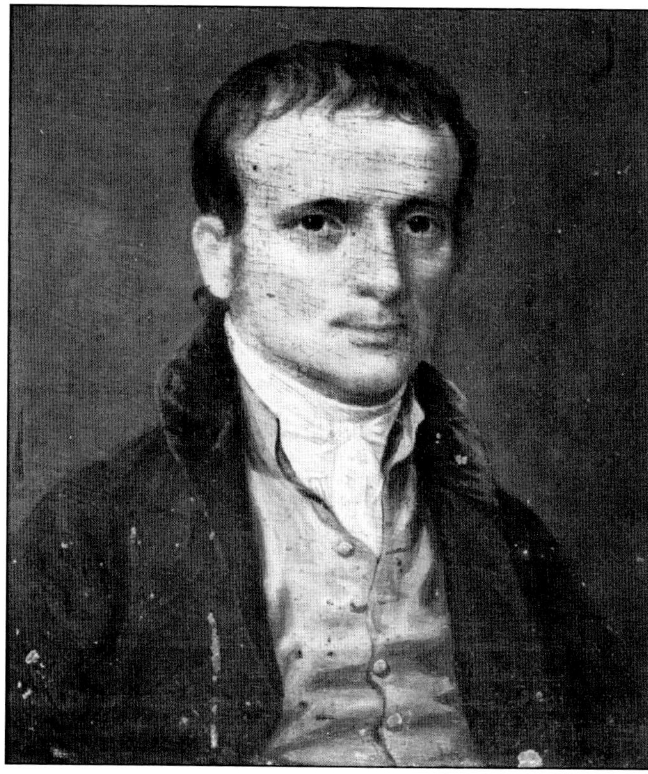

Benjamin Ferris worshiped at Wilmington Friends Meeting and was married and buried there. He and his wife, Fanny Canby, had eight children. (Courtesy of Historical Society of Delaware.)

This was the home of Edward Tatnall on Fifth Street near Shipley, which was built in 1740. Edward Tatnall was born in 1704 in England and immigrated to the Unites States in 1775. He married Elizabeth Pennock and had five children. Tatnall signed the petition for a charter of incorporation of Willingtown. He is buried in the Wilmington and Brandywine Cemetery. (Courtesy of Historical Society of Delaware.)

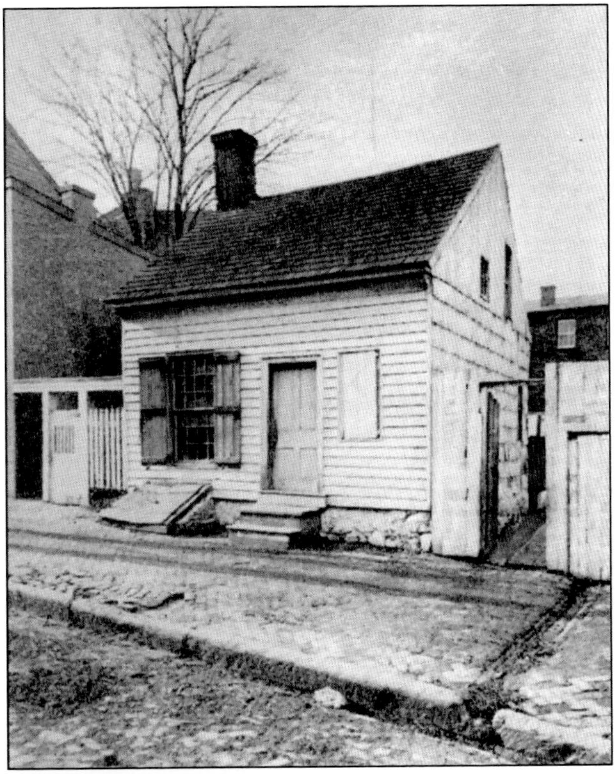

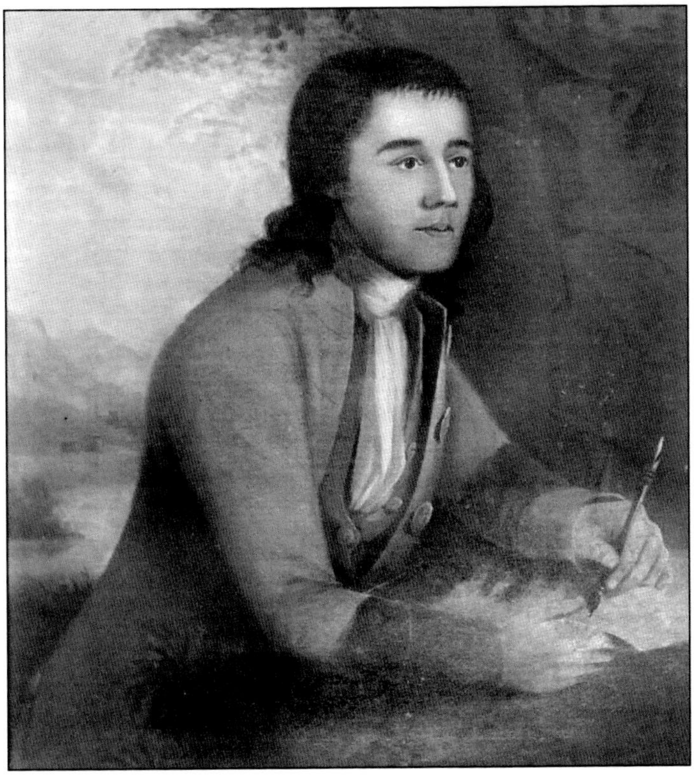

Joseph Bringhurst was born in 1767 and died in 1834. He resided in Rockwell, a mansion now open to the public. He was the first druggist and the first postmaster in Wilmington. Several members of his family are buried in the graveyard at Wilmington Friends Meeting. (Courtesy of Historical Society of Delaware.)

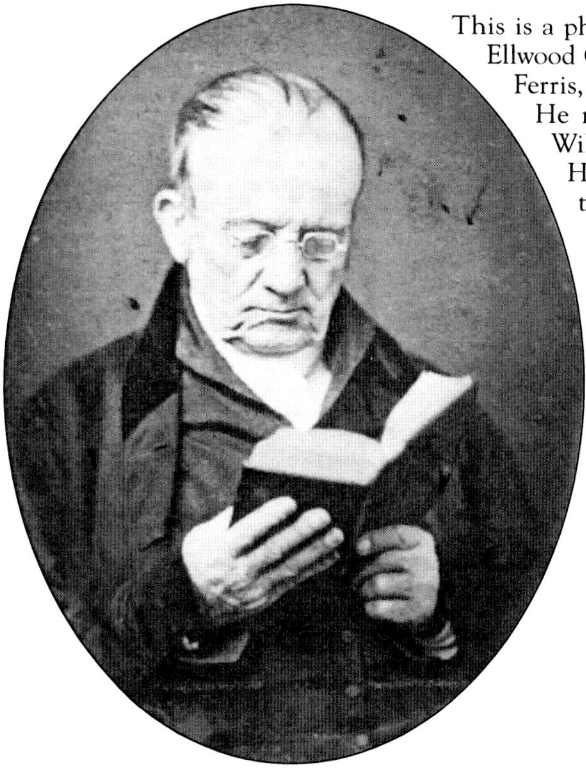

This is a photograph of Benjamin Ferris taken by Ellwood Garrett. Ferris was a descendent of John Ferris, one of the first settlers of Wilmington. He married Fanny Canby (1778–1833) at Wilmington Friends Meeting on May 7, 1804. He was a Hicksite Friend who advocated for the American Indians and helped restore some of their land to them. (Courtesy of Historical Society of Delaware.)

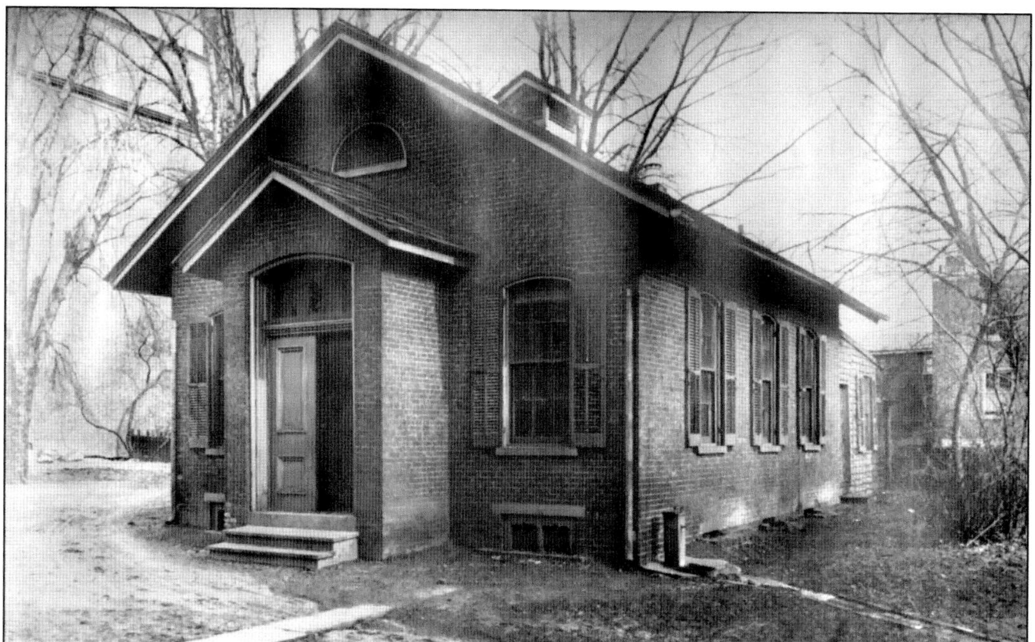

This is the Orthodox Friends School. The Religious Society split into the Orthodox Friends and the Hicksites in the 1820s. The Hicksites generally were more in favor of movements like the abolition of slavery than Orthodox Friends. Each group had its own meetinghouse and school. The Wilmington groups reunited in the 1940s. (Courtesy of Wilmington Friends School.)

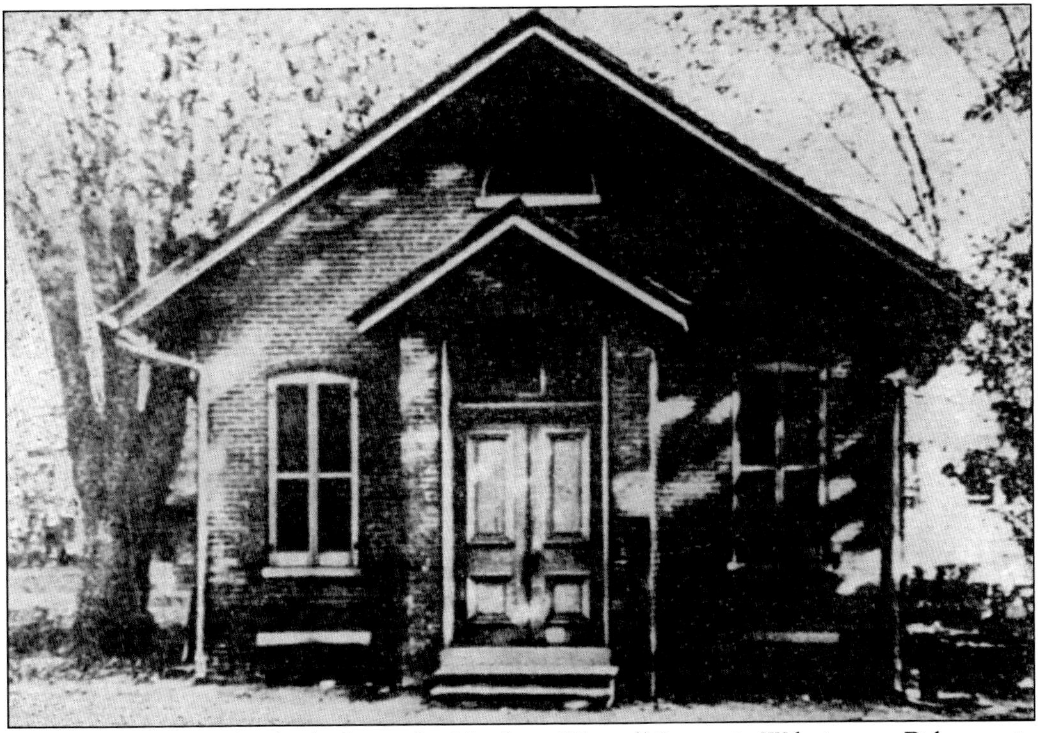

This is the Friends School, which stood at Ninth and Tatnall Streets in Wilmington, Delaware, in 1913. This was a school for the children of Orthodox Friends who worshipped at the meetinghouse at Tenth and Harrison Streets, also in Wilmington, Delaware. (Courtesy of Wilmington Friends Meeting.)

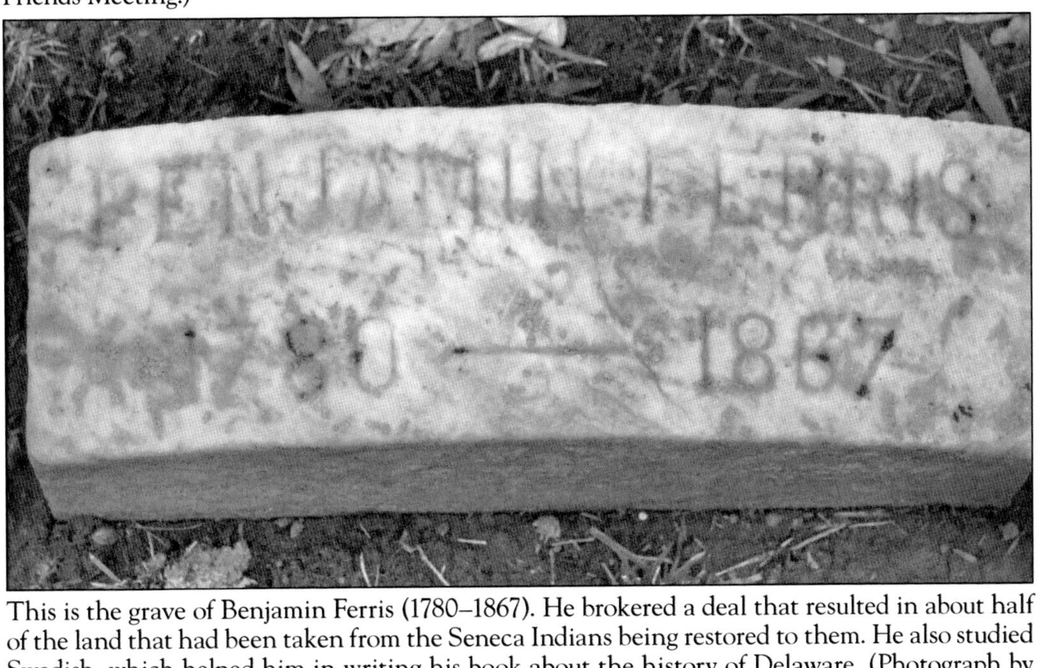

This is the grave of Benjamin Ferris (1780–1867). He brokered a deal that resulted in about half of the land that had been taken from the Seneca Indians being restored to them. He also studied Swedish, which helped him in writing his book about the history of Delaware. (Photograph by James Bierbaum.)

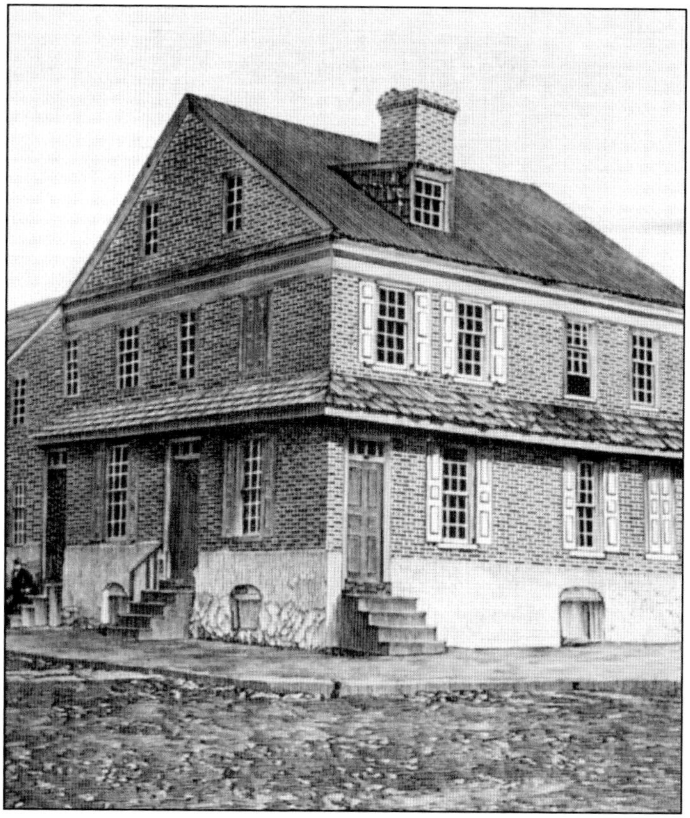

This is a building constructed in 1738 by Thomas West, one of the first settlers of Wilmington, Delaware. He was a relative of Benjamin West, the famous painter of the Revolutionary War era. A house built by Cyrus Stern, great-great-grandson of Thomas West, now stands here. (Courtesy of Historical Society of Delaware.)

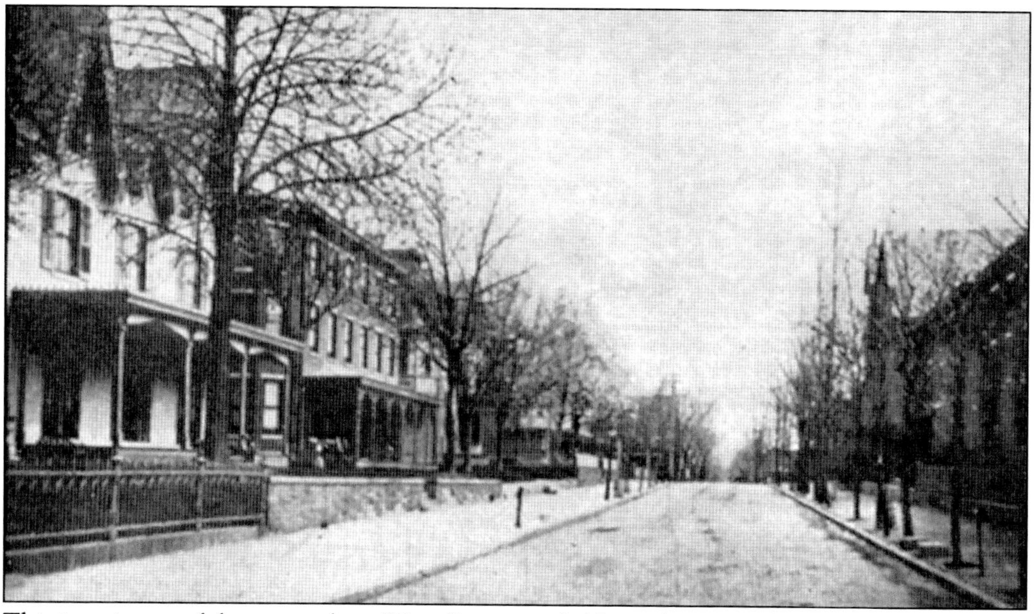

This is a picture of the scene along West Street, probably at the turn of the 20th century. Note the breadth of the street. West Street was one of the first laid out by its founders in Wilmington, Delaware. The Wilmington Friends Meetinghouse stands on West Street. (Courtesy of Historical Society of Delaware.)

This is the Williams School, a public school then on Quaker Hill. The picture was taken in April 1943 and shows the school nurse dispensing medicine. This was during a time when it was more common for public school nurses to dispense medicine to students. (Courtesy of Historical Society of Delaware.)

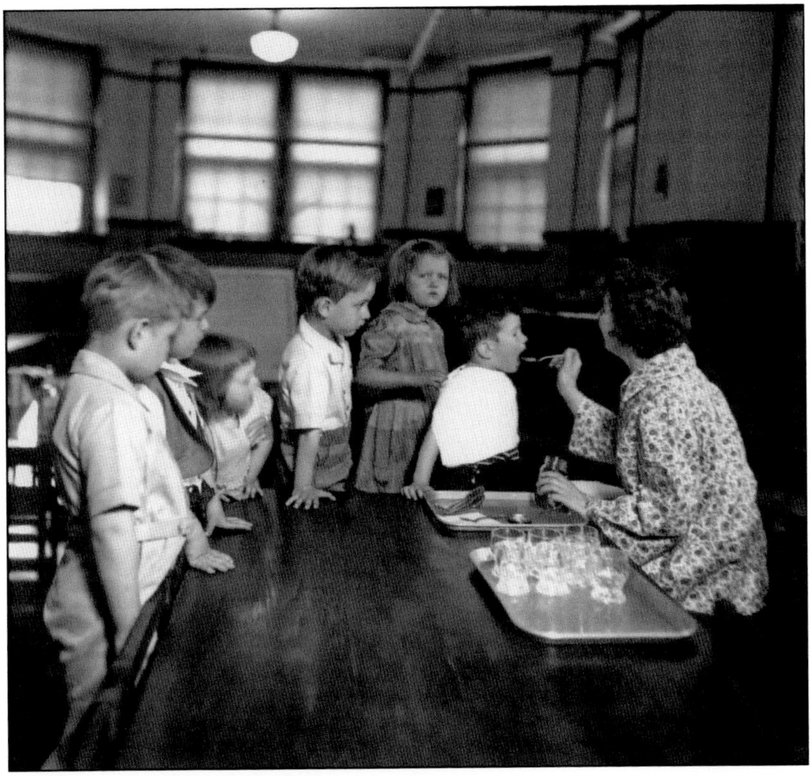

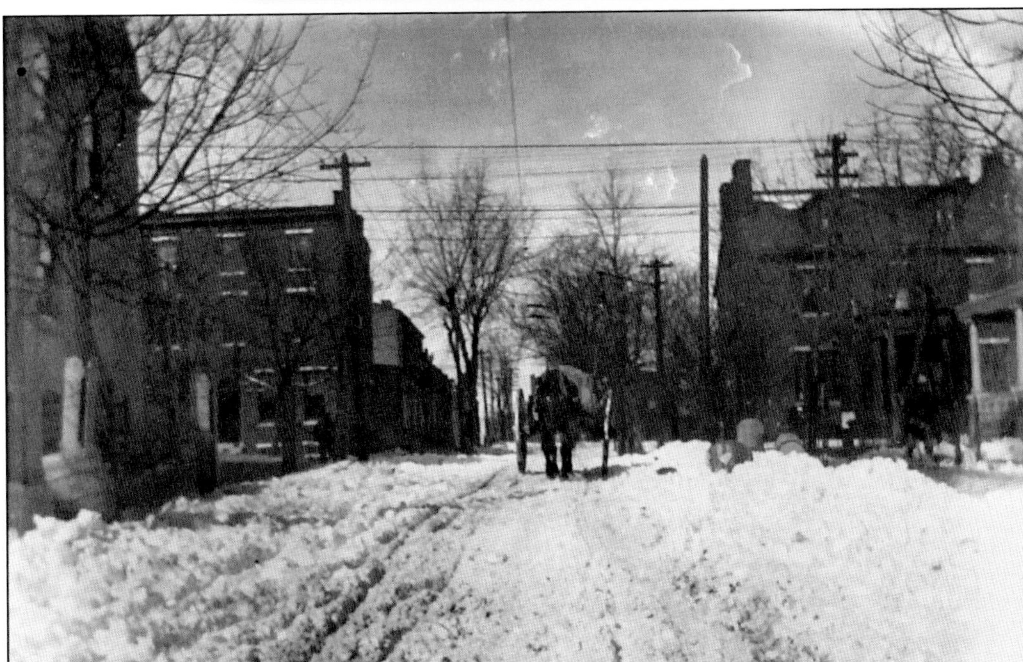

This photograph, which was apparently taken at some time around the beginning of the 20th century, shows a street covered in snow in Quaker Hill. Note the horse drawing the wagon. This is a picture from the Sanborne Collection. (Courtesy of Historical Society of Delaware.)

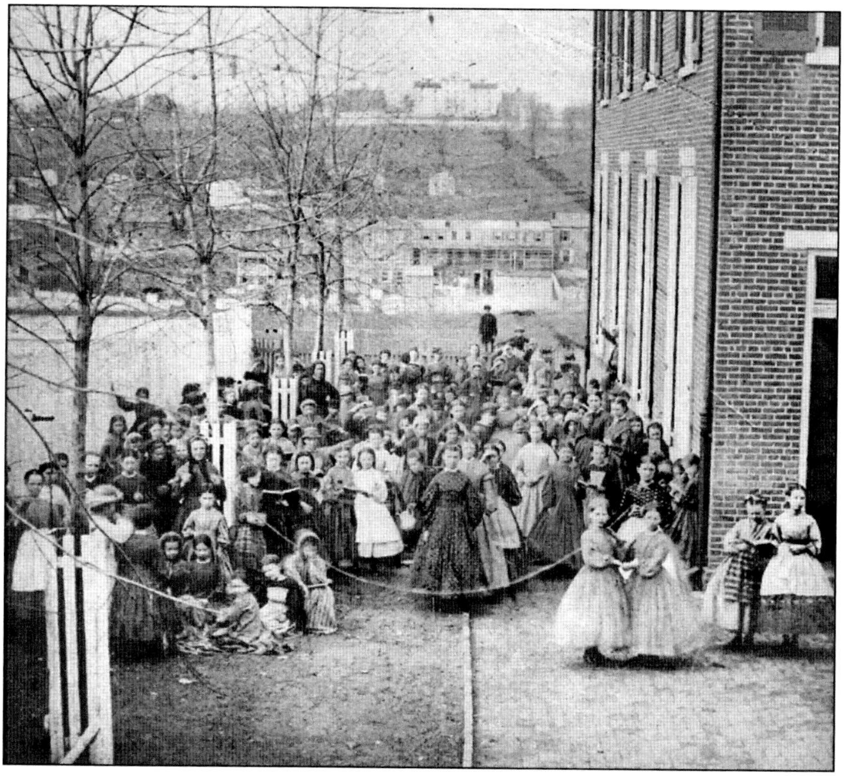

A large group of people is posed outside the No. 4 School in Quaker Hill in Wilmington, Delaware, at some time in the 19th century. At an earlier time, some of the public schools in Wilmington bore numbers instead of proper names. (Courtesy of Historical Society of Delaware.)

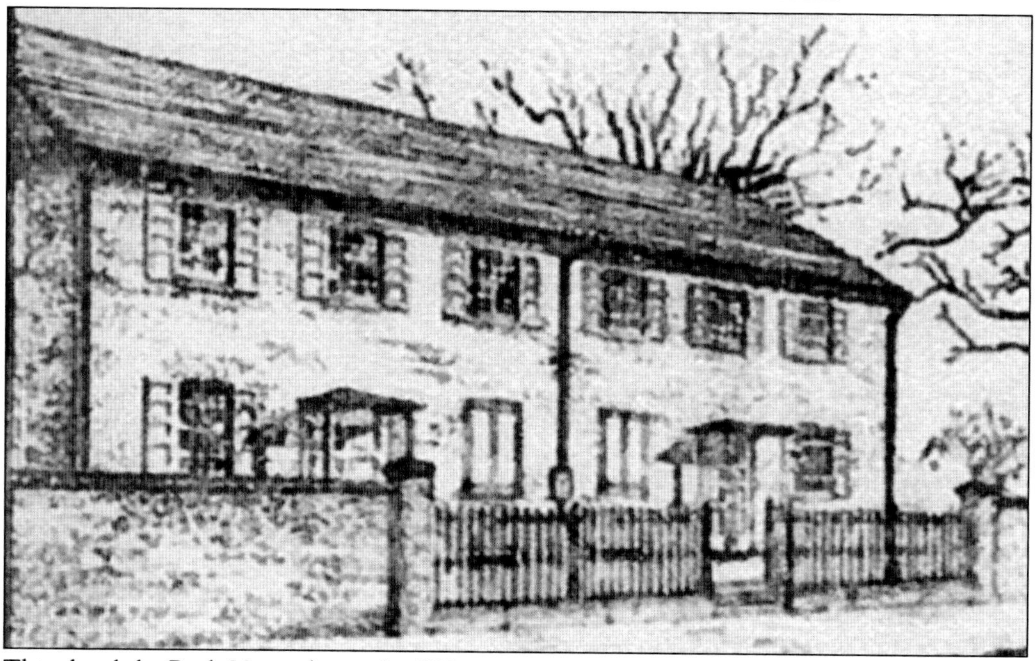

This sketch by Ruth Vesey shows the Wilmington Friends Meetinghouse as it looked in 1818, shortly after it was planned in 1816 and built in 1817. As was typical of Quaker meetinghouses, it followed along simple lines in accordance with the Quaker principle of simplicity. (Courtesy of Wilmington Friends Meeting.)

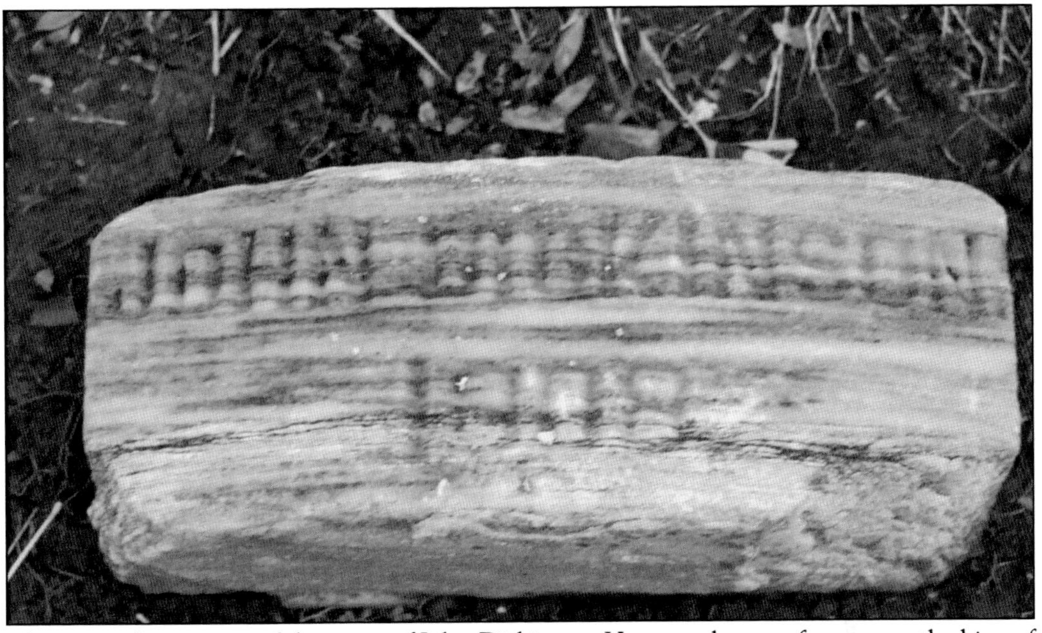

This is another picture of the grave of John Dickinson. He wrote letters of protest to the king of England for a farmer in Pennsylvania. He was a delegate to the First Continental Congress and a founder of Dickinson College. (Photograph by James Bierbaum.)

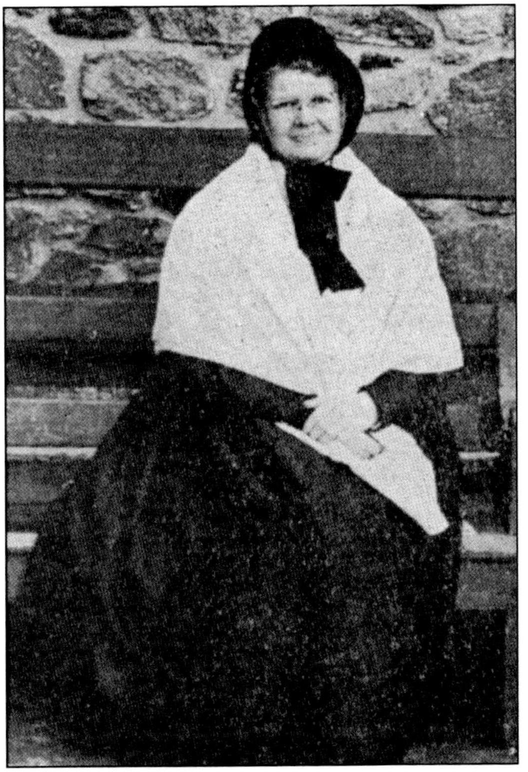

This is Edith Rhoads, a weighty Friend of Wilmington Friends Meeting, dressed to look like a Friend from an earlier time during the celebration of the 300th anniversary of the founding of Wilmington. Rhoads came from a Quaker family who arrived in the time of William Penn. (Courtesy of Wilmington Friends Meeting.)

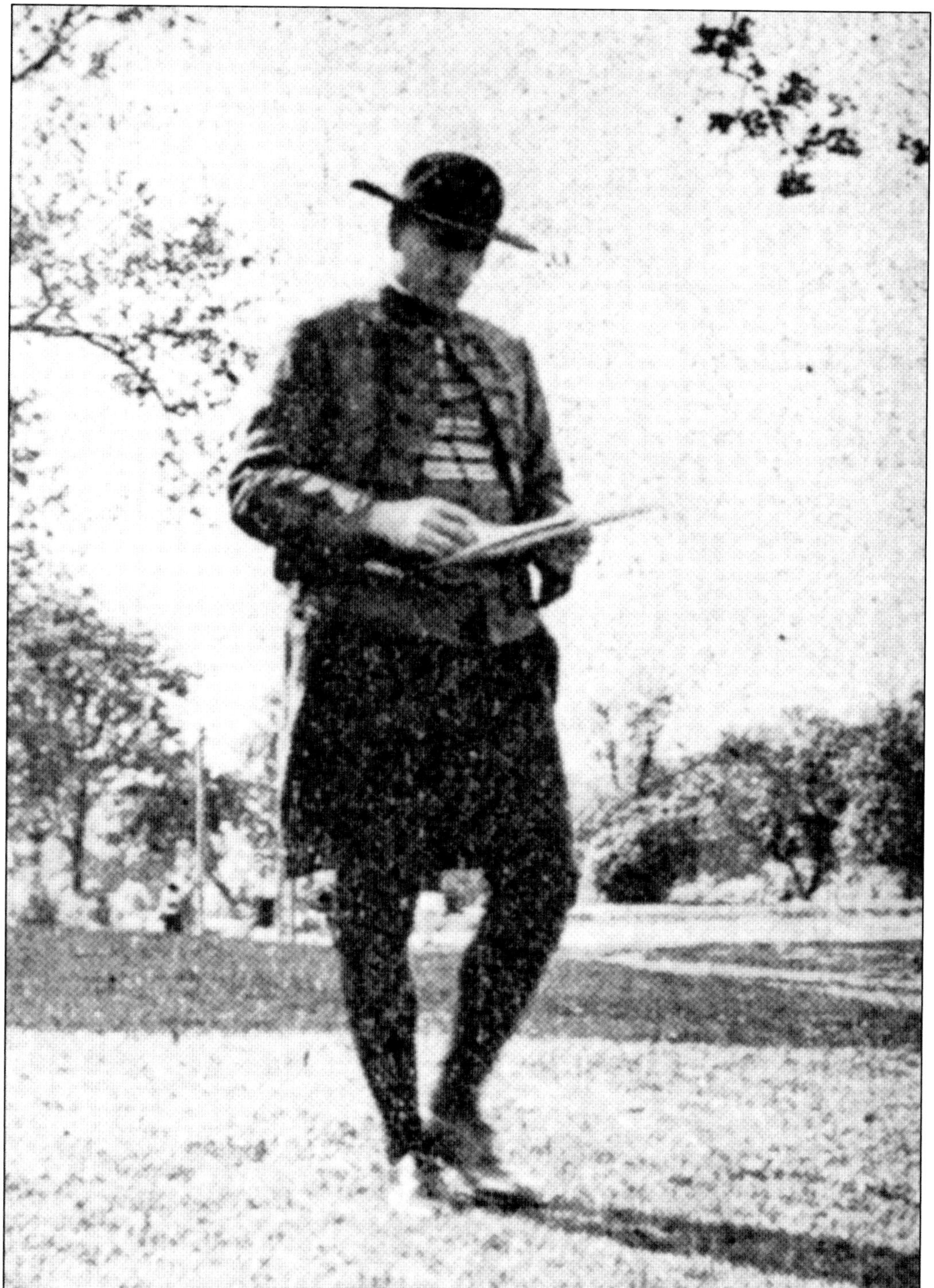

This is a weighty Friend of Wilmington Friends Meeting dressed for the 300th anniversary of Wilmington's founding in 1938. Walter Dew, who is pictured here, was a much-valued Quaker in his own right. (Courtesy of Wilmington Friends Meeting.)

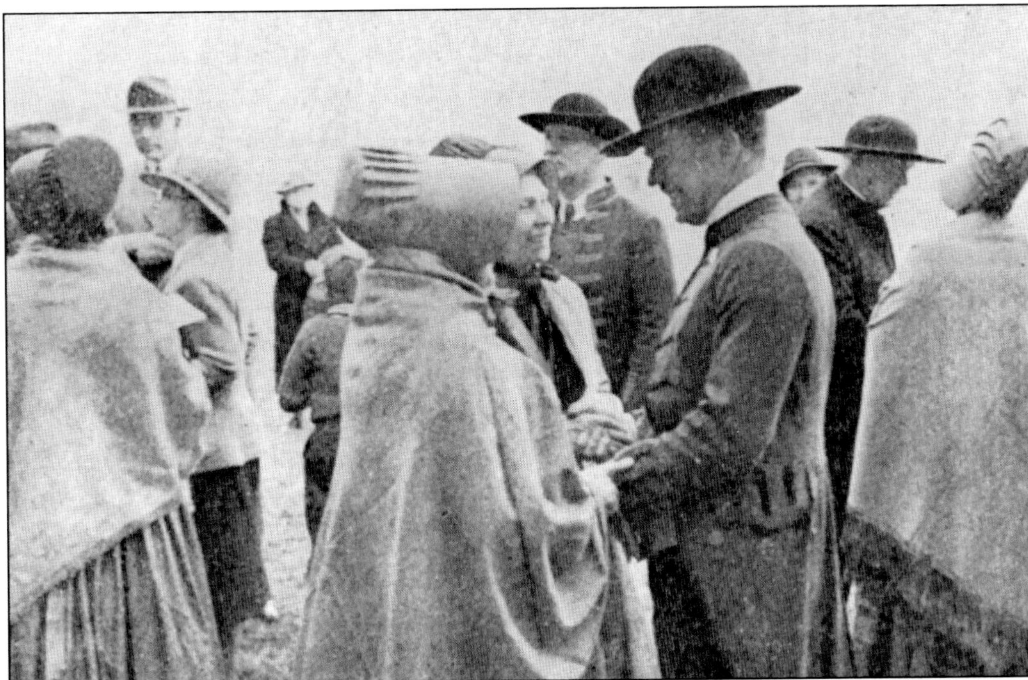

This image shows several other weighty Friends of Wilmington Friends Meeting in period costume during the 300th anniversary celebration. Wilmington's founding closely coincided with the establishment of Wilmington Friends Meeting. (Courtesy of Wilmington Friends Meeting.)

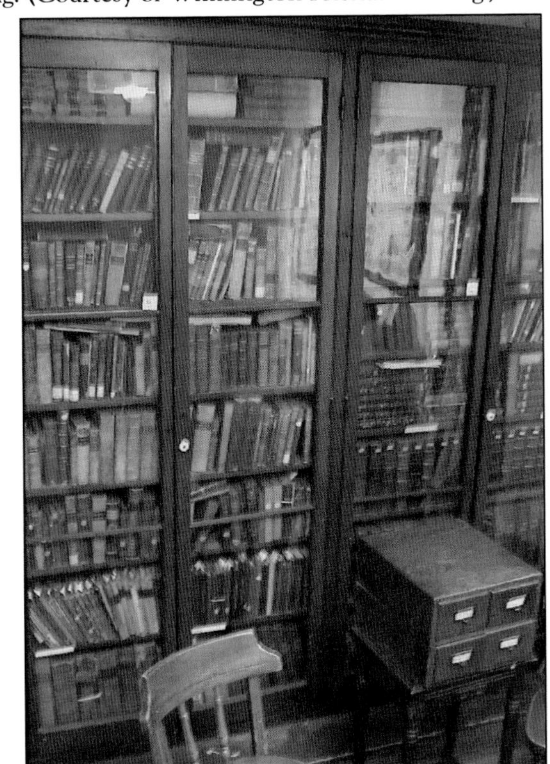

The old library was located in the original portion of the Wilmington Friends Meetinghouse, at 401 North West Street in Wilmington, Delaware. This portion of the building dates from 1817. The old books it contains appear to be even older. (Photograph by James Bierbaum.)

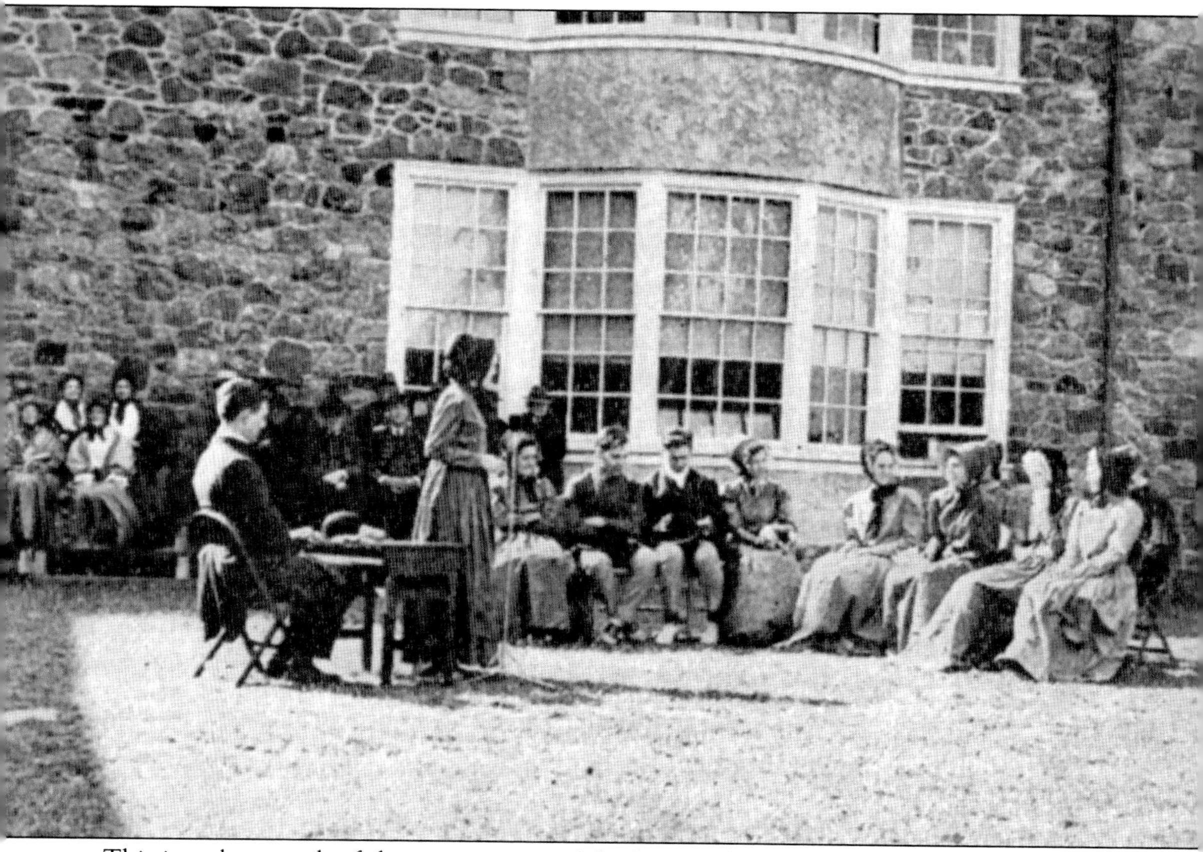

This is a photograph of the reenactment of the Lyceum by members of the Religious Society of Friends in the Historical Pageant of March 14 and 15 of 1938, celebrating Friends' 200 years in Wilmington. The Lyceum was one of the educational events. (Courtesy of Wilmington Friends Meeting.)

This image shows the interior of the Wilmington Friends Meetinghouse at Fourth and West Streets in Wilmington, Delaware, in 1938. Friends worship in silence punctuated by the divinely inspired messages, which can arise from any member of the congregation at any time. (Photograph by James Bierbaum.)

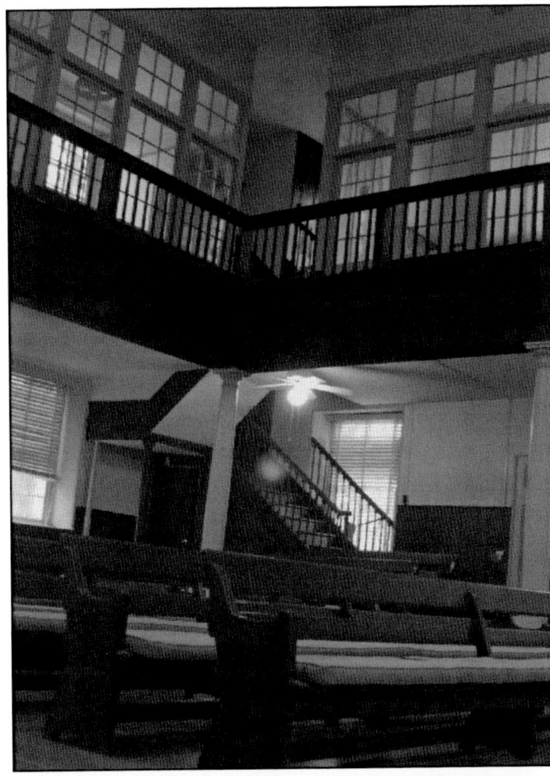

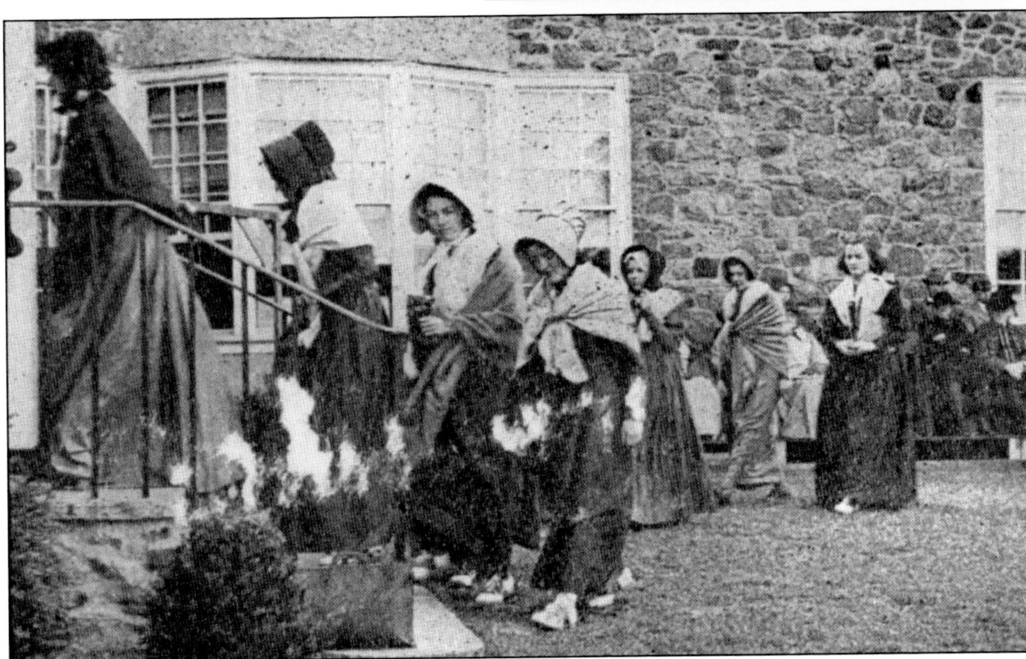

This is a photograph of the members of the Wilmington Monthly Meeting of the Religious Society of Friends acting the parts of early members of the Female Benevolent Society. The Female Benevolent Society was founded in 1800 and continues to this day to award grants to needy social service agencies. (Courtesy of Wilmington Friends Meeting.)

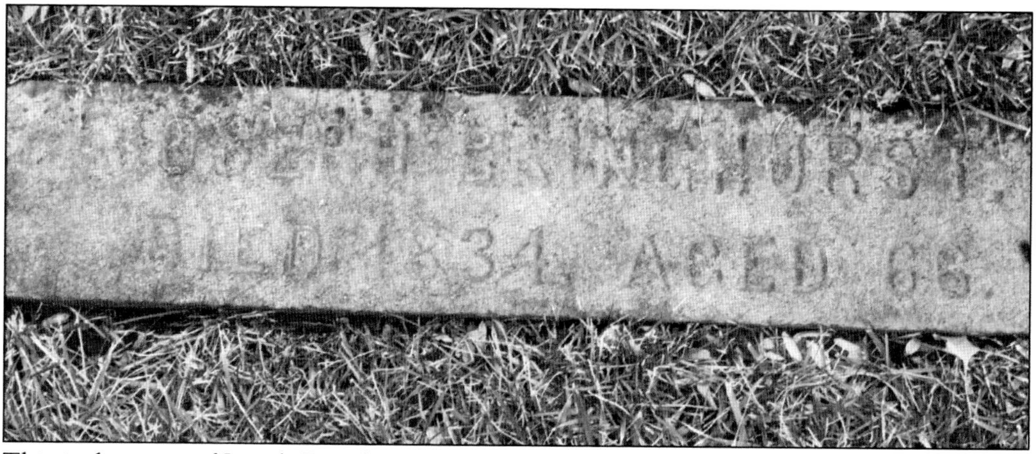

This is the grave of Joseph Bringhurst, who was born in 1767 and died in 1834. He resided in Rockwell, a mansion now open to the public. He was the first druggist and the first postmaster in Wilmington. Several members of his family are buried in the graveyard at Wilmington Friends Meeting. (Photograph by James Bierbaum.)

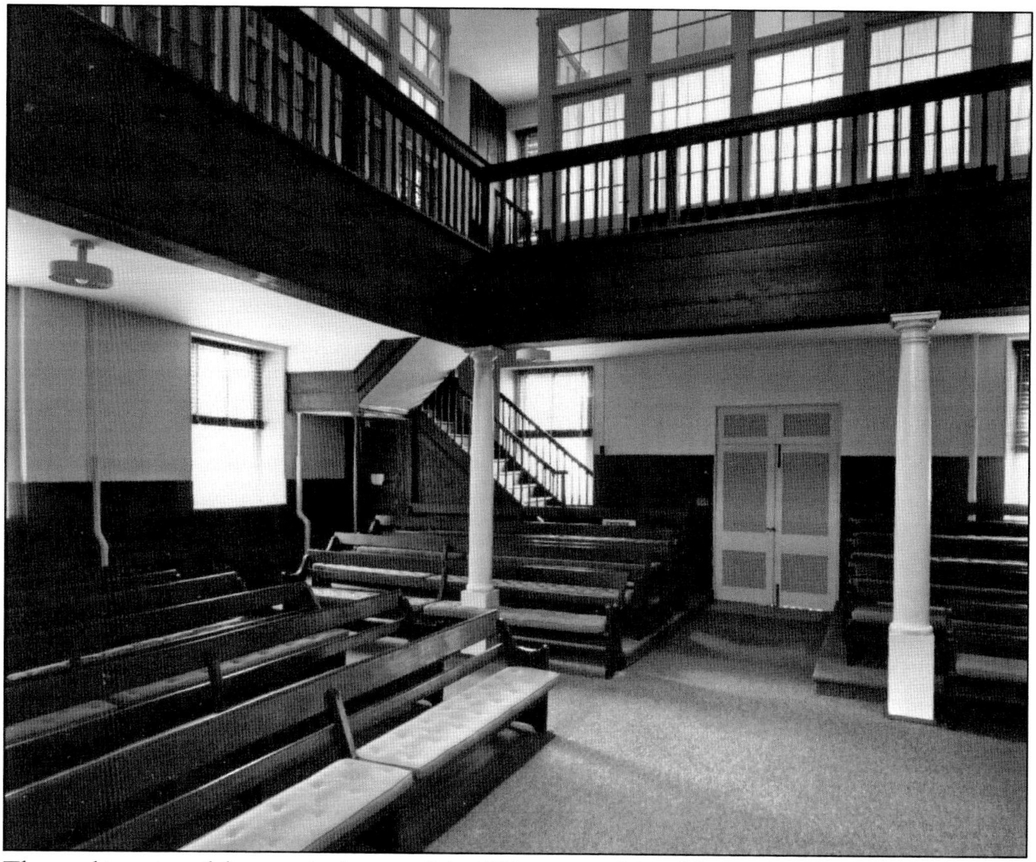

The cool interior of the meetinghouse of the Wilmington Monthly Meeting of Friends, designed in 1816 and built in 1817, reflects the beauty of simplicity, a Quaker principle, and is an ideal place for prayer and meditation, two hallmarks of traditional Quaker worship. (Photograph by Thomas F. Bayard IV.)

This is an interior shot of the meetinghouse of Wilmington Monthly Meeting of Friends, taken from the balcony. Note the benches and that, in lieu of an altar, there is a small table in the center on which flowers can be placed. (Photograph by Thomas F. Bayard IV.)

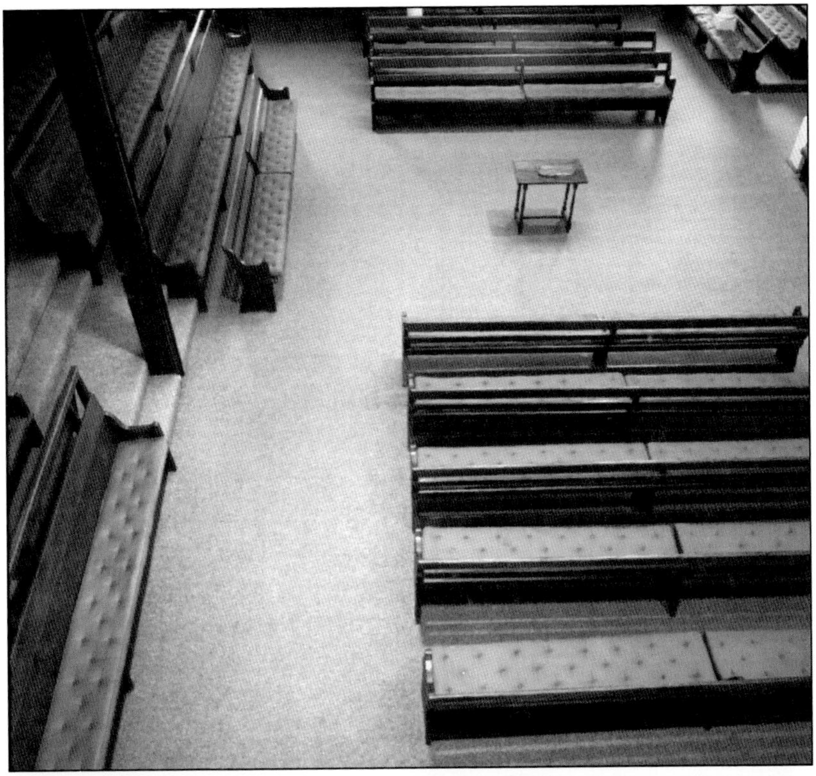

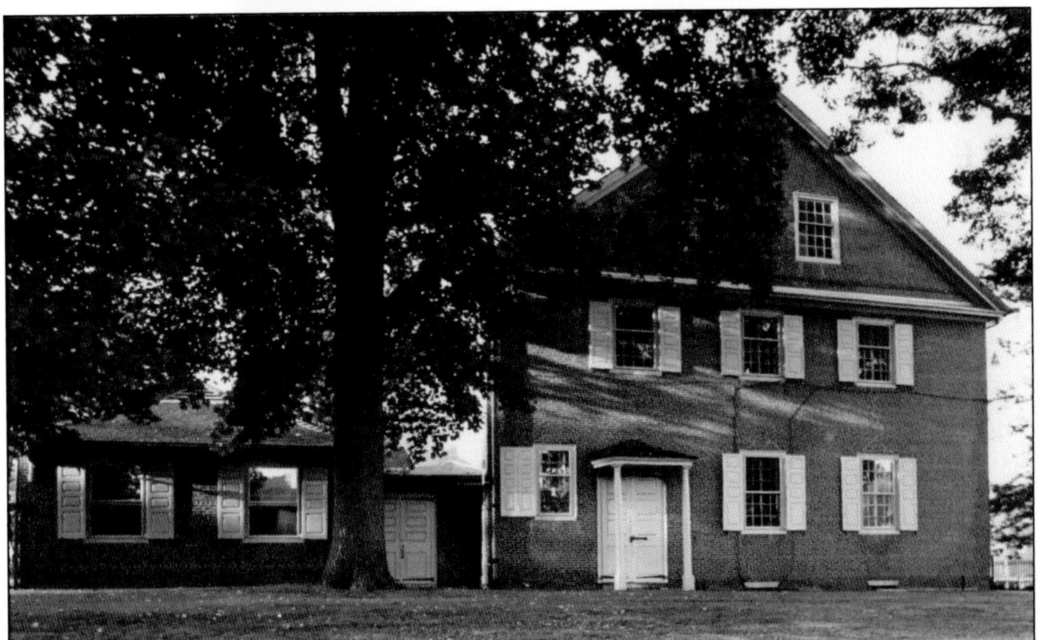

This is the meetinghouse of the Wilmington Monthly Meeting of Friends, taken from the side of the building that faces Fourth Street. Note the simple lines of the porch on the brick building. This is one of the few places in the yard where there are no graves. (Photograph by Thomas F. Bayard IV.)

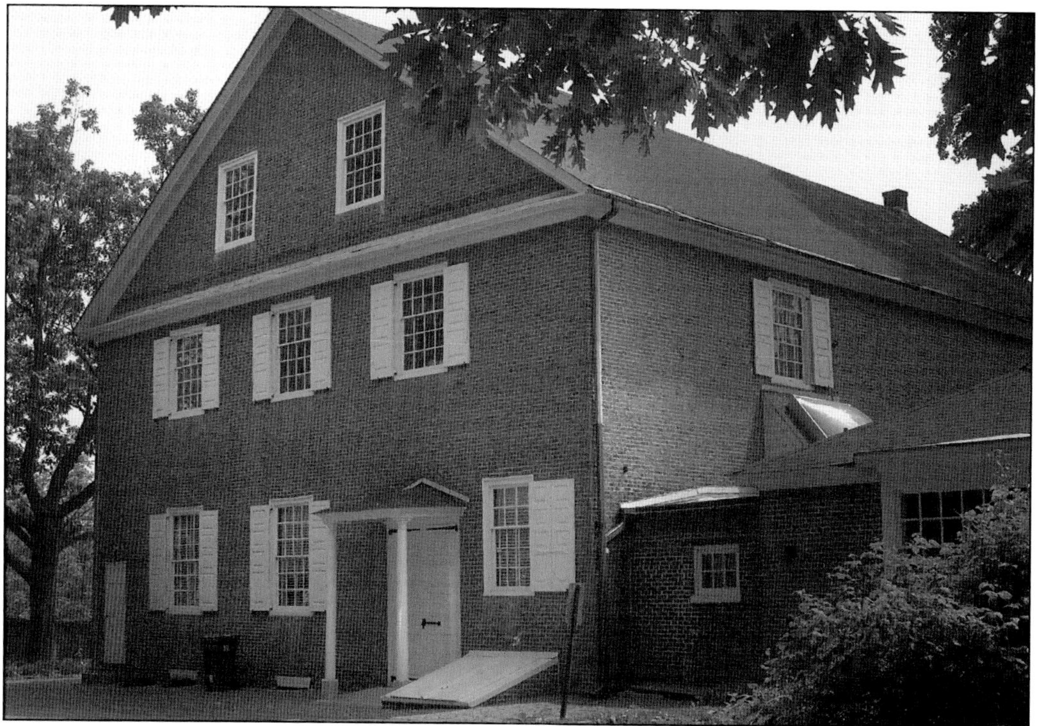

This is an exterior picture of the meetinghouse of the Wilmington Monthly Meeting of Friends, taken from the back of the Fifth Street side. Note the simple lines of the porch. Just behind this spot is the grave of John Dickinson, signer of the U.S. Constitution. (Photograph by James Bierbaum.)

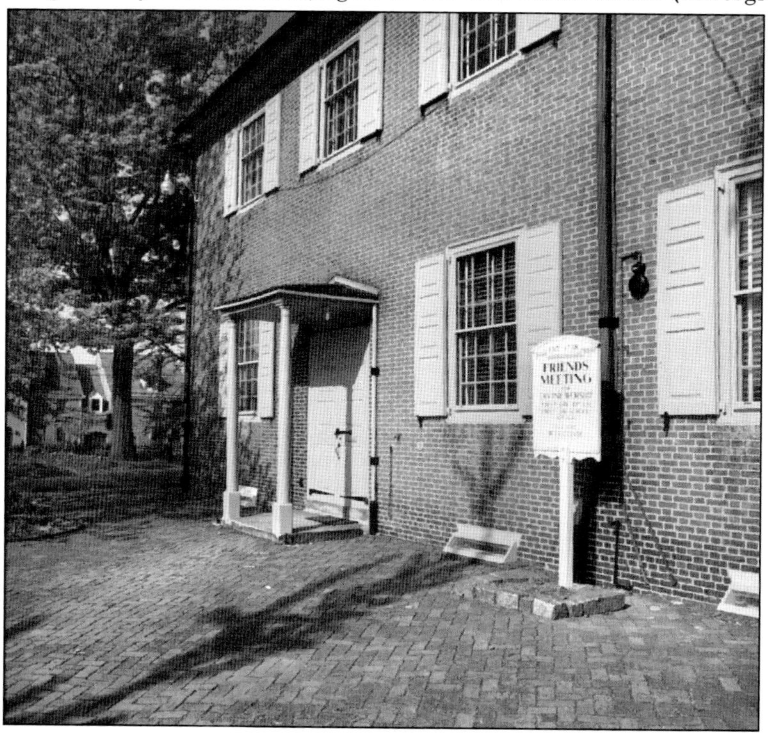

This is an exterior picture of the meetinghouse of the Wilmington Monthly Meeting of Friends, which shows one of the two front porches and doorways of the building. Note the sign declaring that the Wilmington Monthly Meeting of Friends was established in 1738. (Photograph by Thomas F. Bayard IV.)

Two

THOMAS GARRETT

Thomas Garrett, who was born August 21, 1789, and died January 25, 1871, has been called one of the greatest "stationmasters" on the Underground Railroad.

When he was still a young teen in Upper Darby, Pennsylvania, an incident happened that was to change the course of his life. A free African American cook employed by his parents was kidnapped out of their home by slave catchers to be sold into captivity in the South. Young Thomas Garrett followed the trail left by the slave catchers' wagon wheel ruts and was able to rescue the cook. He decided then to make helping runaway slaves to freedom on the Underground Railroad his life's work.

As an adult, he moved to Quaker Hill in Wilmington in the border state of Delaware to be in a better position to help freedom-seekers escape into the North. While working as a merchant of hardware, he also worked diligently with William Still of the Philadelphia Vigilance Committee, which helped freedom-seekers find new roots in the North, and the great Underground Railroad conductor, Harriet Tubman, called the "Moses of her people." He greatly admired her courage and her faith. He related stories of how God had alerted her to opportunities and warned her of dangers.

There were perils for Thomas Garrett in his work on the Underground Railroad as well. He and fellow Underground Railroad stationmaster John Hunn were tried in the courthouse in New Castle, Delaware, for helping a family of runaways escape. He was fined almost all his property as a result. However, he made a speech in court, saying that since he had been relieved of all his property, he had nothing left to lose, and he invited everyone to send runaway slaves to him so that he could assist them.

When he died in 1871, having seen the abolition of slavery, a great funeral was held at Wilmington Friends Meeting, with an estimated 1,500 people attending. His pallbearers, who bore his coffin up Quaker Hill, were from the same African American community that he had championed. His legacy lives on in Quaker Hill and the nation.

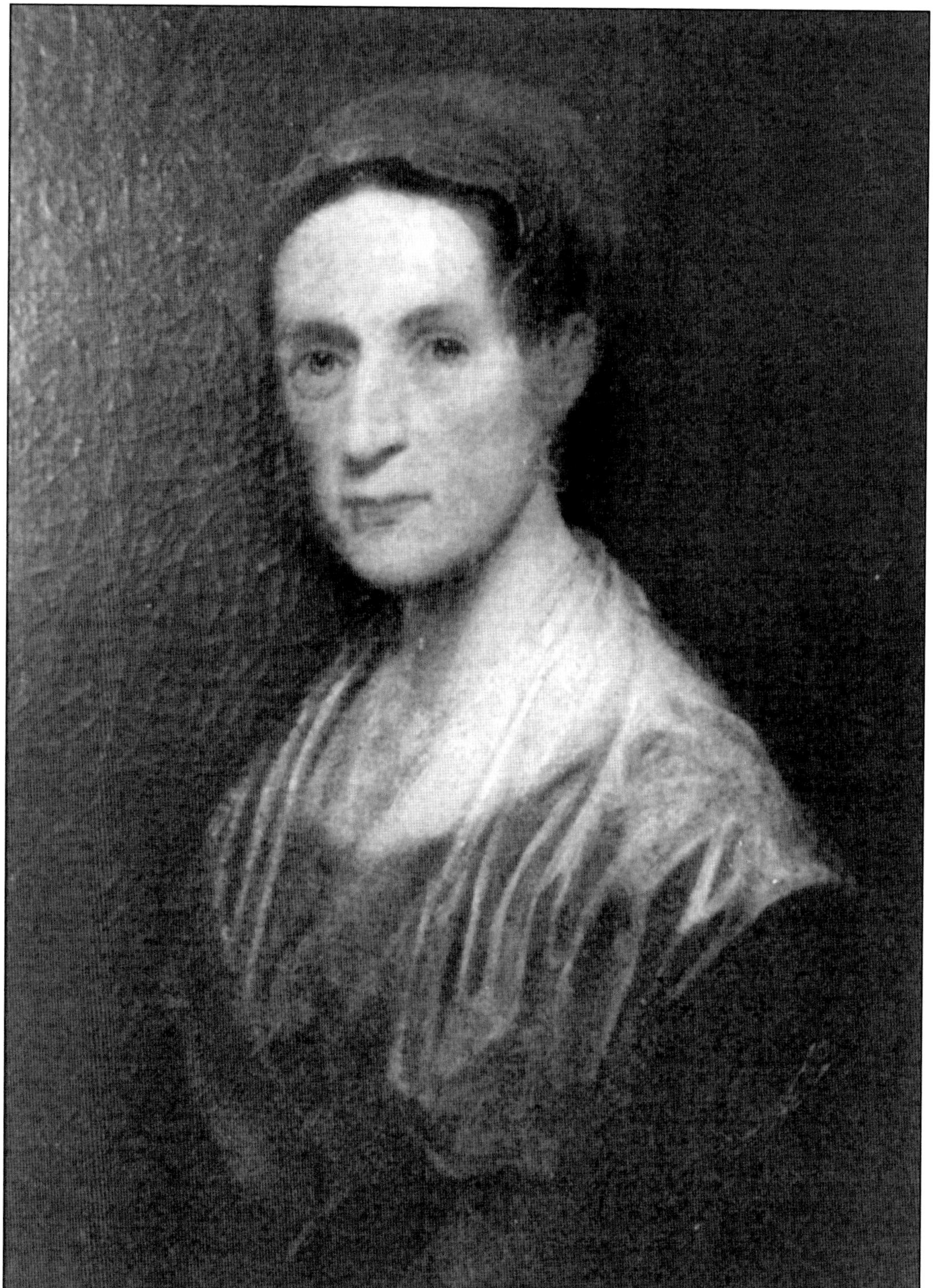

This portrait shows Rachel Mendinall Garrett, the second wife of abolitionist Thomas Garrett. She and her parents assisted Thomas Garrett in helping fugitive slaves escape on the Underground Railroad. This portrait was painted in the 1830s by Bass Otis. (Courtesy of Robert Seeley.)

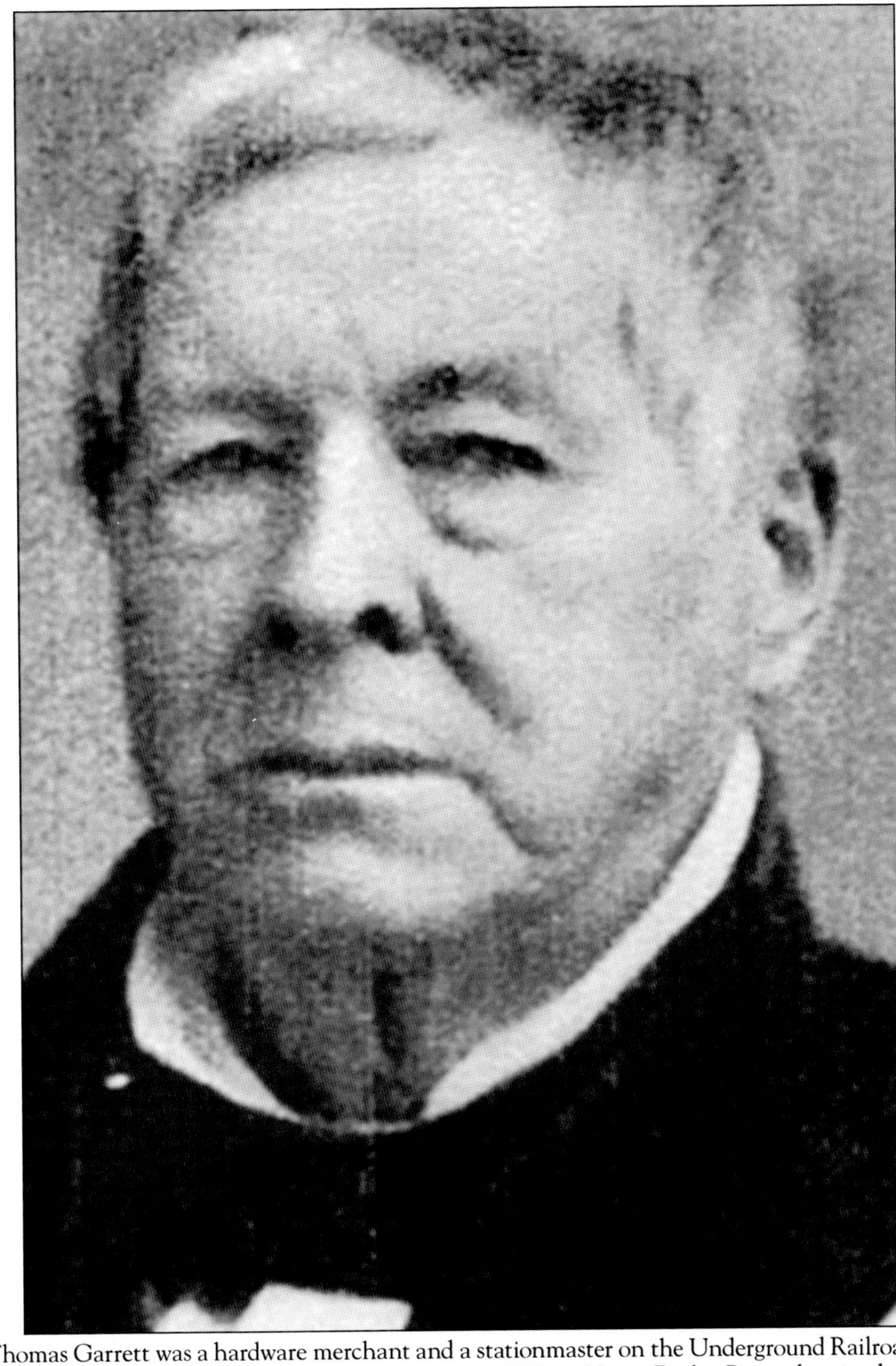

Thomas Garrett was a hardware merchant and a stationmaster on the Underground Railroad in Wilmington, Delaware. He was born on August 21, 1789, in Upper Darby, Pennsylvania, the son of Thomas Garrett Sr., and Sarah Price Garrett, and he died on January 25, 1871, in Wilmington, Delaware. (Courtesy of Historical Society of Delaware.)

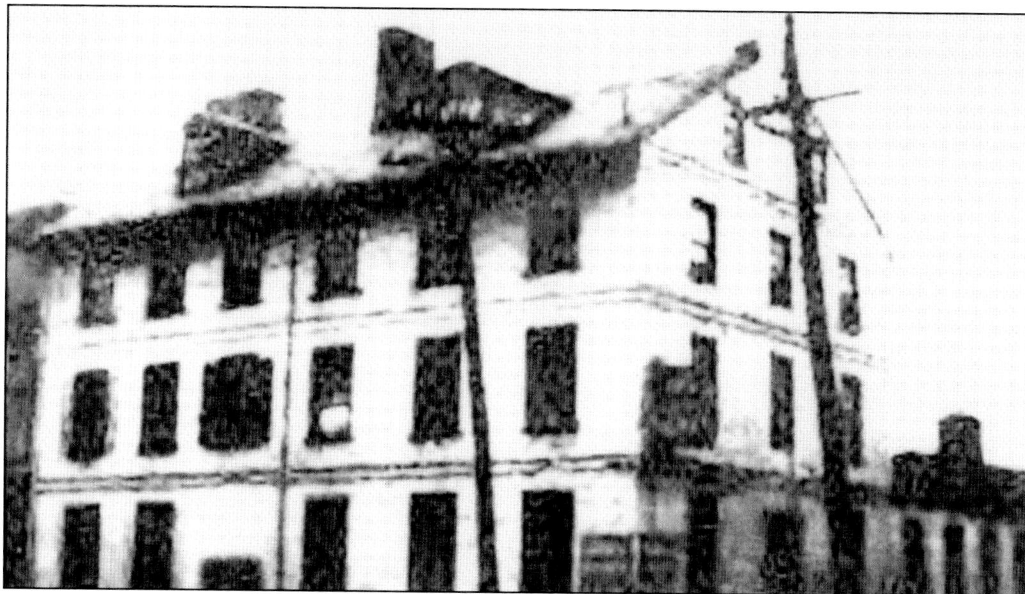

This was the home of Thomas Garrett and Rachel Mendinhall Garrett at 227 Shipley Street in Quaker Hill. When he was fined in court for helping runaway slaves escape, Thomas threatened to add another story to his house to hide additional runaway slaves. (Courtesy of Robert Seeley, from Wilbur H. Siebert Collection.)

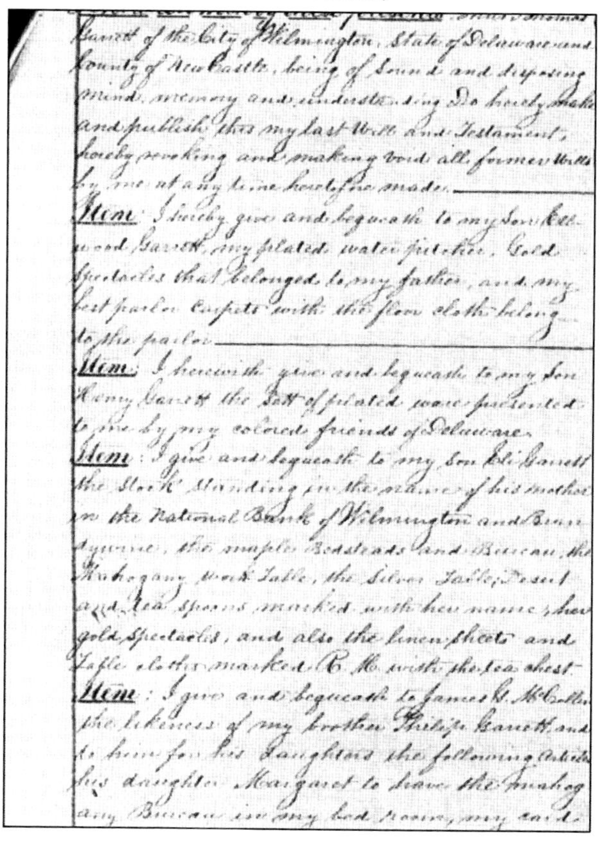

… Thomas
Garrett of the City of Wilmington, State of Delaware and
County of New Castle, being of sound and disposing
mind, memory and understanding Do hereby make
and publish this my last Will and Testament,
hereby revoking and making void all former Wills
by me at any time heretofore made.
Item: I hereby give and bequeath to my son Ell-
wood Garrett my plated water pitcher, Gold
Spectacles that belonged to my father, and my
best parlor carpets with the floor cloth belong
to the parlor.
Item: I herewith give and bequeath to my son
Henry Garrett the sett of plated ware presented
to me by my colored friends of Delaware.
Item: I give and bequeath to my son Eli Garrett
the Stock standing in the name of his mother
in the National Bank of Wilmington and Bran-
dywine, the maple Bedsteads and Bureau, the
Mahogany work table, the Silver Table, Desert
and tea spoons marked with her name, her
gold Spectacles, and also the linen sheets and
Table cloths marked R M with the tea chest.
Item: I give and bequeath to James G. McCollin
the likeness of my brother Philip Garrett and
to him for his daughters the following Articles
his daughter Margaret to have the mahog-
any Bureau in my bed room, my card

This is the will of abolitionist Thomas Garrett, who died in 1871. He states therein: "I bequeath to my son Henry Garrett the set of plated ware presented to me by my colored friends of Delaware." The silver tea set presented to Thomas Garrett is now at the Historical Society of Delaware. (Courtesy of Historical Society of Delaware.)

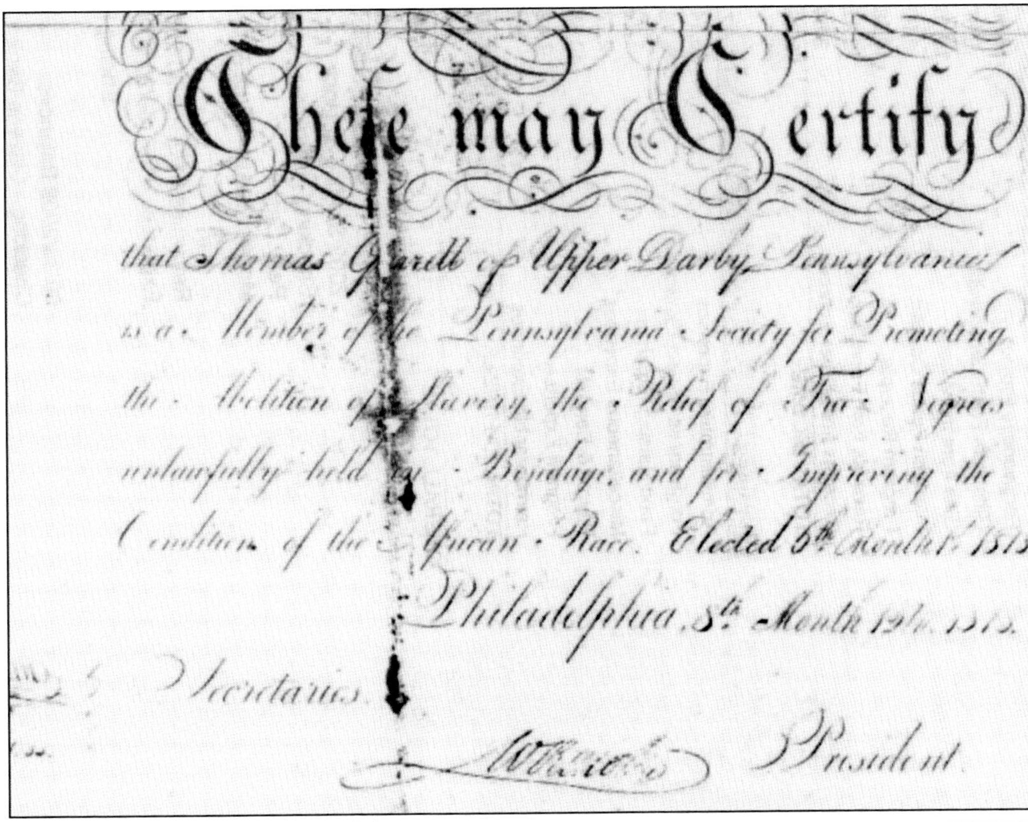

These may Certify

that Thomas Garrett of Upper Darby Pennsylvania

is a Member of the Pennsylvania Society for Promoting the Abolition of Slavery, the Relief of Free Negroes unlawfully held in Bondage, and for Improving the Condition of the African Race. Elected 5th Month [illegible]

Philadelphia 8th Month [illegible]

Secretaries.

President.

This is a picture of the papers of the Pennsylvania Society for Promoting the Abolition of Slavery. Thomas Garrett joined the Pennsylvania Society for Promoting the Abolition of Slavery in 1818. The adherents of the society were largely members of the Religious Society of Friends (Quakers). (Courtesy of Robert Seeley.)

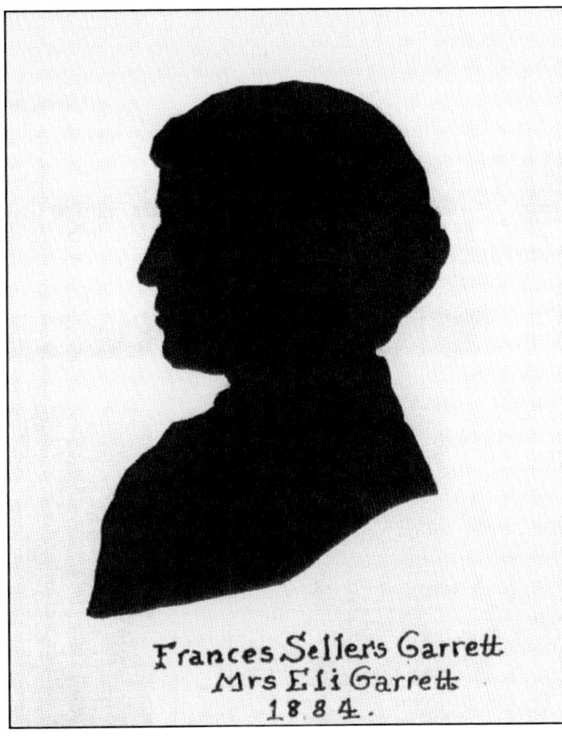

Eli Garrett, son of Thomas Garrett and Rachel Mendinhall Garrett (Thomas' second wife), married Frances Sellers on April 26, 1855, in Millbourne, Pennsylvania, at the home of her parents, John Sellers and Elizabeth Poole Sellers. She was born September 23, 1833, and died August 2, 1918. (Courtesy of Historical Society of Delaware.)

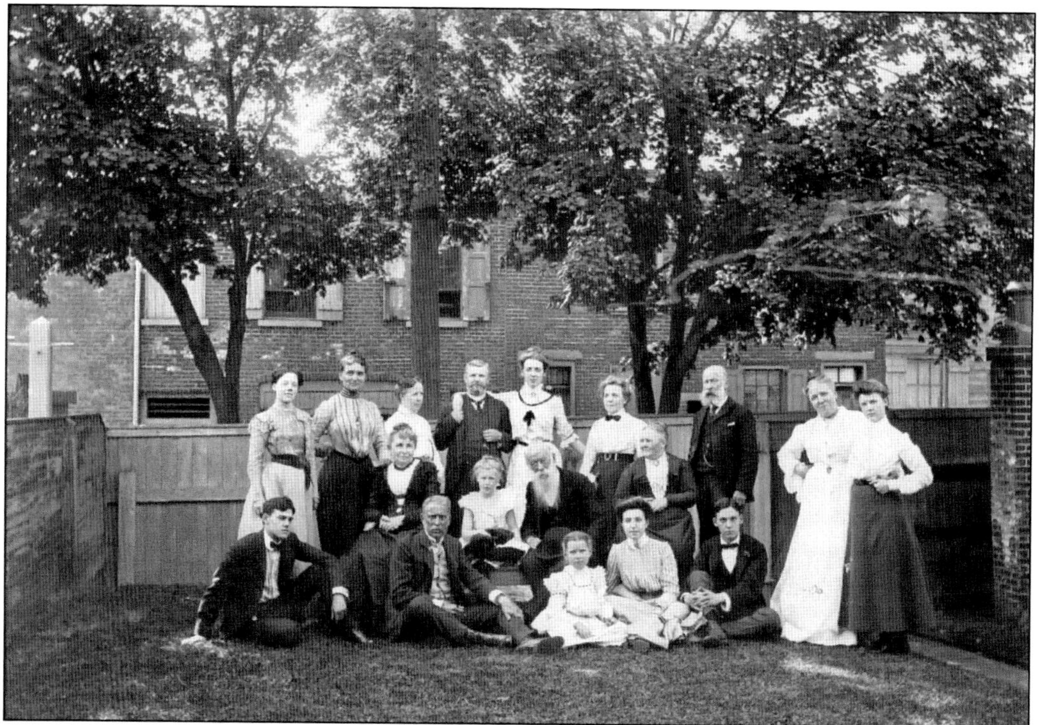

This is a picture of Elwood Garrett and his family around the turn of the 20th century. Ellwood Garrett was the eldest son of Thomas Garrett and lived from December 19, 1815, to May 25, 1910. He married Catharine Wollaston and lived with his family on Washington Street. (Courtesy of Historical Society of Delaware.)

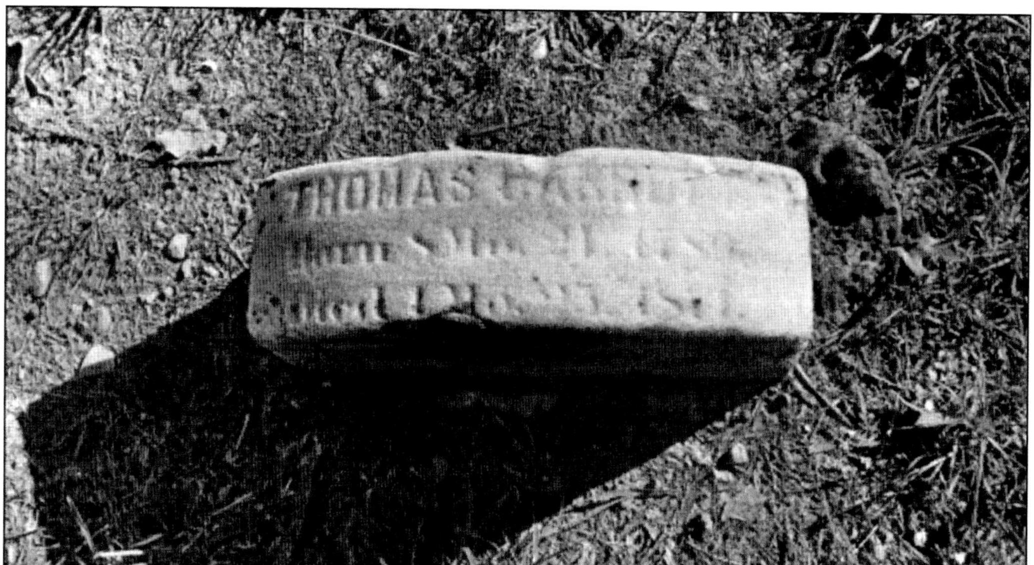

In keeping with Quaker principles of simplicity and equality, the gravestone of Thomas Garrett is small and close to the ground. Thomas Garrett was laid to rest in the graveyard of Wilmington Friends Meeting about January 25, 1871, having seen the completion of his life's work. (Courtesy of Robert Seeley.)

This is the marriage record at Wilmington Friends Meeting. Listed are the marriages of Thomas Garrett and Rachel Mendinhall in 1830; Sarah Garrett to Edward Hewes in 1814; and Ellwood Garrett to Catharine Wollaston in 1839. Note that Elizabeth Wollaston and Albert Smith also married June 5, 1839. (Courtesy of Robert Seeley.)

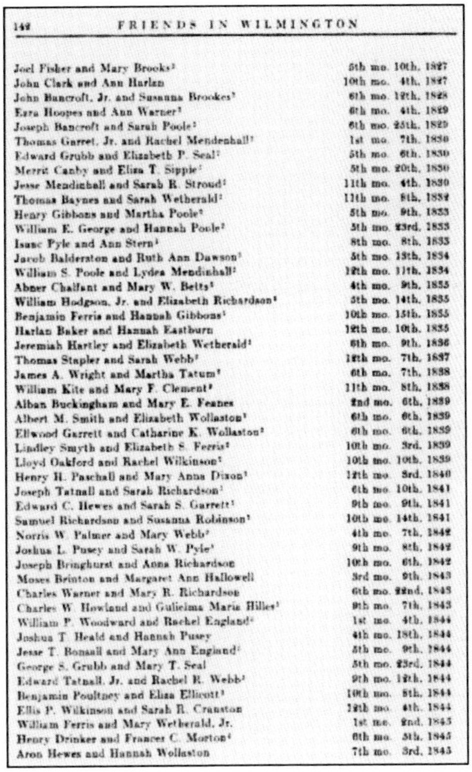

142 FRIENDS IN WILMINGTON

Joel Fisher and Mary Brooks	5th mo. 10th, 1827
John Clark and Ann Harlan	10th mo. 4th, 1827
John Bancroft, Jr. and Susanna Brookes	6th mo. 12th, 1828
Ezra Hoopes and Ann Warner	6th mo. 4th, 1829
Joseph Bancroft and Sarah Poole	6th mo. 25th, 1829
Thomas Garret, Jr. and Rachel Mendenhall	1st mo. 7th, 1830
Edward Grubb and Elizabeth P. Seal	5th mo. 6th, 1830
Merrit Canby and Eliza T. Sippie	5th mo. 20th, 1830
Jesse Mendinhall and Sarah R. Stroud	11th mo. 4th, 1830
Thomas Baynes and Sarah Wetherald	11th mo. 8th, 1832
Henry Gibbons and Martha Poole	5th mo. 9th, 1833
William E. George and Hannah Poole	5th mo. 23rd, 1833
Isaac Pyle and Ann Stern	8th mo. 8th, 1833
Jacob Balderston and Ruth Ann Dawson	5th mo. 15th, 1834
William S. Poole and Lydea Mendinhall	12th mo. 11th, 1834
Abner Chalfant and Mary W. Betts	4th mo. 9th, 1835
William Hodgson, Jr. and Elizabeth Richardson	5th mo. 14th, 1835
Benjamin Ferris and Hannah Gibbons	10th mo. 15th, 1835
Harlan Baker and Hannah Eastburn	12th mo. 10th, 1835
Jeremiah Hartley and Elizabeth Wetherald	6th mo. 9th, 1836
Thomas Stapler and Sarah Webb	12th mo. 7th, 1837
James A. Wright and Martha Tatum	6th mo. 7th, 1838
William Kite and Mary F. Clement	11th mo. 8th, 1838
Alban Buckingham and Mary E. Feanes	2nd mo. 6th, 1839
Albert M. Smith and Elizabeth Wollaston	6th mo. 6th, 1839
Ellwood Garrett and Catharine K. Wollaston	6th mo. 6th, 1839
Lindley Smyth and Elizabeth S. Ferris	10th mo. 3rd, 1839
Lloyd Oakford and Rachel Wilkinson	10th mo. 10th, 1839
Henry H. Paschall and Mary Anna Dixon	12th mo. 3rd, 1840
Joseph Tatnall and Sarah Richardson	6th mo. 10th, 1841
Edward C. Hewes and Sarah S. Garrett	9th mo. 9th, 1841
Samuel Richardson and Susanna Robinson	10th mo. 14th, 1841
Norris W. Palmer and Mary Webb	4th mo. 7th, 1842
Joshua L. Pusey and Sarah W. Pyle	9th mo. 8th, 1842
Joseph Bringhurst and Anna Richardson	10th mo. 6th, 1842
Moses Brinton and Margaret Ann Hallowell	3rd mo. 9th, 1843
Charles Warner and Mary R. Richardson	6th mo. 22nd, 1843
Charles W. Howland and Gulielma Maria Hilles	9th mo. 7th, 1843
William P. Woodward and Rachel England	1st mo. 4th, 1844
Joshua T. Heald and Hannah Pusey	4th mo. 18th, 1844
Jesse T. Bonsall and Mary Ann England	5th mo. 9th, 1844
George S. Grubb and Mary T. Seal	5th mo. 23rd, 1844
Edward Tatnall, Jr. and Rachel R. Webb	9th mo. 12th, 1844
Benjamin Poultney and Eliza Ellicott	10th mo. 8th, 1844
Ellis P. Wilkinson and Sarah R. Cranston	12th mo. 4th, 1844
William Ferris and Mary Wetherald, Jr.	1st mo. 2nd, 1845
Henry Drinker and Frances C. Morton	6th mo. 5th, 1845
Aron Hewes and Hannah Wollaston	7th mo. 3rd, 1845

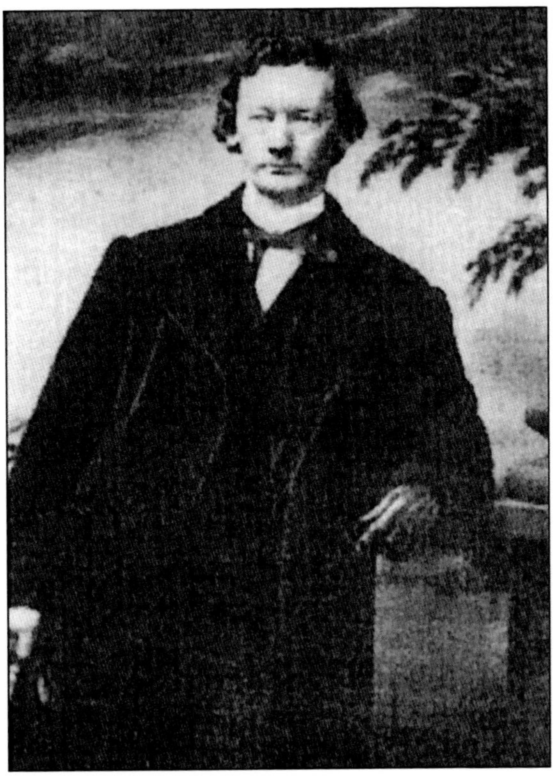

Henry Garrett, Thomas Garrett's son, was born on November 22, 1824, and died on August 25, 1903, both in Wilmington, Delaware. He married Catherine Ann Canby, daughter of Charles Canby and Ann Richards Canby, on May 7, 1846. Henry lived on Shipley Street near his father's home. (Courtesy of Historical Society of Delaware.)

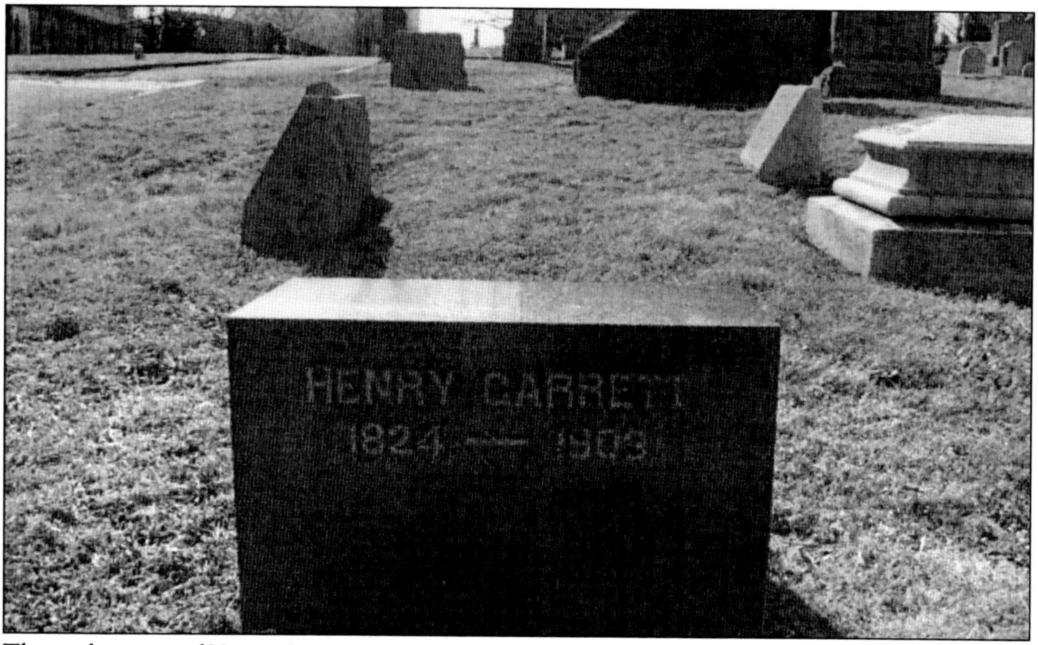

This is the grave of Henry Garrett, son of Thomas Garrett. Dr. Henry Garrett married Catherine Ann Canby, who was born on August 19, 1824, and died on August 4, 1900. Henry graduated from the Philadelphia College of Dental Surgery in 1853. Henry and Catharine Canby Garrett are buried in the family plot at Wilmington and Brandywine Cemetery. (Courtesy of Robert Seeley.)

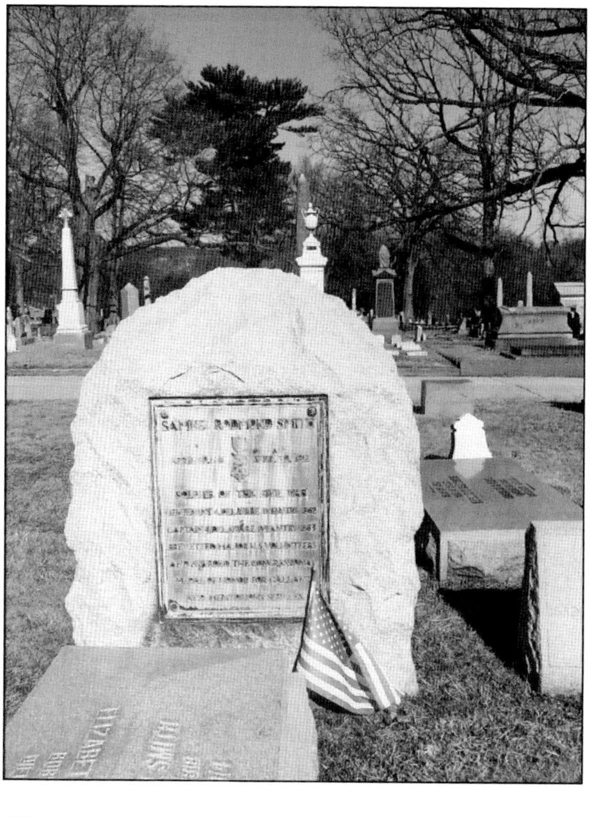

This is the grave of Samuel Rodmond Smith. He was awarded the Congressional Medal of Honor for service in the Civil War. He was present at the surrender of Robert E. Lee at the Appomattox Court House. He is buried in the Garrett/ Wollaston family plot in the Wilmington and Brandywine Cemetery in Wilmington, Delaware. (Courtesy of Robert Seeley.)

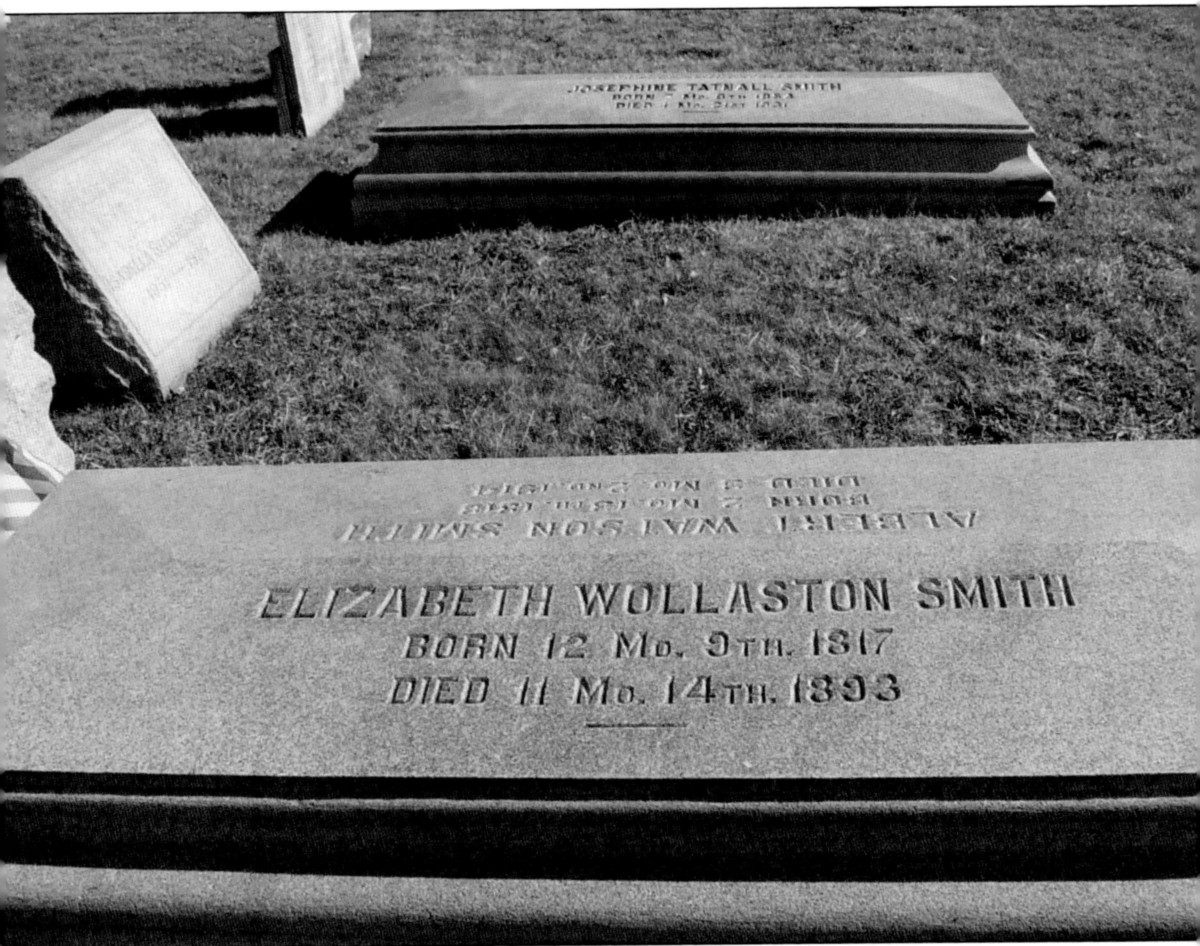

This is the grave of the parents of Samuel Rodmond Smith. They were Elizabeth Wollaston Smith and Albert Smith, who were married in Wilmington Friends Meeting. Elizabeth Wollaston Smith (born December 9, 1817, and died November 14, 1893) was the sister of Catharine Wollaston Garrett, wife of Ellwood Garrett and daughter-in-law of abolitionist Thomas Garrett. (Courtesy of Robert Seeley.)

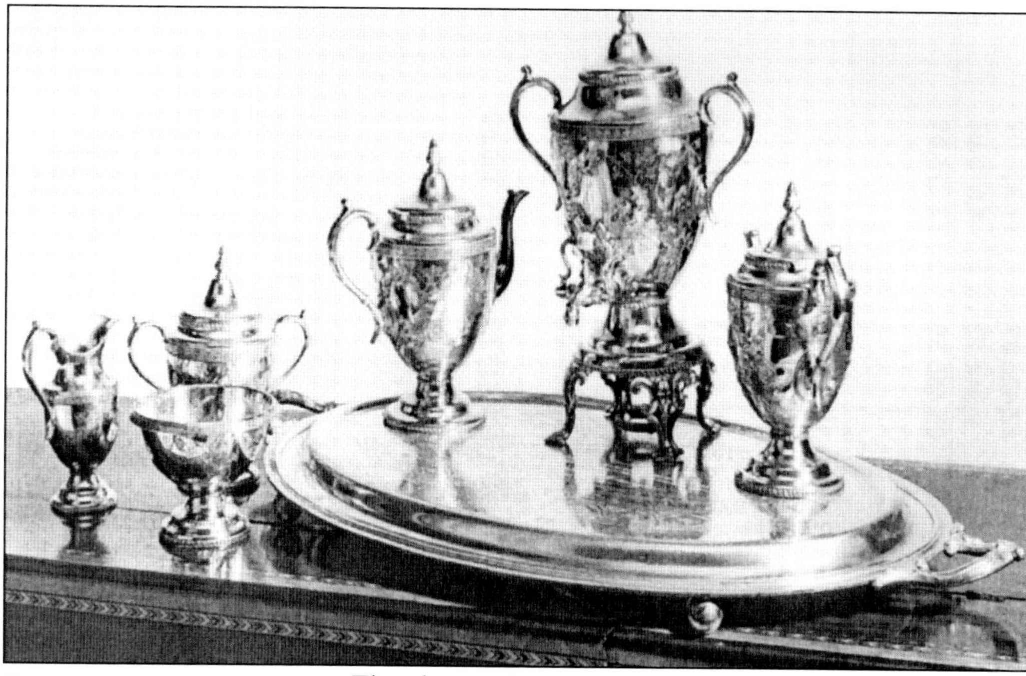

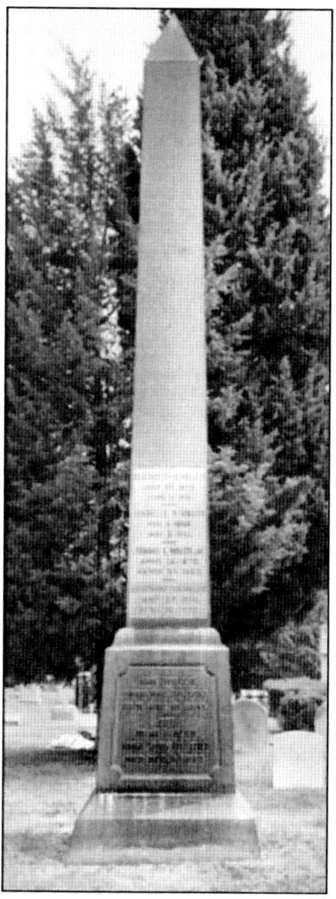

This elegant silver tea set was presented to Thomas Garrett for his pioneering and extremely important work in promoting the abolition of slavery. Note the engraving. The tea set is now on display at the museum of the Historical Society of Delaware. (Courtesy of Robert Seeley.)

This is the monument to John Wales, the attorney who represented Thomas Garrett in his trial in the New Castle Courthouse. Thomas Garrett lost his case and was fined most of his property for helping slaves escape, but he made a speech after the trial that changed some hearts and minds. (Courtesy of Robert Seeley.)

Ellwood Garrett, eldest son of Thomas Garrett, married Catharine K. Wollaston, daughter of Samuel Wollaston (right) and Elizabeth Russell Wollaston, on June 6, 1839, in Wilmington Friends Meeting. She was born August 26, 1813, and died November 6, 1876. Ellwood Garrett and Catharine Wollaston Garrett are buried in the family plot at Wilmington and Brandywine Cemetery. (Courtesy of Historical Society of Delaware.)

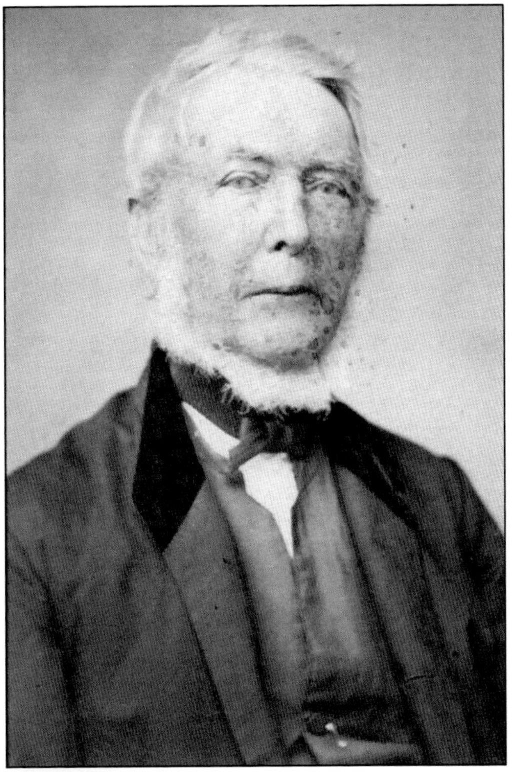

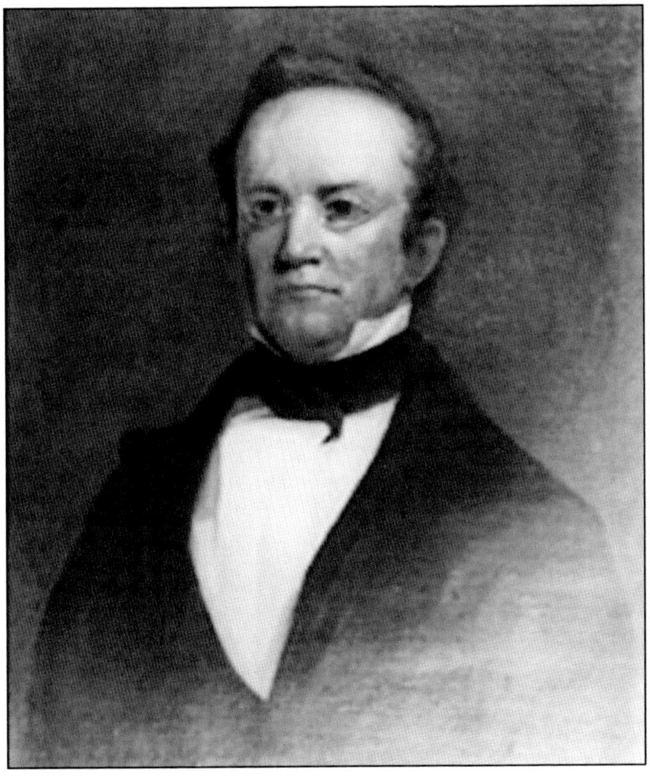

John Walls lived from 1783 to 1863. He was a lawyer and Whig politician from Wilmington, Delaware. He was born in New Haven, Connecticut, and graduated from Yale College in 1801. He represented Thomas Garrett in his trial in New Castle, Delaware. (Courtesy of Historical Society of Delaware.)

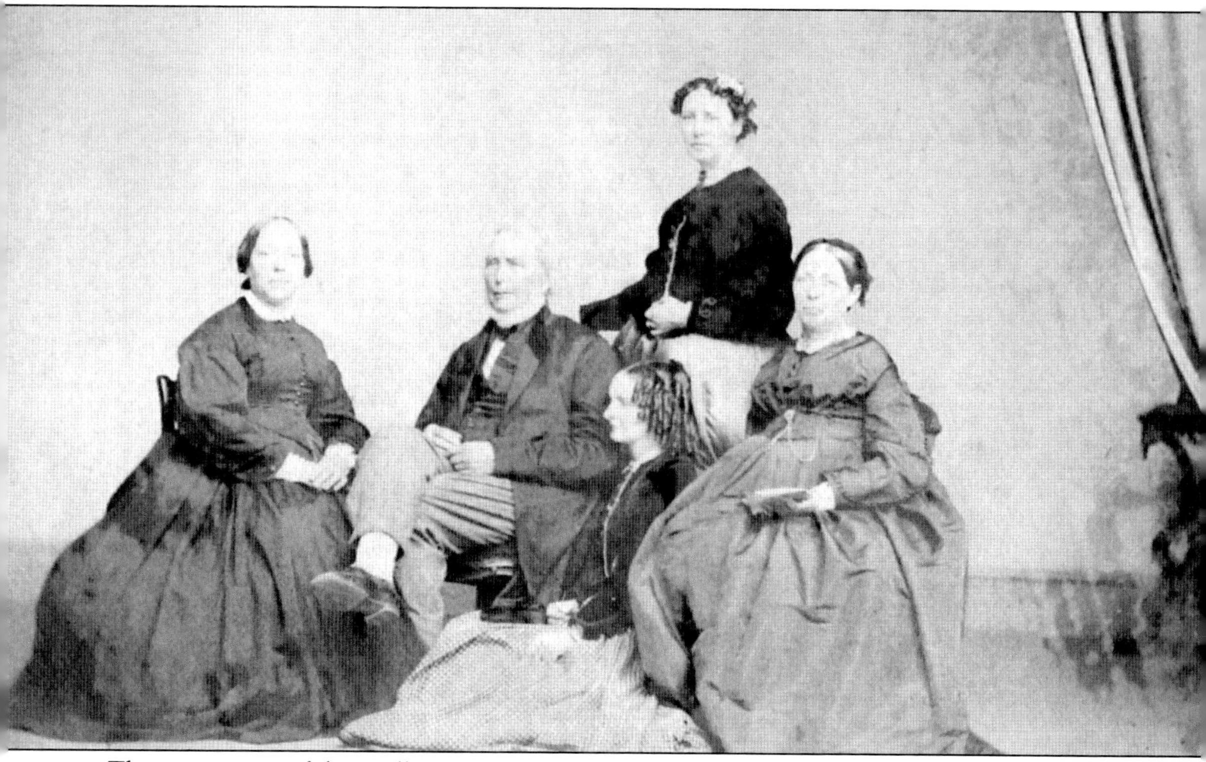

This is a picture of the Wollaston family around the 1860s. The Wollastons were a well-known family belonging to the Wilmington Friends Meeting of the Religious Society of Friends and intermarried with other Quaker families of note, such as the Garretts (of Underground Railroad fame), and the Pennocks and the Puseys, who came to the New World in the time of William Penn. (Courtesy of Historical Society of Delaware.)

Three

Wilmington Friends School on Quaker Hill

George Fox, founder of the Society of Friends (Quakers), believed that there is "that of God" in every person. He therefore urged members to educate all their children, male and female, and those of the neighboring poor. After the Shipleys and other Quaker families moved to Wilmington, they started a school. Of that school, made from the first meetinghouse, historian Benjamin Ferris wrote, "To this useful purpose it has been devoted since 1748, and thousands of children have there received the first rudiments of an English education" (1846.). Originally only 25 feet square, the school across from the meeting steadily grew in size and numbers over the next 189 years.

Through a special fund, the meeting supported local schooling long before public education began in 1827. Over 2,200 "payment vouchers" for the education of poor children were recently discovered, including almost 400 for black children. Teachers such as Emma Worrell, Clarkson Taylor, and William Thomas were not only memorable educators but also leaders of social causes—abolition of slavery, women's rights, and adult literacy, among others.

From 1881–1898, under the leadership of Isaac Johnson, Friends School expanded greatly in faculty, student body, teaching space, and mission. It became a true college preparatory school but also added a kindergarten and teaching school. Under Johnson, Friends School was not only the oldest school in Delaware but also undoubtedly the best, a source of expanding culture and knowledge for the Wilmington community. The literary critic and author Henry Seidel Canby, class of 1895, writes that his school instilled in his generation confidence in "the permanent possibility of good in any man," reflecting fundamental Quaker beliefs.

While the school continued to increase in numbers and offerings, some began advocating its removal from the site of Elizabeth Shipley's vision. Its buildings were old, it lacked sports fields (apart from the informally used Meeting graveyard), and the neighborhood around it was becoming run down. In 1937, on many acres provided by the Bancroft family, among the school's greatest benefactors, Friends School moved to the Wilmington suburb of Alapocas. Its influence on Quaker Hill, however, remains strong.

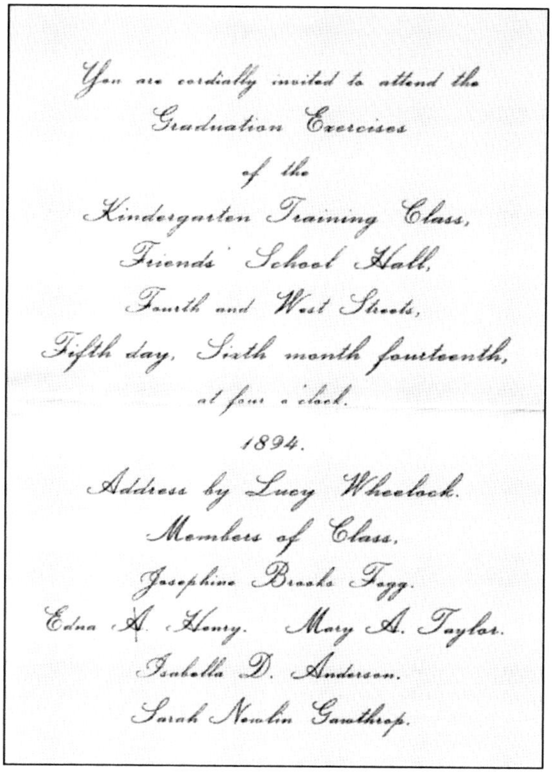

You are cordially invited to attend the
Graduation Exercises
of the
Kindergarten Training Class,
Friends' School Hall,
Fourth and West Streets,
Fifth day, Sixth month fourteenth,
at four o'clock.
1894.
Address by Lucy Wheelock.
Members of Class,
Josephine Brooks Fogg.
Edna A. Henry. Mary A. Taylor.
Isabella D. Anderson.
Sarah Newlin Gawthrop.

This is an invitation to the graduation of the Kindergarten Training Class at Wilmington Friends School on June 5, 1894. The class included Josephine Fogg, Edna Henry, Mary Taylor, Isabelle Anderson, and Sarah Gawthrop. The address was made by Lucy Wheelock, a distinguished educator. (Courtesy of Wilmington Friends School.)

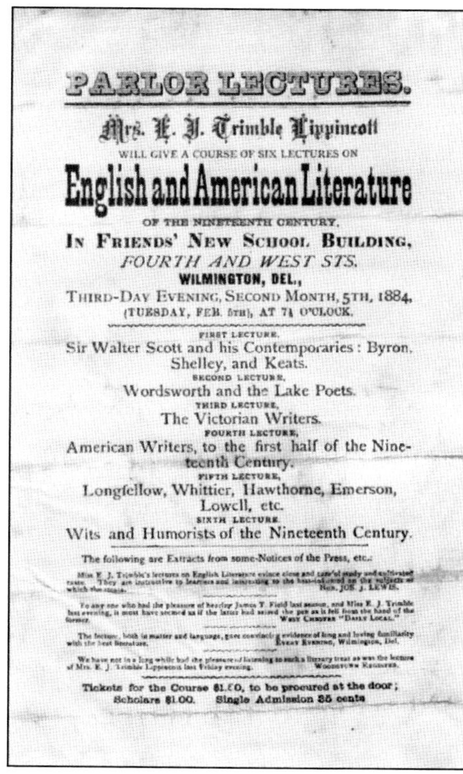

PARLOR LECTURES.
Mrs. E. J. Trimble Lippincott
WILL GIVE A COURSE OF SIX LECTURES ON
English and American Literature
OF THE NINETEENTH CENTURY,
IN FRIENDS' NEW SCHOOL BUILDING,
FOURTH AND WEST STS.
WILMINGTON, DEL.,
THIRD-DAY EVENING, SECOND MONTH, 5TH, 1884,
(TUESDAY, FEB. 5TH), AT 7½ O'CLOCK.

FIRST LECTURE.
Sir Walter Scott and his Contemporaries: Byron, Shelley, and Keats.
SECOND LECTURE.
Wordsworth and the Lake Poets.
THIRD LECTURE.
The Victorian Writers.
FOURTH LECTURE.
American Writers, to the first half of the Nineteenth Century.
FIFTH LECTURE.
Longfellow, Whittier, Hawthorne, Emerson, Lowell, etc.
SIXTH LECTURE.
Wits and Humorists of the Nineteenth Century.

The following are Extracts from some Notices of the Press, etc.:

Miss E. J. Trimble's lectures on English Literature evince close and careful study and cultivated taste. They are instructive to learners and interesting to the [illegible] on the subjects of which [illegible]. Hon. JOS. J. LEWIS.

To any one who had the pleasure of hearing James T. Field last season, and Miss E. J. Trimble last evening, it must have seemed as if the latter had seized the pen as it fell from the hand of the former. WEST CHESTER "DAILY LOCAL."

The lecture, both in matter and language, gave convincing evidence of long and loving familiarity with the best literature. EVERY EVENING, Wilmington, Del.

We have not in a long while had the pleasure of listening to such a literary treat as was the lecture of Mrs. E. J. Trimble Lippincott last Friday evening. WOODSTOWN REGISTER.

Tickets for the Course $1.50, to be procured at the door; Scholars $1.00. Single Admission 35 cents

This is an advertisement for some parlor lectures offered by Wilmington Friends School on English and American literature just before the turn of the 20th century. Wilmington Friends School was instrumental in bringing in an amount of high culture to the Wilmington community. (Courtesy of Wilmington Friends School.)

This is a letter from Wilmington Friends School principal Frederick Eden Bach to the School Committee in June of 1880. He states that he feels he has failed to win over the boys as a good teacher should but that there is an improvement in their conduct. (Courtesy of Wilmington Friends School.)

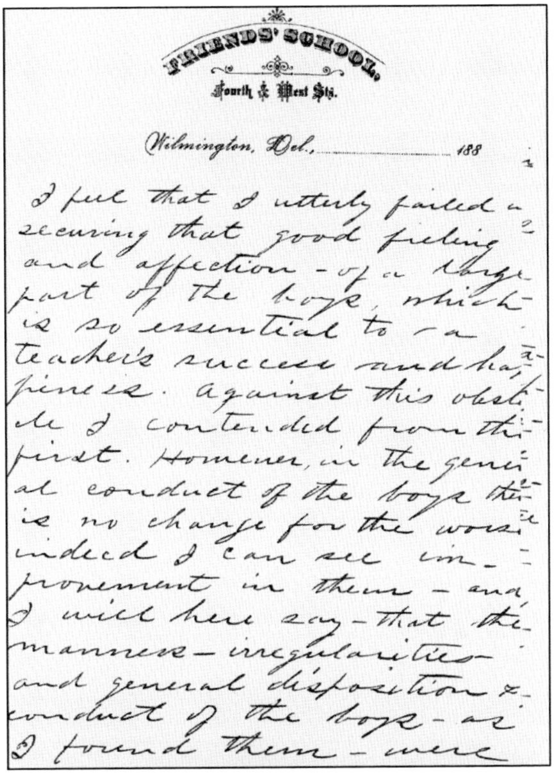

FRIENDS' SCHOOL,
Fourth & West Sts.
Wilmington, Del., 188

I feel that I utterly failed in
securing that good feeling
and affection—of a large
part of the boys, which
is so essential to a
teacher's success and hap-
piness. Against this obsta-
cle I contended from the
first. However, in the gener-
al conduct of the boys there
is no change for the worse
indeed I can see im-
provement in them—and
I will here say—that the
manners—irregularities—
and general disposition &
conduct of the boys—as
I found them—were

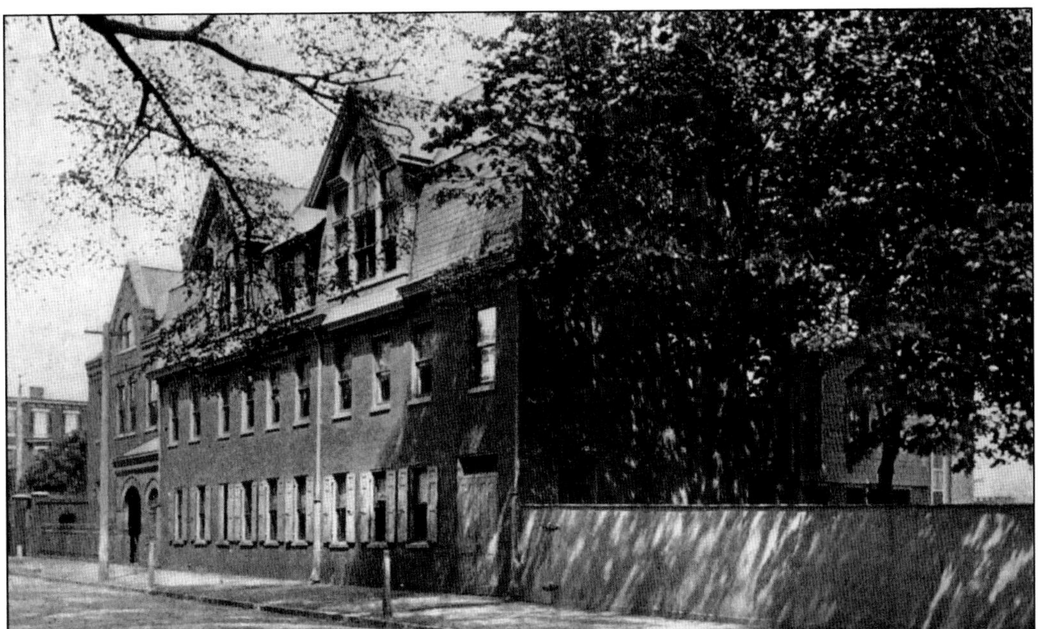

This is a picture of the Wilmington Friends School taken in 1897. Several additions were later made to the building. These additions include the "new" gymnasium of 1907 and the final addition of 1913. The school stood across West Street from the venerable Wilmington Friends Meetinghouse. (Courtesy of Wilmington Friends School.)

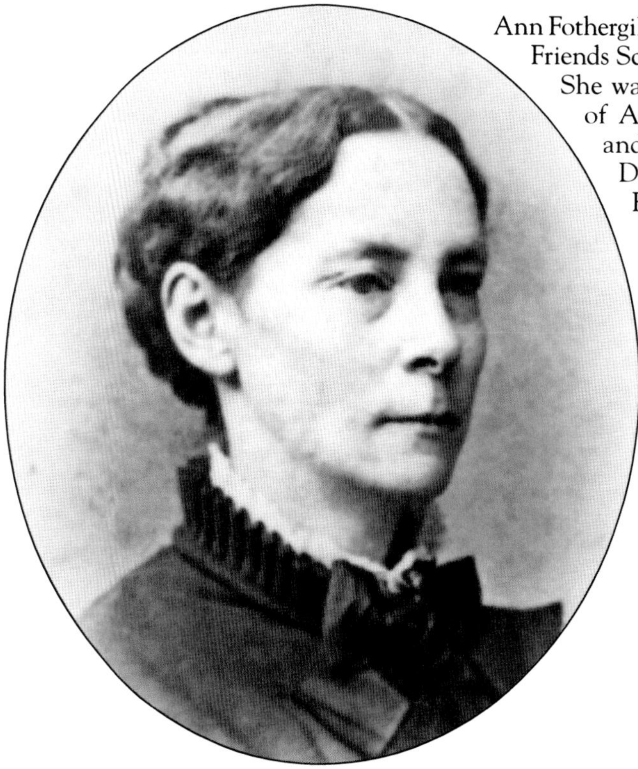

Ann Fothergill was the principal of the Wilmington Friends School girls' school from 1858 to 1882. She was born in 1830, one of 11 children of Alexander Fothergill, in England, and the family moved to Wilmington, Delaware. (Courtesy of Wilmington Friends School.)

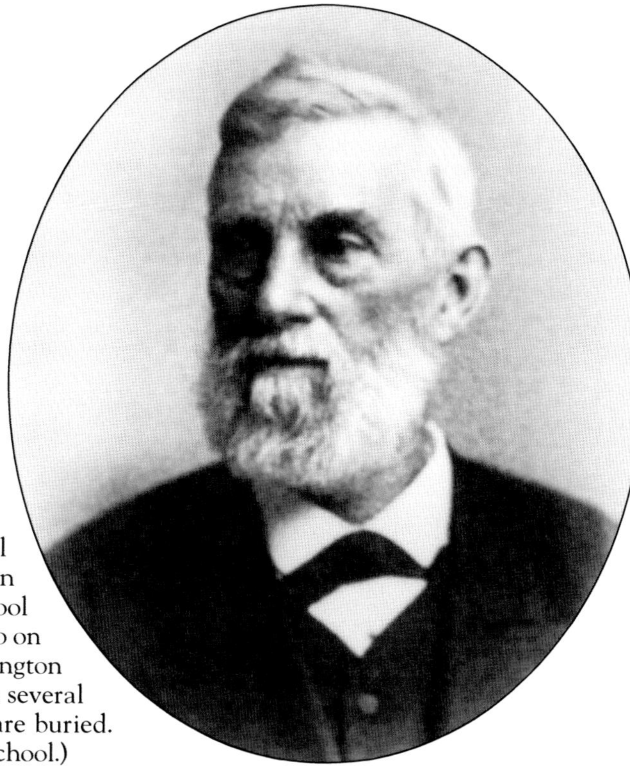

Albert W. Smith was the principal of the boys' school at Wilmington Friends School. He was later a School Committee member, and he was also on the board of directors of the Wilmington and Brandywine Cemetery, where several prominent Wilmington Quakers are buried. (Courtesy of Wilmington Friends School.)

FRIENDS' SCHOOL.

This school is pleasantly situated on West Street between Fourth and Fifth Streets. The provisions for light, heat, and ventilation are excellent. The furniture, which is modern, was selected with special reference to comfort and convenience. A large playground is provided for the boys, and a separate one for the girls.

INSTRUCTION.

The pupils are divided into Four (4) Grades, with such subdivisions as necessity dictates.

The boys and girls of the advanced grades sit and study in separate rooms, but recite together.

Pupils ignorant of the alphabet cannot be admitted.

The Primary pupils are thoroughly drilled in the elements of Reading, Spelling, Writing, and Arithmetic. Object Lessons, Oral Geography, Elements of Drawing, and talks on Natural History constitute a part of their instruction.

Believing that culture and true utility are ever combined, it is aimed to create in the pupil a genuine love for study as well as the power of useful application.

COURSE OF STUDY.

Reading,	Written Arithmetic,	Botany,
Etymology,	Mental "	Chemistry,
Orthography,	Algebra,	Nat. Philosophy,
English Grammar,	Geometry,	Physiology,
Composition,	Book-keeping,	Phys. Geography,
Eng. Literature,	Drawing,	Political "
History,	Penmanship,	Political Science,
Latin,	German,	French.

As aids to instruction, the blackboard surface is ample; and a necessary supply of maps, charts, globes, geometrical forms, and reference books are provided. The school contains a considerable collection of minerals, and also apparatus for scientific illustrations.

RULES AND REQUESTS.

Pupils known to have contracted vicious habits will not be received; those who develop such habits after admission, and incorrigibly adhere to them, cannot be retained.

It is again urged that early entrance, and regularity and punctuality of attendance, are absolutely necessary for the progress of the pupils.

ADVANTAGES.

All text books, paper, pens, pencils, slates, ink, and, in fact, all necessary materials for school work, are supplied by the school.

The school is under the kindly supervision of the Committee of the Monthly Meeting.

There are absolutely no extras.

The school affords an exclusiveness, an attention to the individual, and a freedom from the evils of a rigid classification, not found in Normal or Public schools.

TIME.

Fall term begins on 2nd day, 9th month 8th, 1879. (Vacation from evening of 12th month 24th, 1879, until the morning of 1st month 2nd, 1880.)

Fall term ends on 6th day, 1st month 30th, 1880.

Spring term begins on 2nd day, 2nd month 2nd, 1880.

Spring term ends on 6th day, 6th month 18th, 1880.

The school year thus affords two (2) terms of twenty (20) weeks each.

TERMS,

Per session of twenty weeks.

First Grade,	$25.00
Second Grade,	20.00
Third Grade,	15.00
Fourth Grade,	10.00

This is an annual circular of 1879 that spelled out the Friends School program, rules, and so on. Note the subjects: reading, etymology, orthography, English grammar, composition, English literature, history, Latin, written arithmetic, mental arithmetic, algebra, geometry, bookkeeping, drawing, penmanship, German, botany, chemistry, natural philosophy, physiology, physical geography, political geography, political science, French. Note the cost—$10. (Courtesy of Wilmington Friends School.)

This is a photograph of the meetinghouse of the Wilmington Monthly Meeting of Friends, which was taken from the Fifth Street side of the building. Children from the Wilmington Friends School frequently played ball games and other games with large groups of schoolchildren on this site. (Photograph by James Bierbaum.)

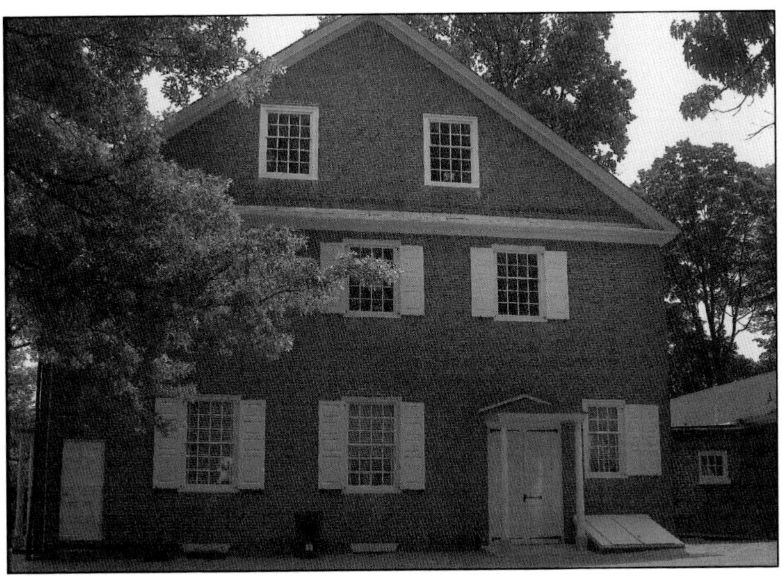

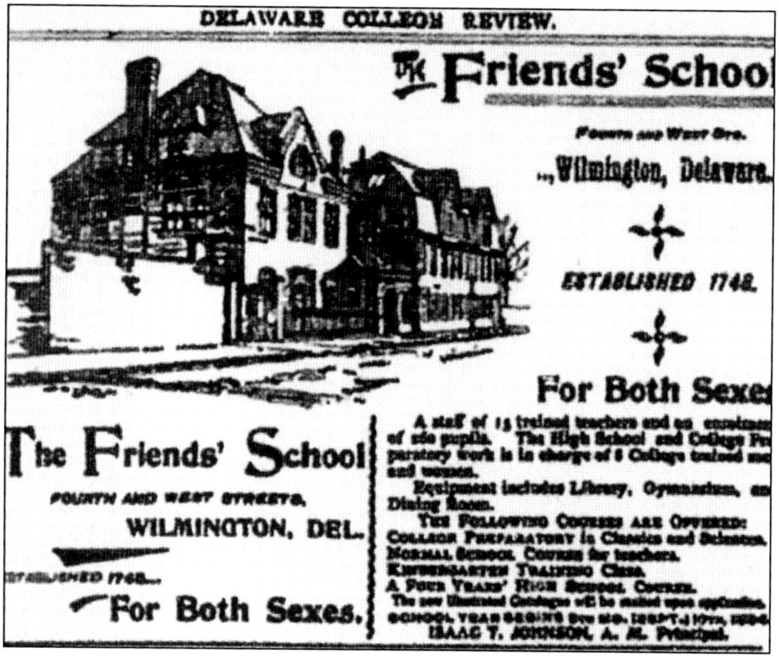

This is an advertisement for Wilmington Friends School that appeared in the Delaware College Review in 1894. It advertises offerings of college preparatory classes, normal school training for teachers, and kindergarten teacher training. It states that the school was founded in 1748 and offers four years of high school for both sexes. (Courtesy of Wilmington Friends School.)

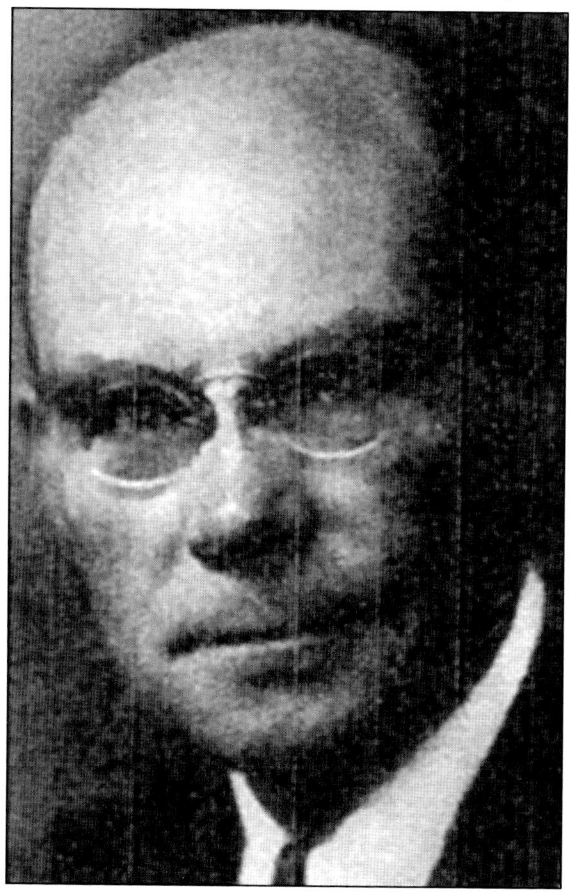

Charles Bush enjoyed a distinguished career as a principal of Wilmington Friends School. He was also active in the Young Men's Christian Association, and after retirement from Wilmington Friends School, he became the director of admissions at the University of Delaware. (Courtesy of Wilmington Friends School.)

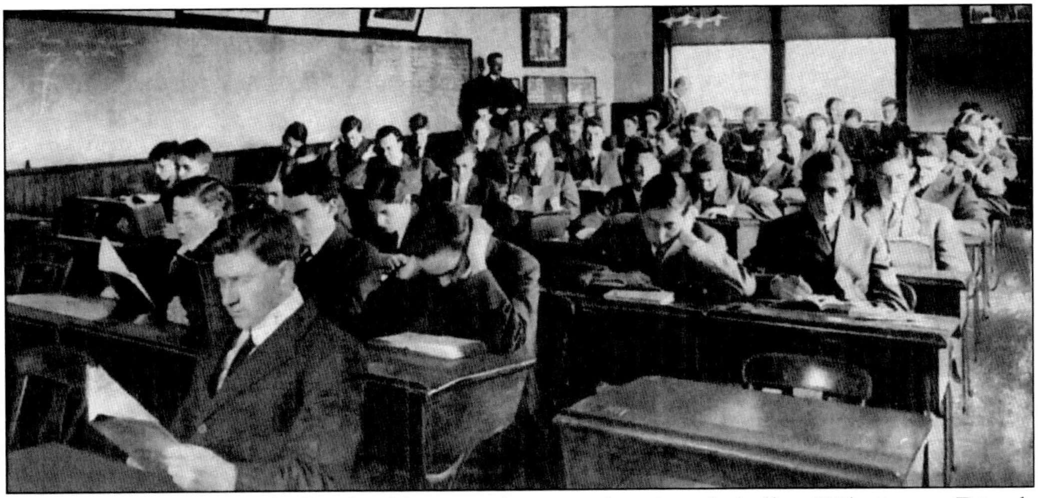

This is a picture of the high school boys in the upper boys' study hall at Wilmington Friends School in 1912. You will note that the boys are studying carefully under the watchful eyes of the boys' then high school principal, Floyd Johnson, in the classroom. (Courtesy of Wilmington Friends School.)

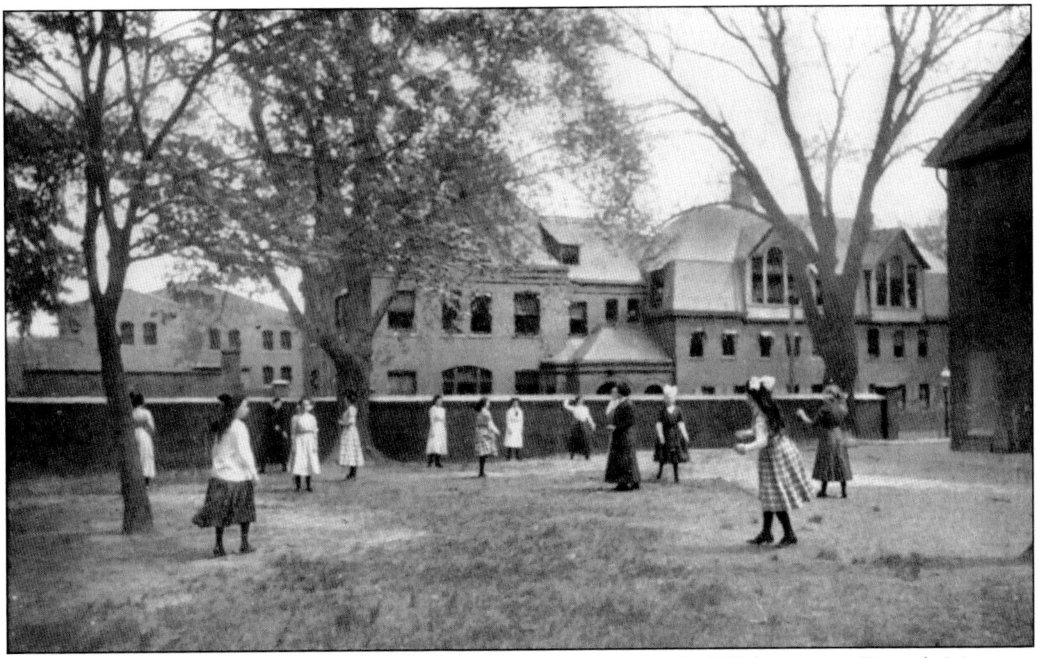

This is a picture of several girls playing games in the graveyard of Wilmington Friends Meeting across from Wilmington Friends School in 1910. True to Quaker principles of simplicity and equality, the graves are low to the ground and offer no impediment to the games. (Courtesy of Wilmington Friends School.)

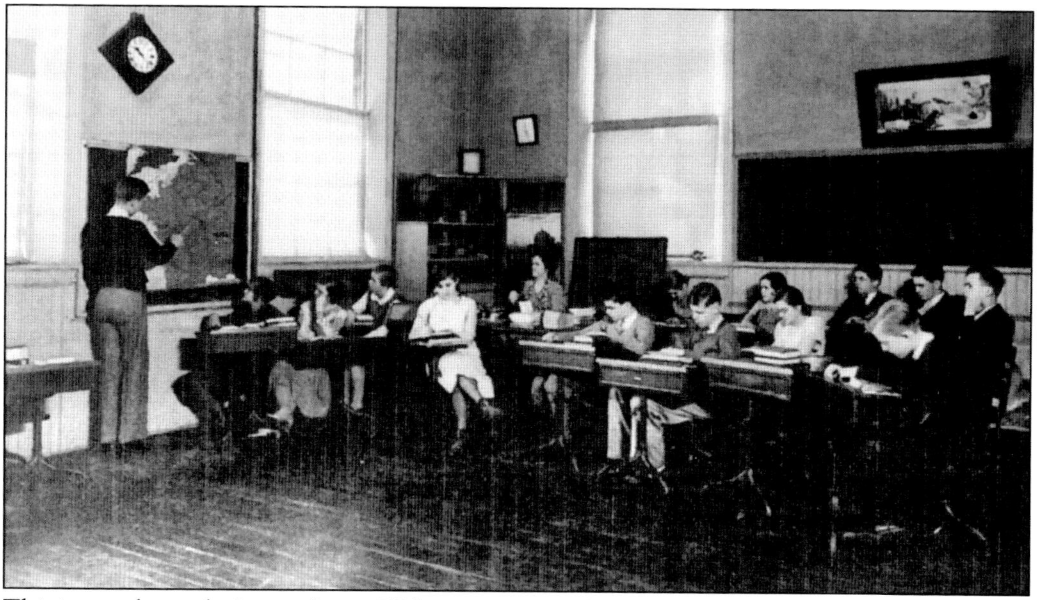

This image shows the Latin class at Wilmington Friends School. Student J. Albert Marshall Jr. is standing and pointing out the three parts of Gaul on the map, while teacher Frances Baird, who graduated from Wilmington Friends School in 1913, looks on (fifth from the left). (Courtesy of Wilmington Friends School.)

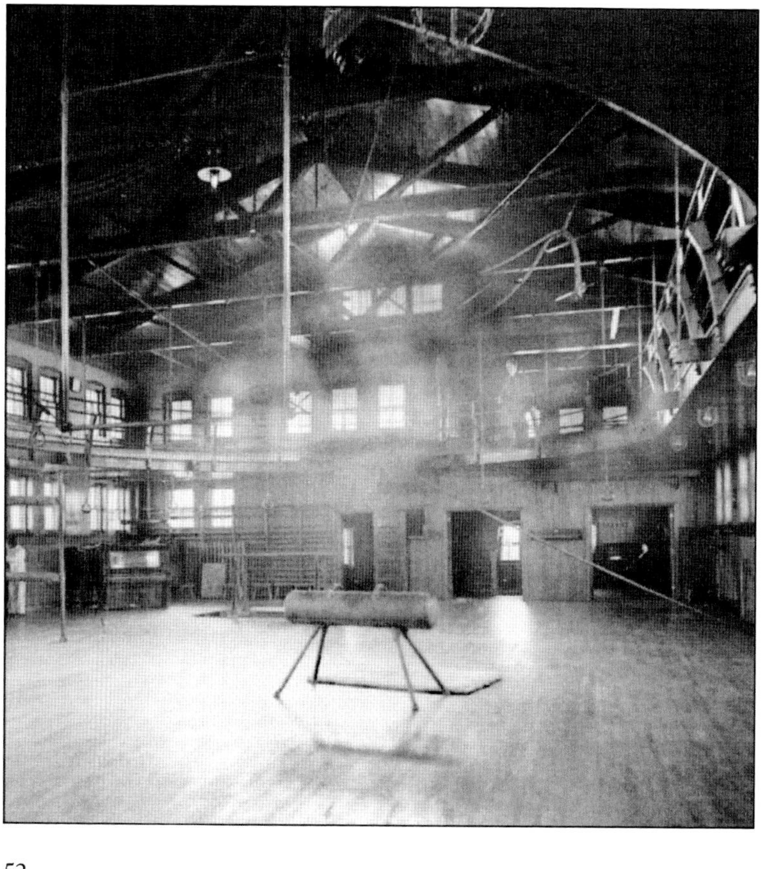

This is the interior of the "new" gymnasium at Wilmington Friends School. The gymnasium was one of the last additions to the building in Quaker Hill and was built in 1905. Note the elevated track running around the inside of the gymnasium. (Courtesy of Wilmington Friends School.)

Henry Dettwyler taught at Wilmington Friends School until 1952. Among other things, he taught Latin and higher level mathematics, including algebra and geometry. His main teaching career consisted of teaching in the upper school of Wilmington Friends School. (Courtesy of Wilmington Friends School.)

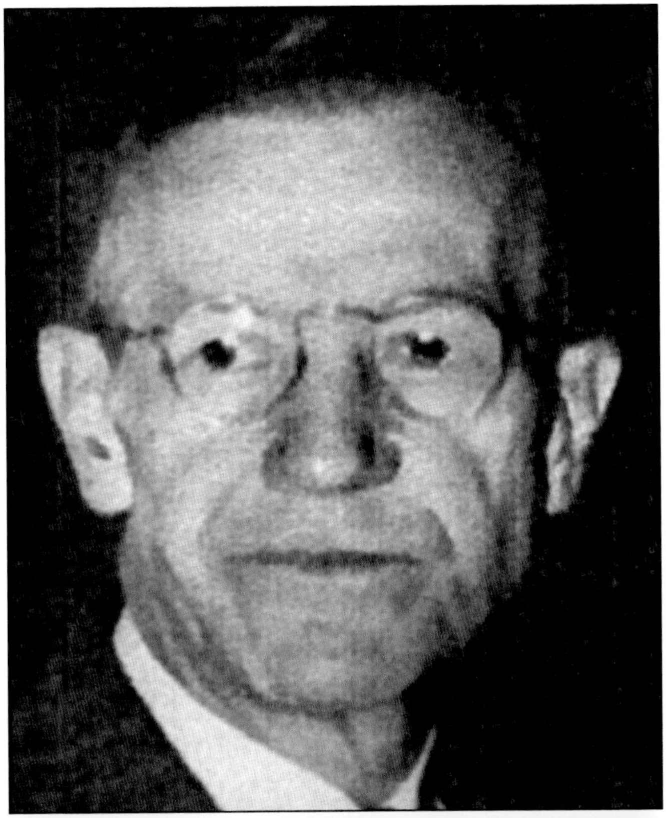

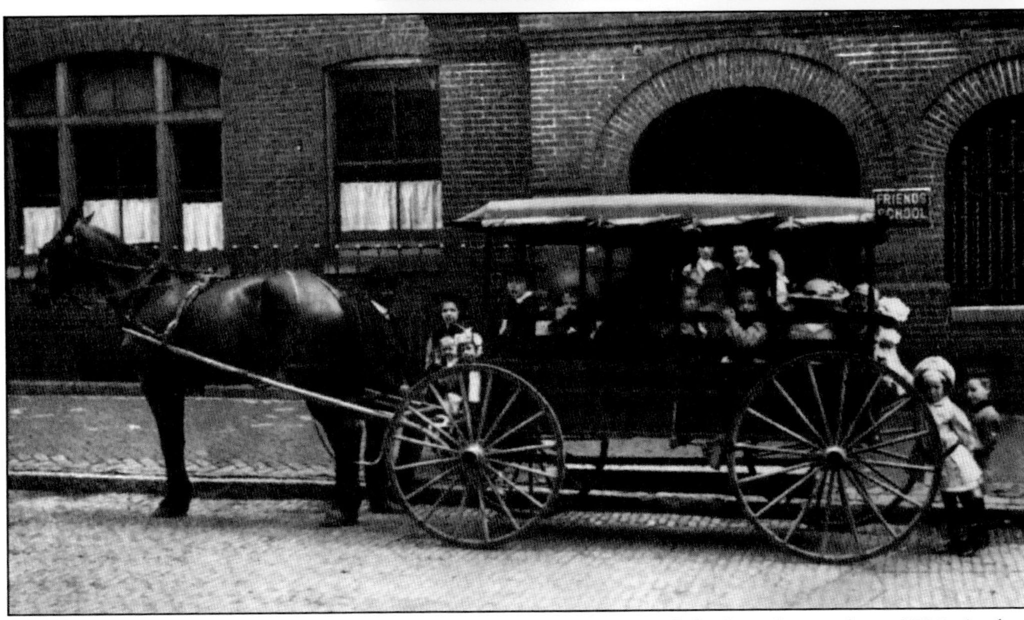

This is a picture of the Wilmington Friends School students and the bus they rode in 1908. Arthur Harrison (far left) drove the first wagon of primary students to Wilmington Friends School, and later in 1916 he drove the students in a motor-driven vehicle. (Courtesy of Wilmington Friends School.)

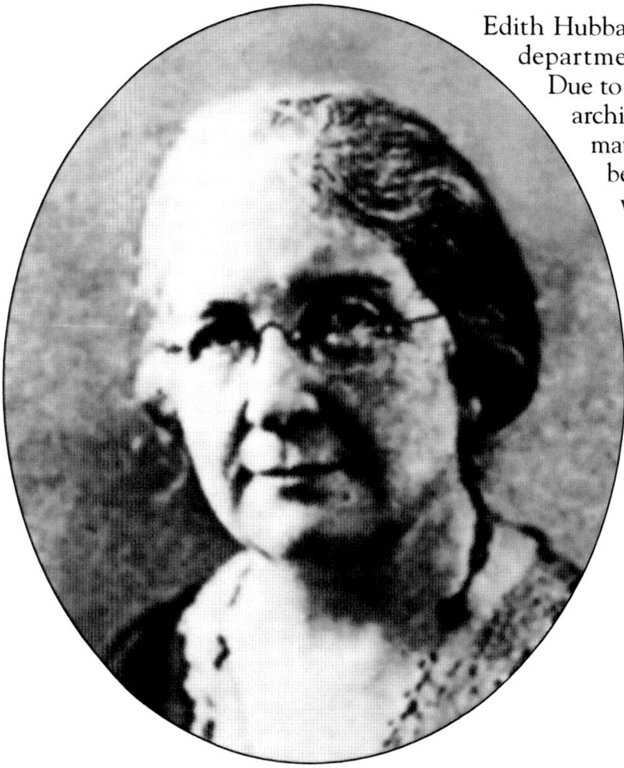

Edith Hubbard was the head of the mathematics department at Wilmington Friends School. Due to her trips abroad, she had a passion for architecture and in turn gave the teaching of mathematics an international and practical bend at Wilmington Friends School. She was remembered for quiet wisdom and concern for human dignity. (Courtesy of Wilmington Friends School.)

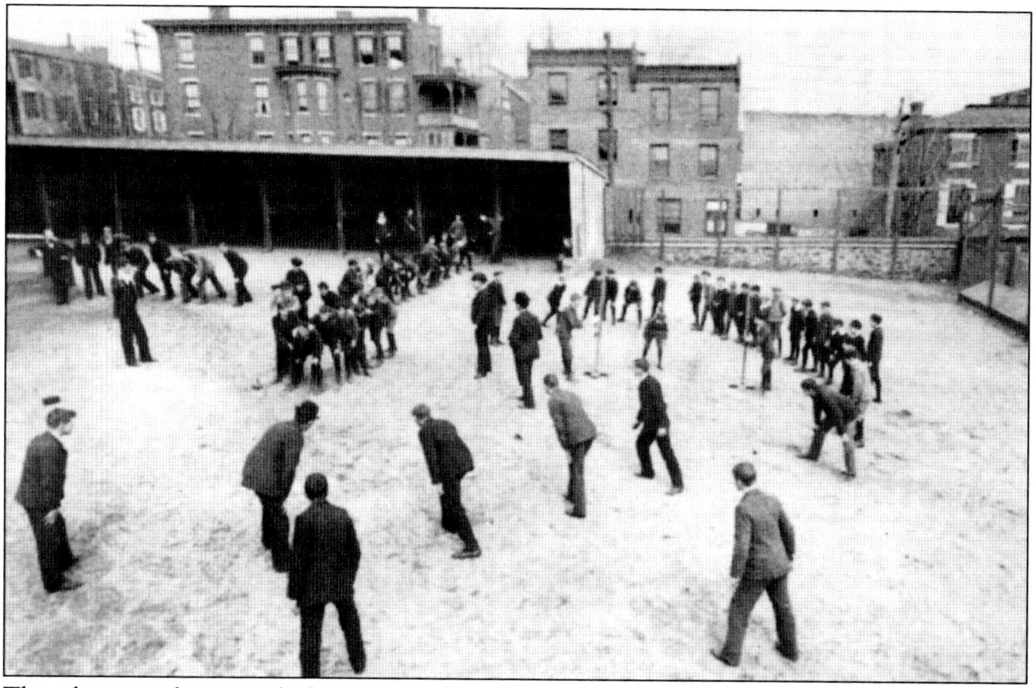

These boys are playing in the boys' yard at Wilmington Friends School in 1905. Note that the boys are wearing much more formal clothes than would be normal for boys playing today. Doubtless, they were enjoined to keep their clothes clean, too. (Courtesy of Wilmington Friends School.)

T. Clarkson Taylor was reputed to be a popular boys' schoolteacher at Wilmington Friends School from 1862 to 1857. Some educators believed that popular teachers created good morale in the classroom. (Courtesy of Wilmington Friends School.)

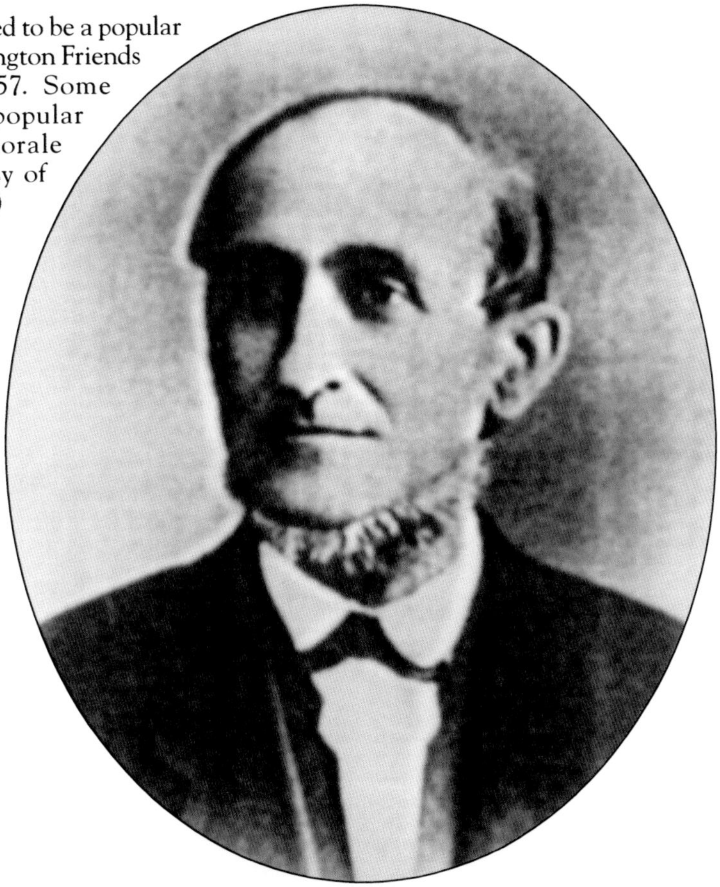

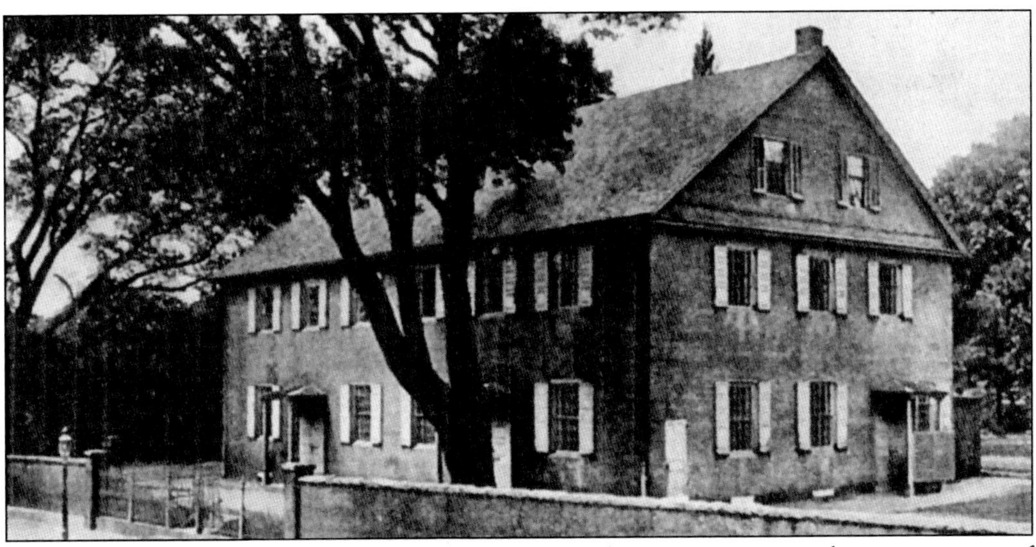

This is a picture of the Wilmington Friends Meetinghouse as it appeared to generations of Wilmington Friends School students who studied at Wilmington Friends School across the street. All the students and faculty would cross the street to the meetinghouse for weekly worship. (Courtesy of Wilmington Friends School.)

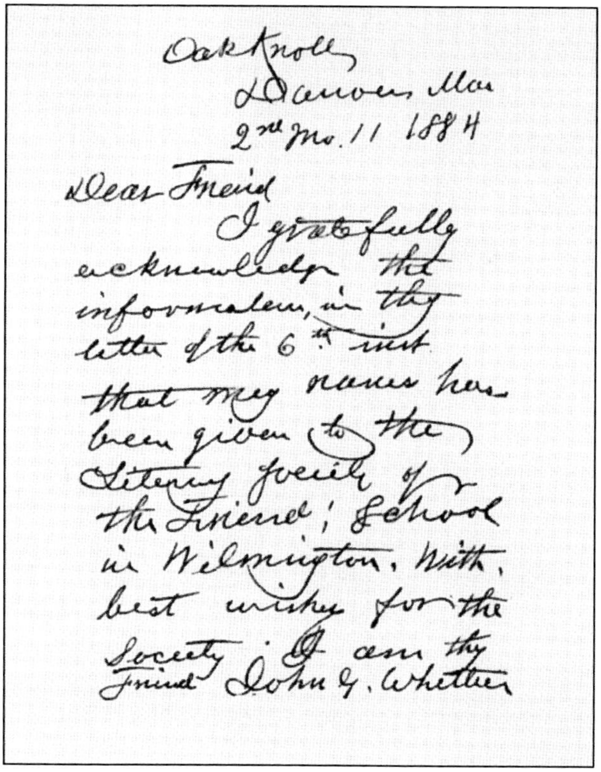

Oak Knoll
Danvers Mass
2nd Mo. 11 1884

Dear Friend
I gratefully acknowledge the information in thy letter of the 6th inst that my name has been given to the Literary Society of the Friends' School in Wilmington. With best wishes for the Society I am thy friend John G. Whittier

This is a picture of a letter from the Quaker poet John Greenleaf Whittier to Wilmington Friends School. He states: "I gratefully acknowledge the information in thy letter of the sixth month instant that my name has been given to the literary journal of the Friends School in Wilmington. With best wishes for the Society, I am thy Friend, John G. Whittier." (Courtesy of Wilmington Friends School.)

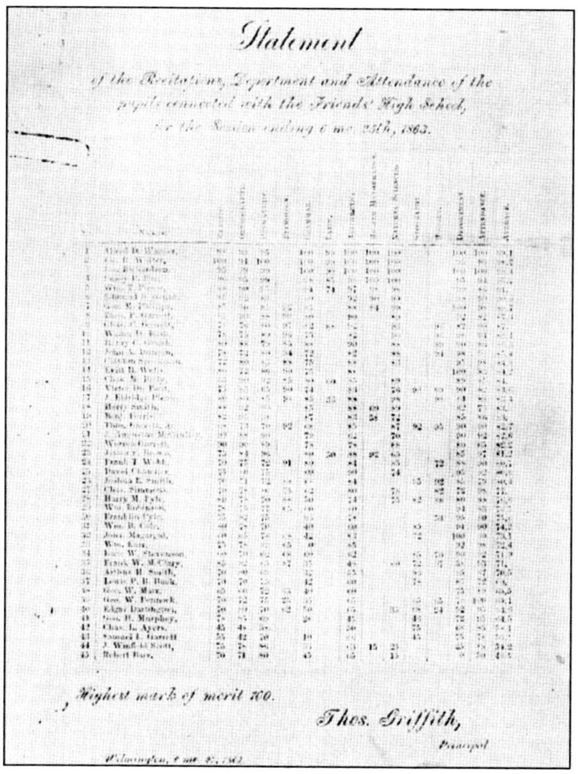

Statement

of the Recitations, Deportment and Attendance of the pupils connected with the Friends' High School, for the Session ending 6 mo. 25th, 1863.

Highest mark of merit 100.

Thos. Griffith,
Principal

This is a picture of the final grades of high school boys at Wilmington Friends School in 1863. The subjects included were reading, orthography, penmanship, etymology, grammar, Latin, arithmetic, higher mathematics, natural sciences, geography, history, and deportment. The grades vary widely yet were available to the public. (Courtesy of Wilmington Friends School.)

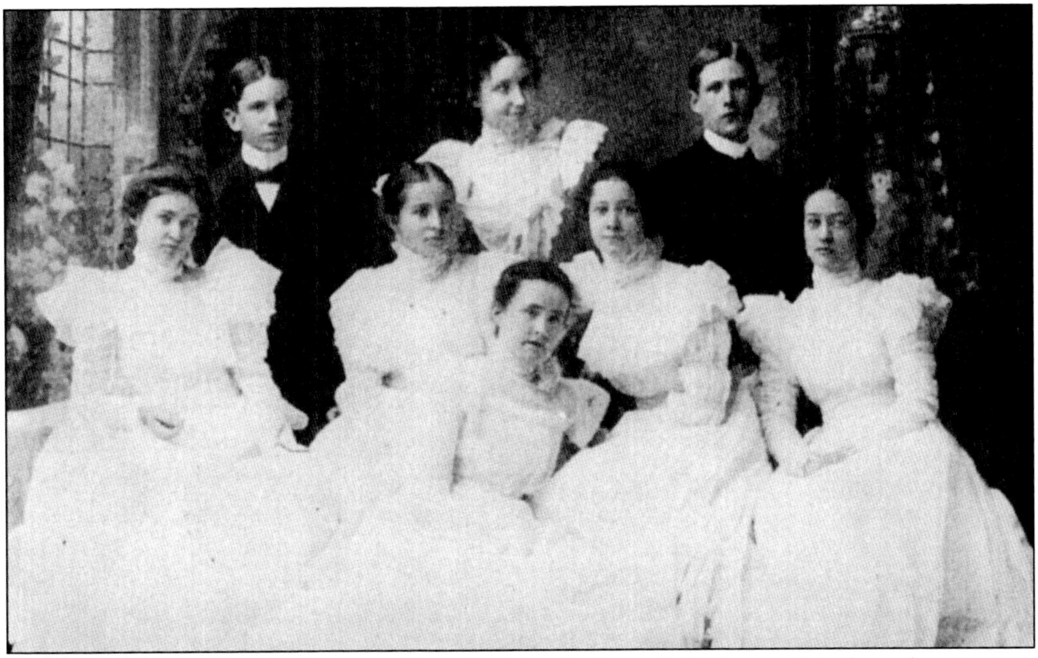

This image shows the Wilmington Friends School class of 1898, posed in formal attire in a formal setting. The year of 1898 marked the 150th anniversary of the school. Note the size of the graduating class of 1898—just two young men and six young women. (Courtesy of Wilmington Friends School.)

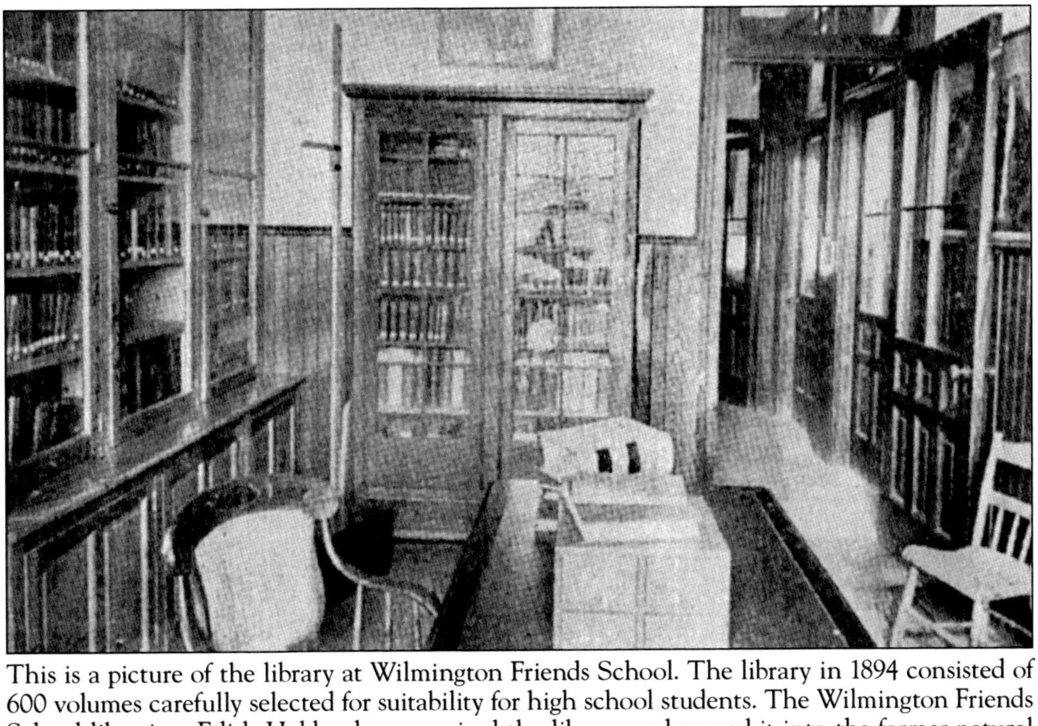

This is a picture of the library at Wilmington Friends School. The library in 1894 consisted of 600 volumes carefully selected for suitability for high school students. The Wilmington Friends School librarian, Edith Hubbard, reorganized the library and moved it into the former natural history museum. (Courtesy of Wilmington Friends School.)

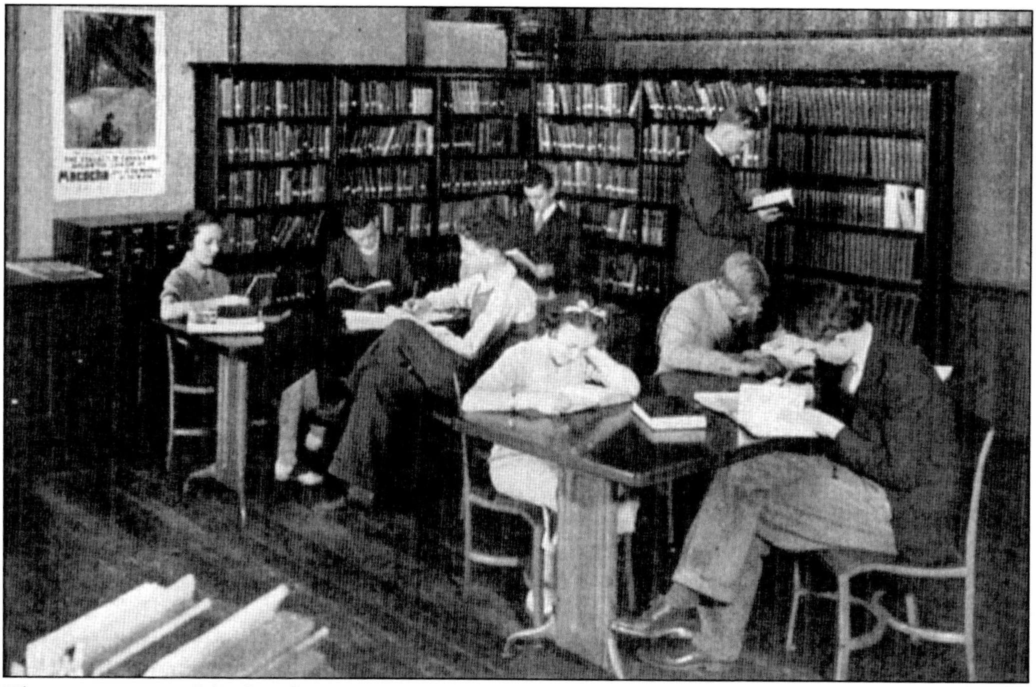

This is a picture of the lunchroom at Wilmington Friends School in the early 1900s, when it was located on the third floor. Pupils were encouraged to do as follows: "Pupils may or may not bring their lunch or any portion of their lunch." (Courtesy of Wilmington Friends School.)

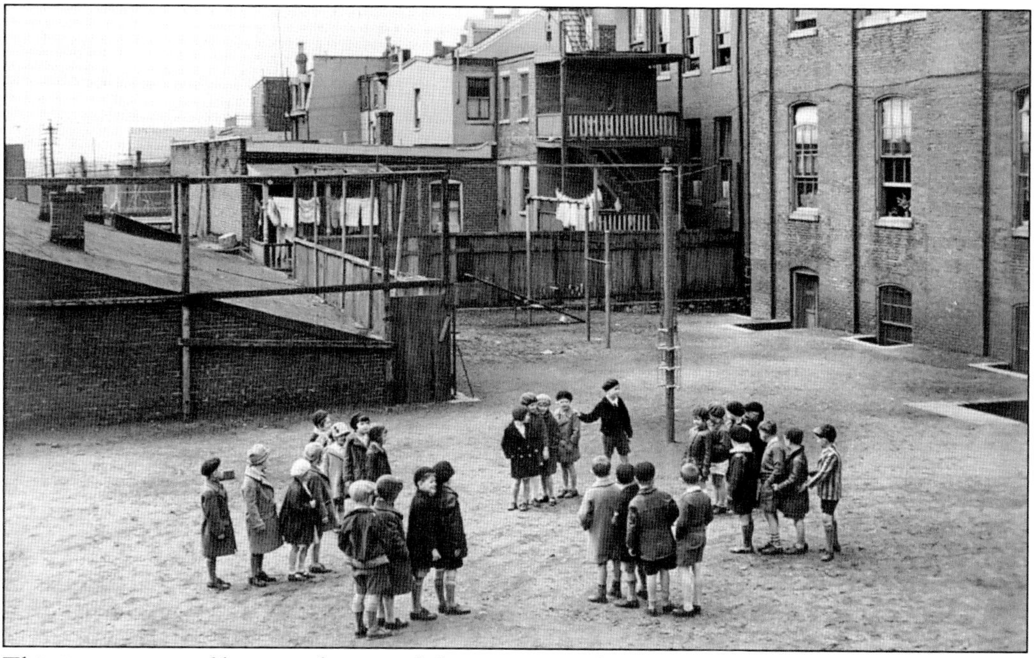

This is a picture of boys in the act of choosing up sides in the primary playground in 1932. The Wilmington Friends School was surrounded by poverty in the city in the depths of the Depression. In 1937, the school moved into the suburbs of Wilmington. (Courtesy of Wilmington Friends School.)

This is a picture of two members of the Wilmington Friends School. Alumna Mary Kent Wyatt was a member of the class of 1900, attending her 65th high school reunion. Her younger friend, Alumnus Edmund G. Robinson, was a member of the class of 1901. (Courtesy of Wilmington Friends School.)

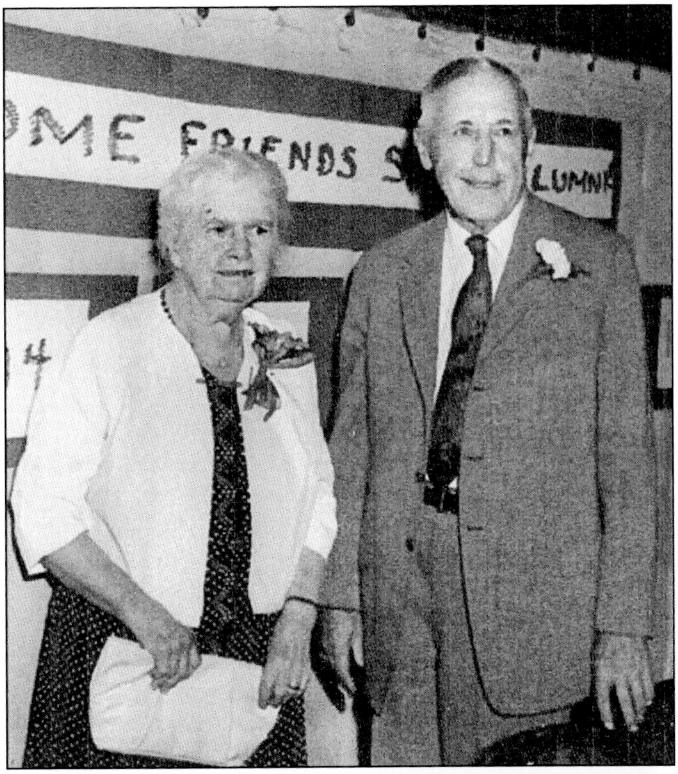

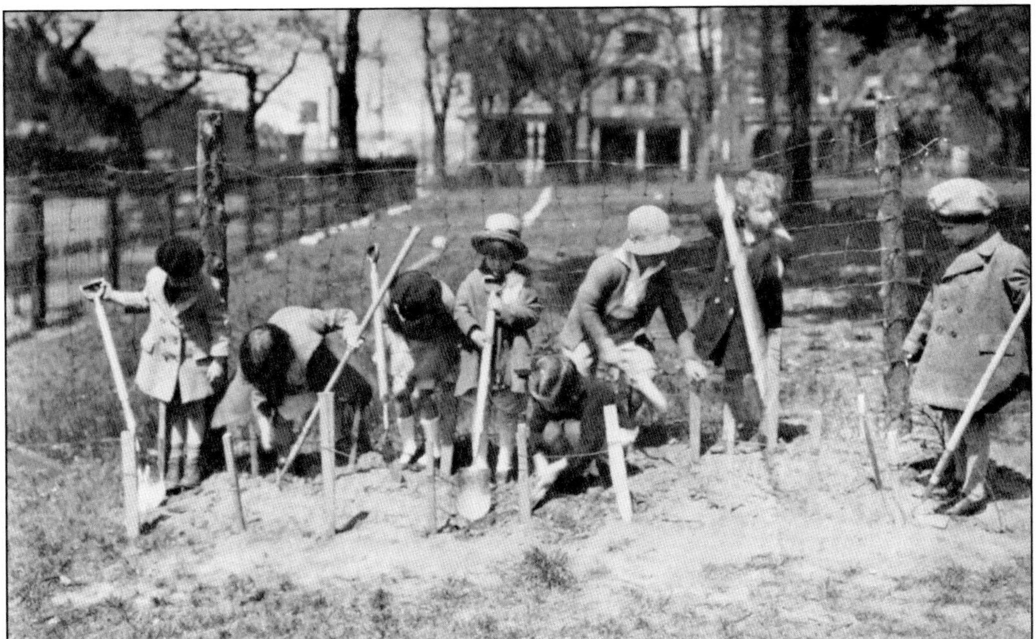

These Wilmington Friends School children are gardening near the graveyard of Wilmington Friends Meeting. Young children of the First Day School (Sunday school) continue to garden near the graveyard today and have recently won prizes in local horticulture competitions. (Courtesy of Wilmington Friends School.)

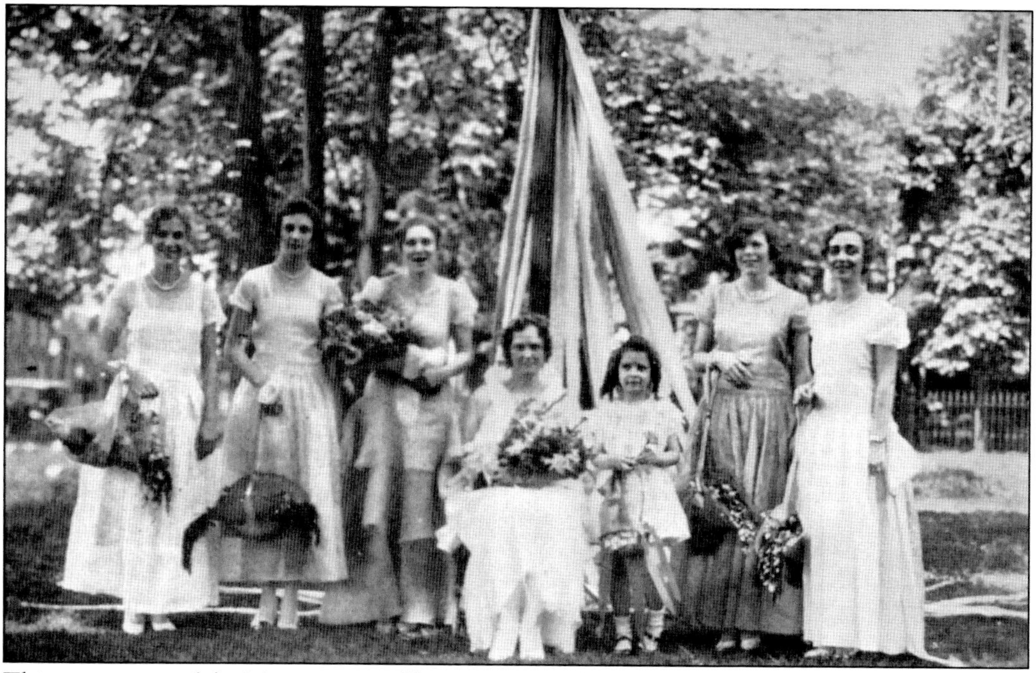

This is a picture of the May queen and her court at Wilmington Friends School. The celebration of May Day and dancing around the maypole (pictured) came from the British Isles. The May Day institution persists in nearby colleges with Quaker roots such as Bryn Mawr College. (Courtesy of Wilmington Friends School.)

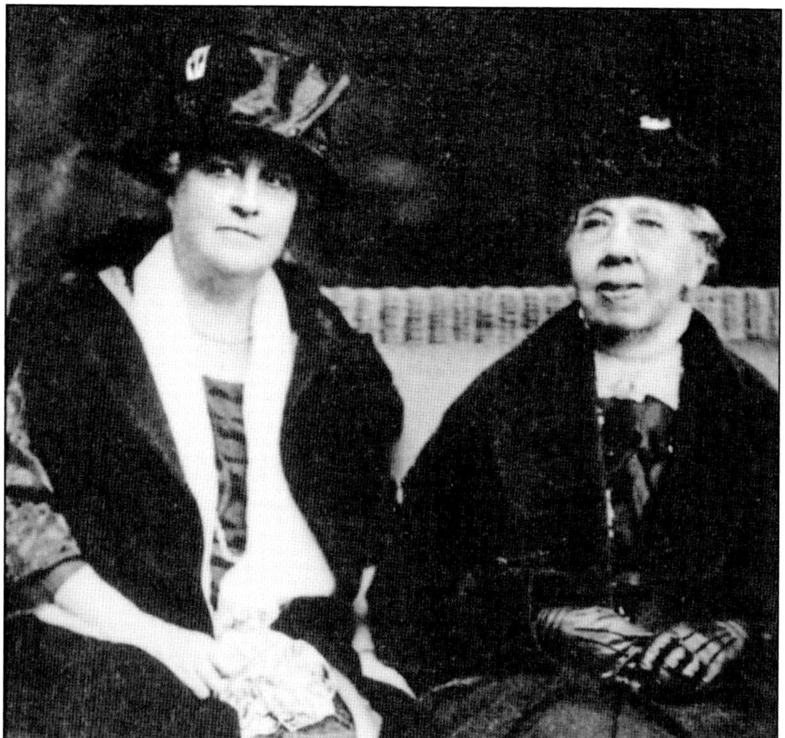

This is a picture of Emma Worrell, who was a principal of Wilmington Friends School. She spoke at the state constitutional convention in 1896 in favor of women's suffrage and helped lead the antislavery movement together with other Wilmington Quakers like Thomas Garrett. (Courtesy of Wilmington Friends School.)

Herschel Norris was the principal of Wilmington Friends School from 1899 to 1923. He came with a graduate degree from Princeton University and, during his tenure, oversaw the expansion of Wilmington Friends School. A new gymnasium was built in 1907 and a new primary building was added in 1913. (Courtesy of Wilmington Friends School.)

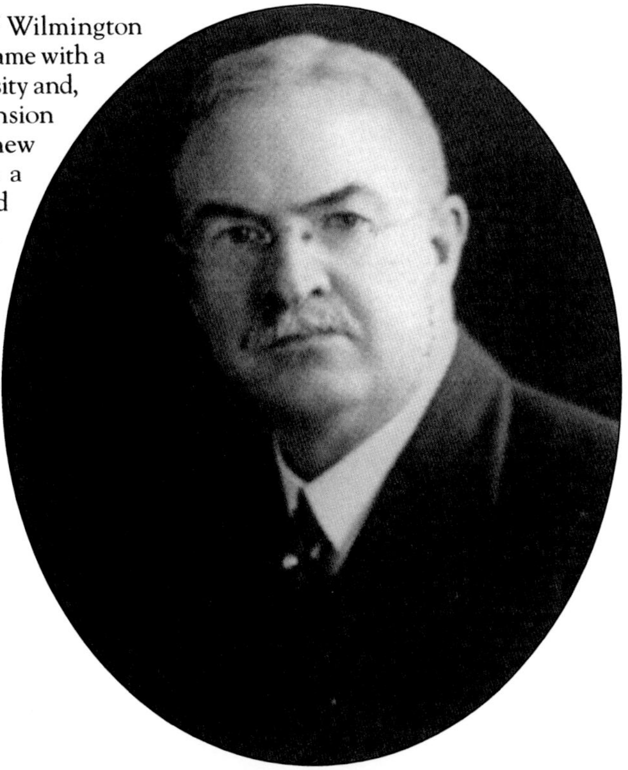

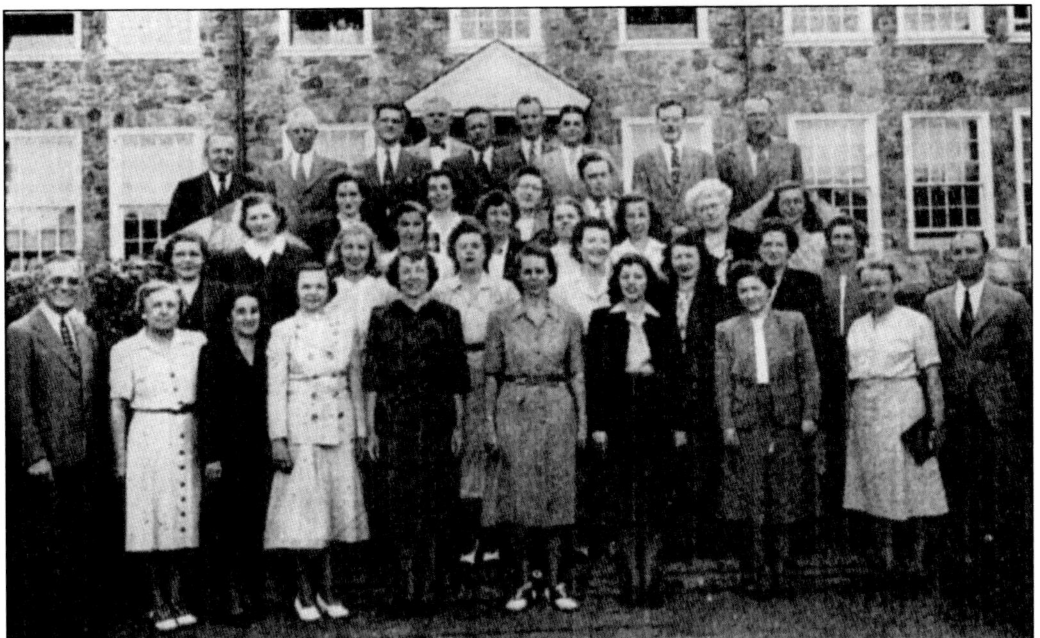

This is a picture of the staff of Wilmington Friends School standing before the new building in 1947 or 1948. The staff included 32 teachers as well as officers and secretaries. Several of these also worked in the old building that stood on Quaker Hill in Wilmington, Delaware. (Courtesy of Wilmington Friends School.)

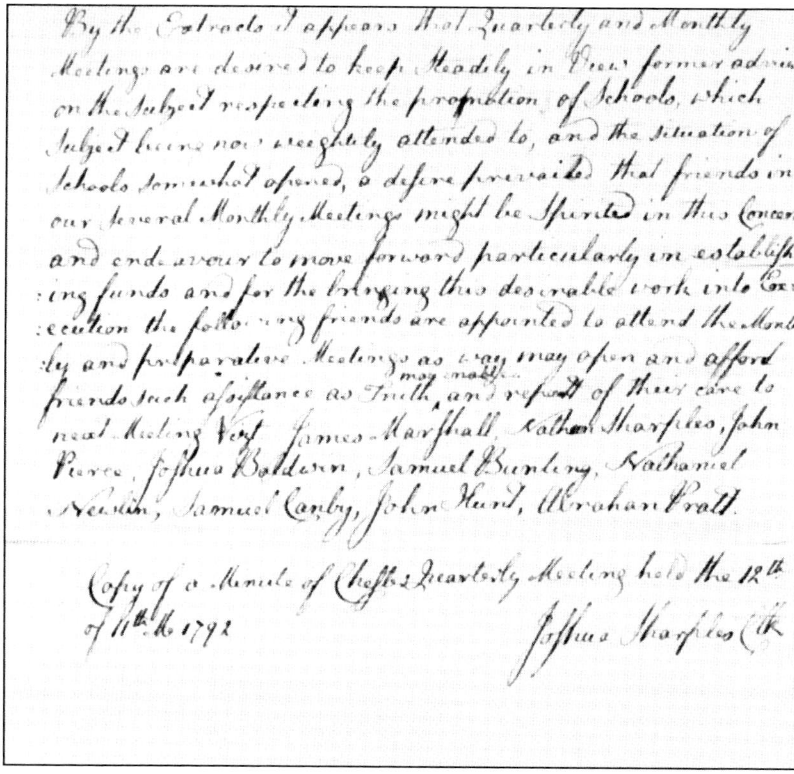

By the Extracts it appears that Quarterly and Monthly Meetings are desired to keep steadily in View former advice on the Subject respecting the promotion of Schools, which Subject being now weightily attended to, and the situation of Schools somewhat opened, a desire prevailed that friends in our several Monthly Meetings might be Spirited in this Concern and endeavour to move forward particularly in establishing funds and for the bringing this desirable work into Execution the following friends are appointed to attend the Monthly and preparative Meetings as way may open and afford friends such assistance as Truth may enable, and report of their care to next Meeting Viz. James Marshall, Nathan Sharples, John Pierce, Joshua Baldwin, Samuel Bunting, Nathaniel Newlin, Samuel Canby, John Hunt, Abraham Pratt.

Copy of a Minute of Chester Quarterly Meeting held the 12th of 11th Mo 1792

Joshua Sharples Clk

This is a minute from Chester Quarterly Meeting of November 12, 1792, signed by Joshua Sharples as clerk of the meeting. Quarterly meetings were composed of several monthly meetings of Friends who worshiped weekly in meetinghouses. This minute concerns the establishment of Friends Schools. (Courtesy of Wilmington Friends School.)

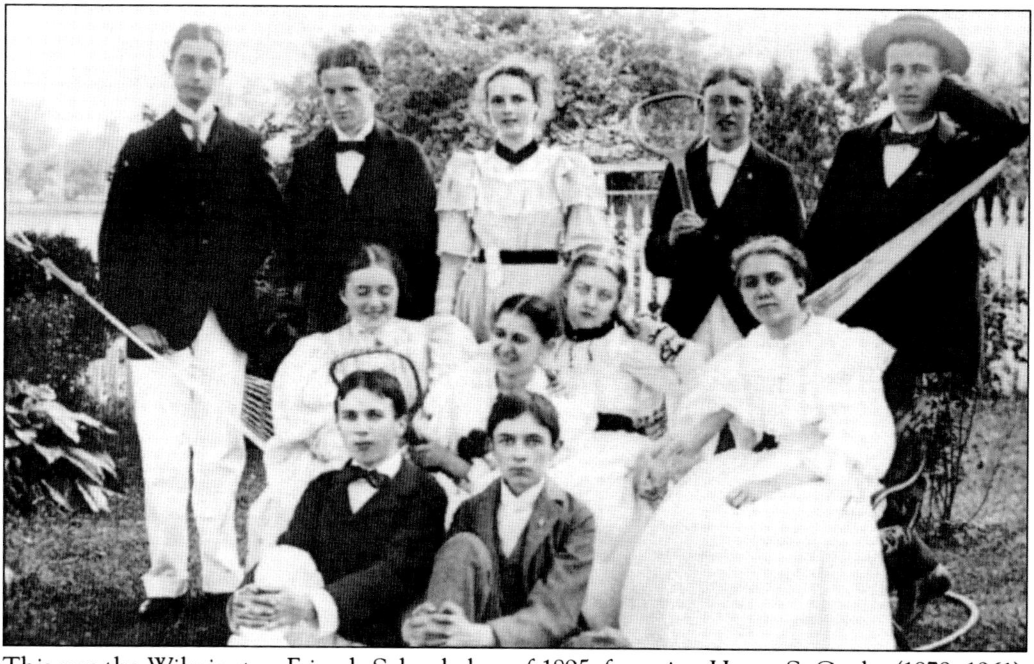

This was the Wilmington Friends School class of 1895, featuring Henry S. Canby (1878–1961), who taught at Yale and edited the Literary Review of the New York Evening Post and the Saturday Review of Literature. He also wrote books about Thoreau, Whitman, Mark Twain, Henry James, and the Brandywine. (Courtesy of Wilmington Friends School.)

This is a catalogue from Wilmington Friends School from the year 1912. Every year, Wilmington Friends School published a catalogue of its programs and its staff. This one follows along classical or art nouveau lines. (Courtesy of Wilmington Friends School.)

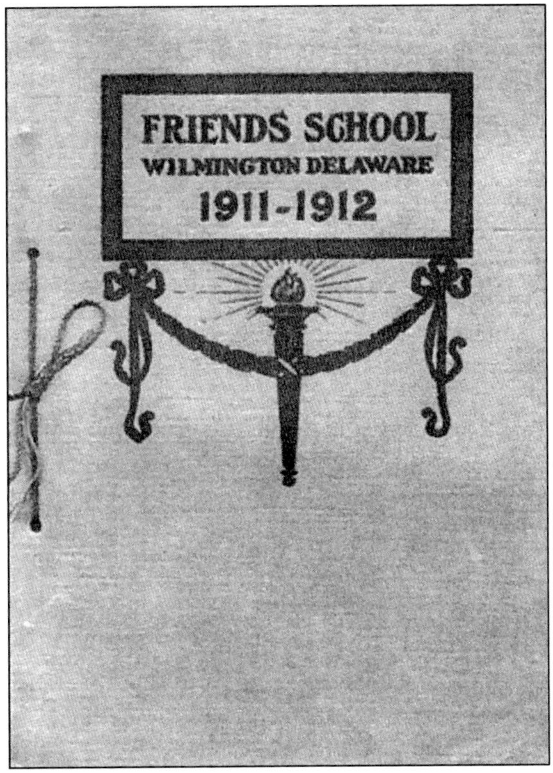

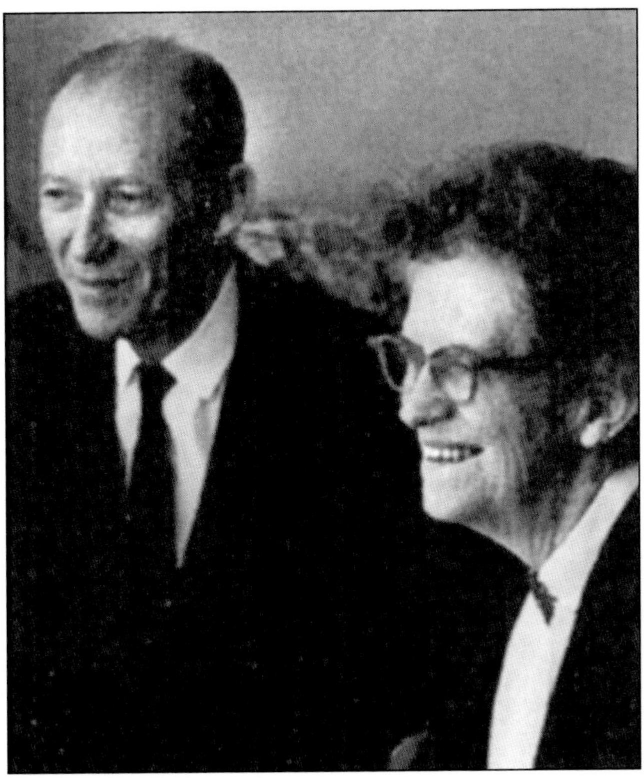

This is a picture of two Wilmington Friends School teachers. George Reeser, a history teacher, retired after a tenure of 36 years. Frances Baird, who was a Latin teacher, retired after a tenure of 42 years, having served Wilmington Friends School almost half a century. (Courtesy of Wilmington Friends School.)

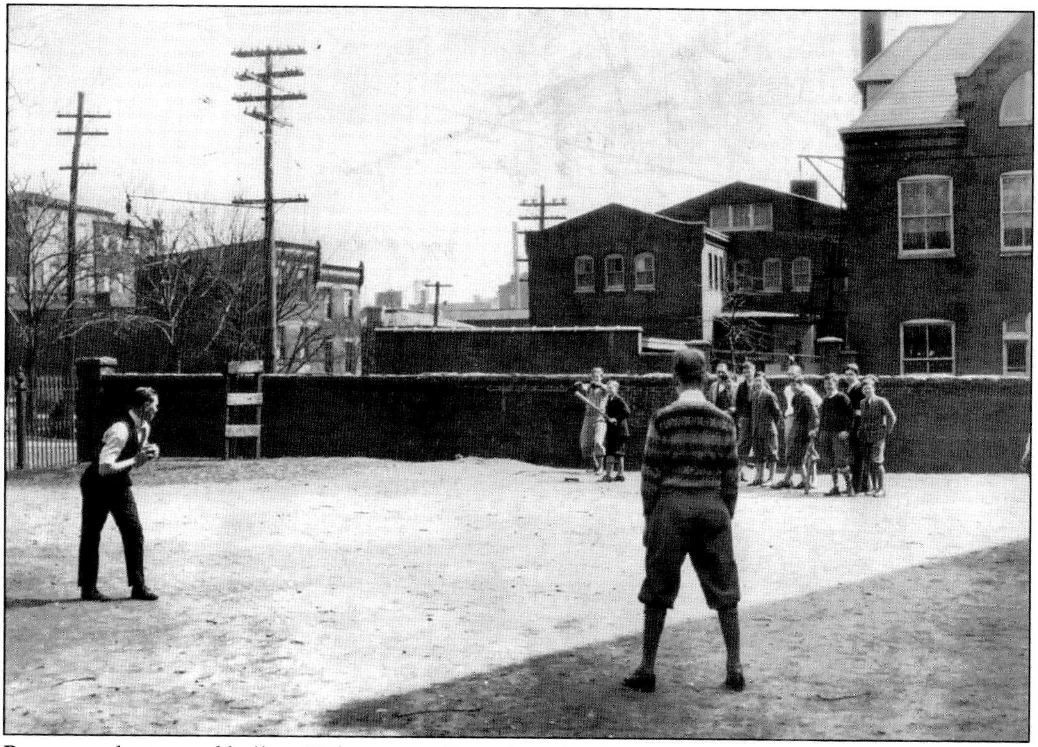

Boys are playing softball at Wilmington Friends School at the beginning of the 20th century. Although Quakers are pacifists and do not believe in any kind of aggression, there has long been a place for sports in Wilmington Friends School. (Courtesy of Wilmington Friends School.)

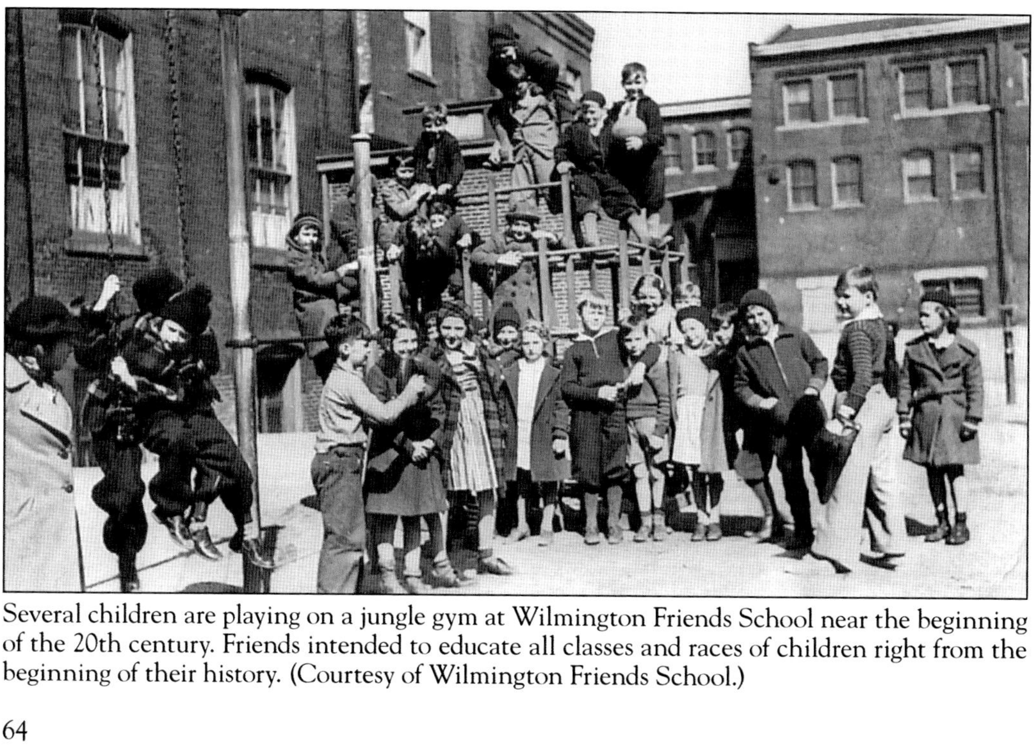

Several children are playing on a jungle gym at Wilmington Friends School near the beginning of the 20th century. Friends intended to educate all classes and races of children right from the beginning of their history. (Courtesy of Wilmington Friends School.)

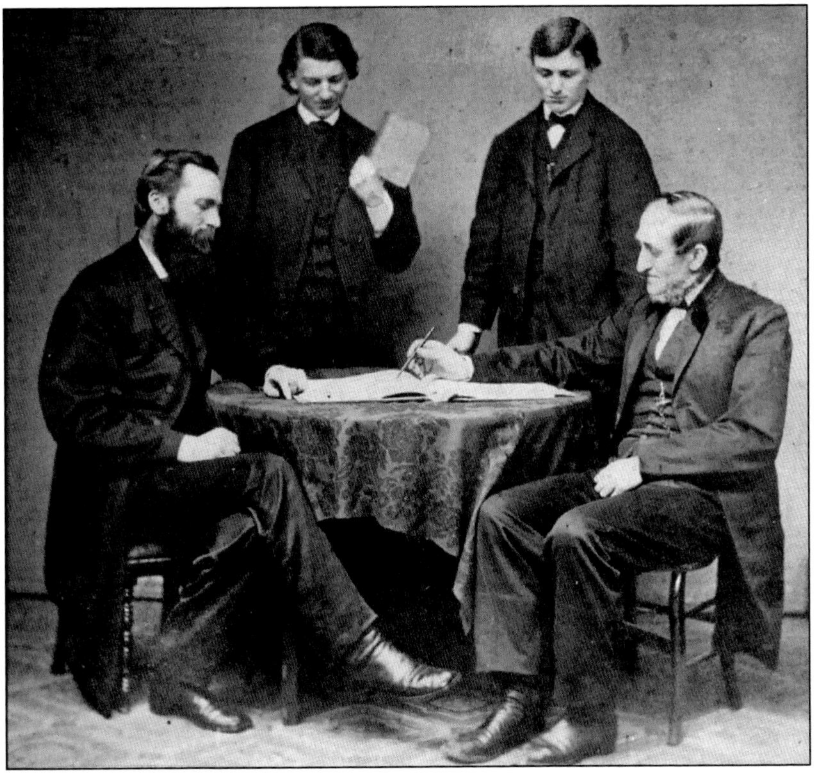

This is a picture of T. Clarkson Taylor. He is the person seated on the right. He was said to be a popular boys' schoolteacher at Wilmington Friends School from 1857 to 1862. One 19th-century principal opined that popular teachers created good morale in the classroom. (Courtesy of Historical Society of Delaware.)

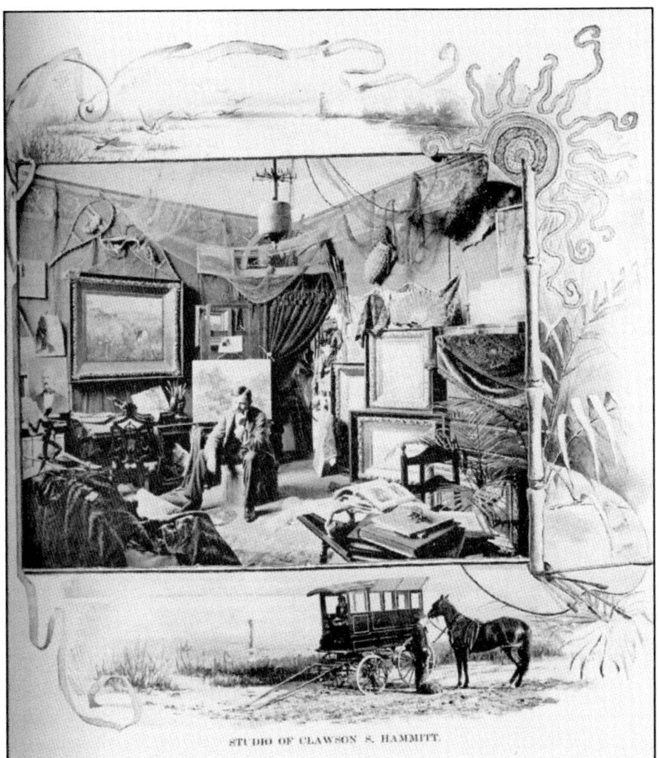

STUDIO OF CLAWSON S. HAMMITT.

This is a picture of the art studio of Clawson Hammitt, who was a favorite art teacher at Wilmington Friends School at the beginning of the 20th century. He is pictured here at the Institute Building at Eighth and Market Streets in Wilmington, Delaware. (Courtesy of Historical Society of Delaware.)

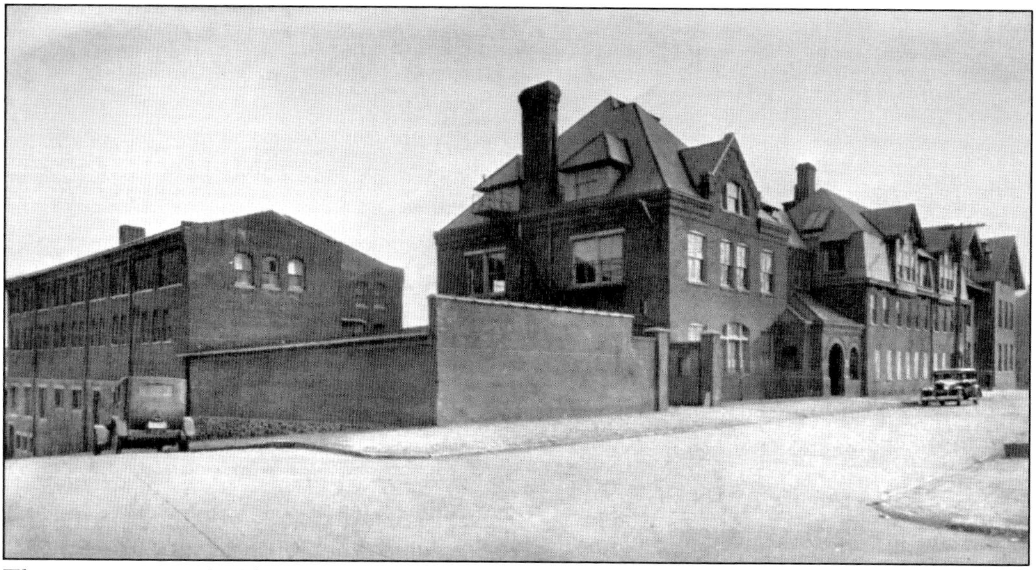

This is a picture of Wilmington Friends School as it appeared in the 1920s. At that time, all the additions had been built. In the 1930s, the school was moved to Alapocas in the suburbs of Wilmington. Most of the building in Quaker Hill was torn down. (Courtesy of Wilmington Friends School.)

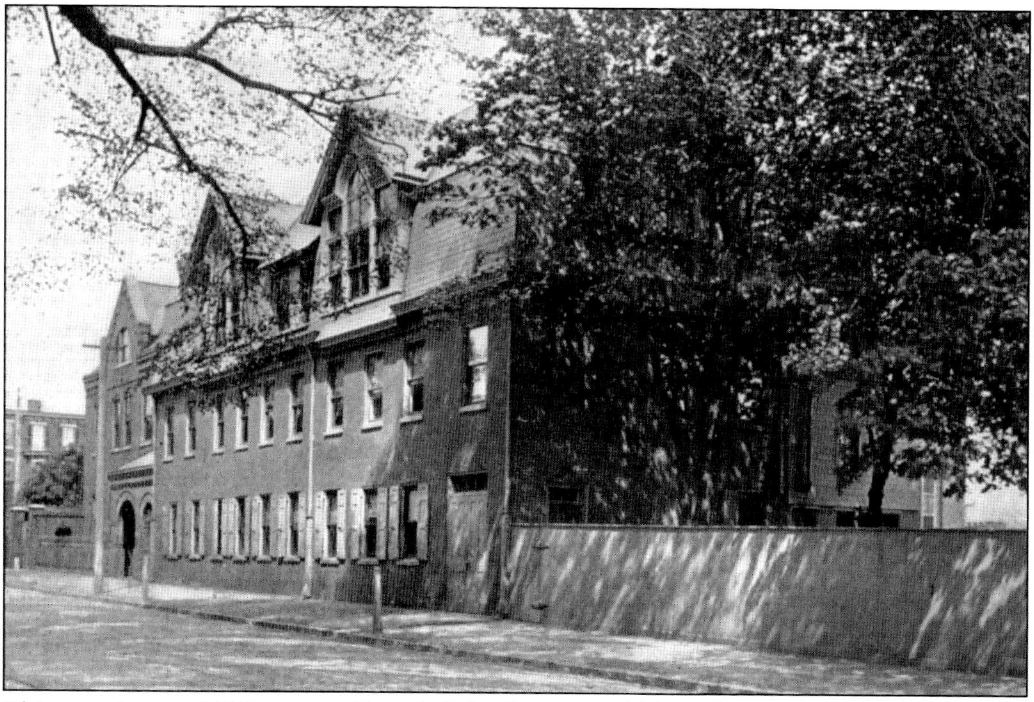

This is a picture of Wilmington Friends School as it would have looked seen from the Fourth Street side. The school had undergone several additions over the years. Most of the original school building is now gone, although a portion was later used to house apartments. (Courtesy of Wilmington Friends School.)

This is the front door of Wilmington Friends School as it stood in Quaker Hill. Students walked through this door for almost two centuries. Note the plaque, which states that the school was founded in 1748. (Courtesy of Wilmington Friends School.)

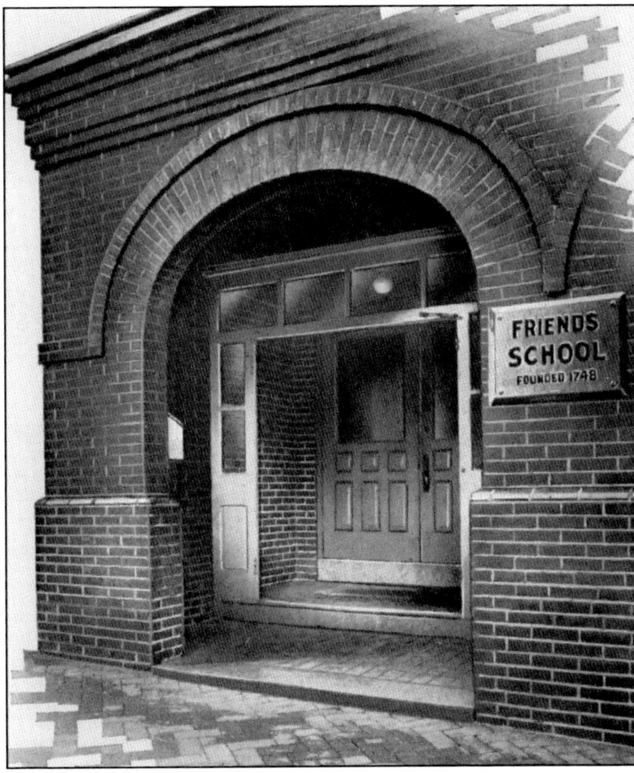

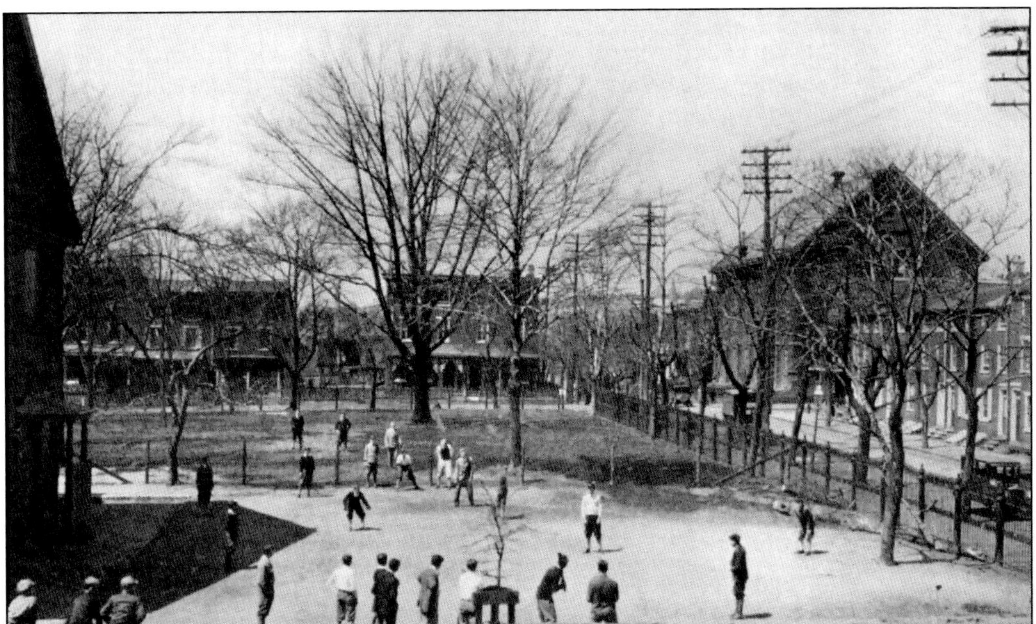

This playground was located in the graveyard of the Wilmington Friends Meetinghouse, across from the Wilmington Friends School, in 1927. The playground is located on the Fifth Street side of the Wilmington Friends Meetinghouse. The old playground area is now a parking lot. (Courtesy of Wilmington Friends School.)

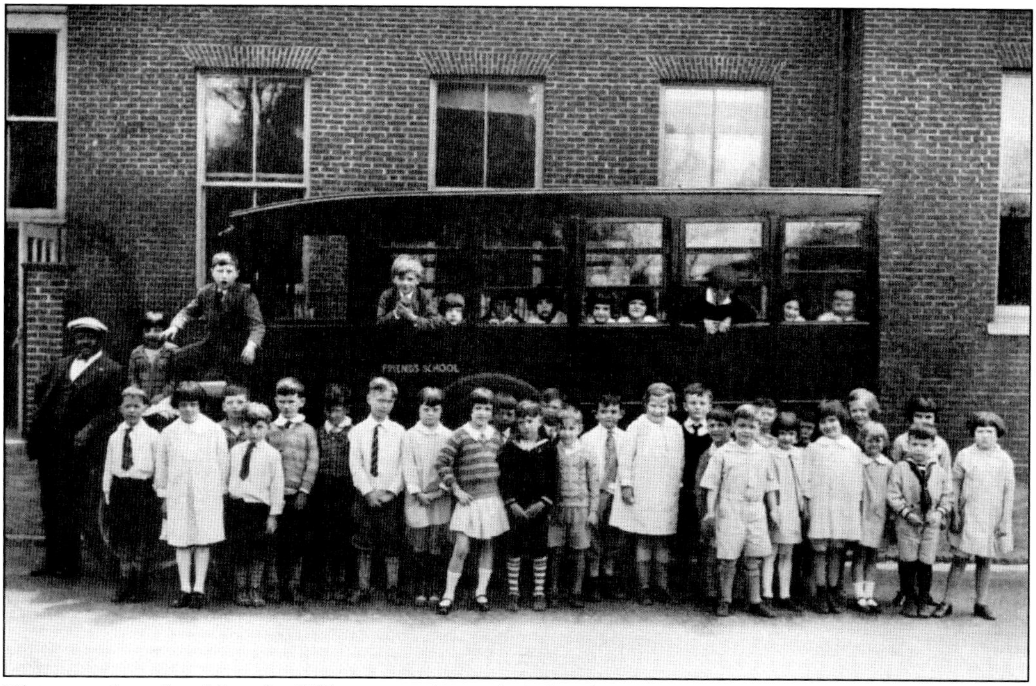

This was the school bus for Wilmington Friends School in 1927. By this time the bus was motor-driven, but the bus driver remained the same. Most of the children who rode the school bus were of primary-school age. (Courtesy of Wilmington Friends School.)

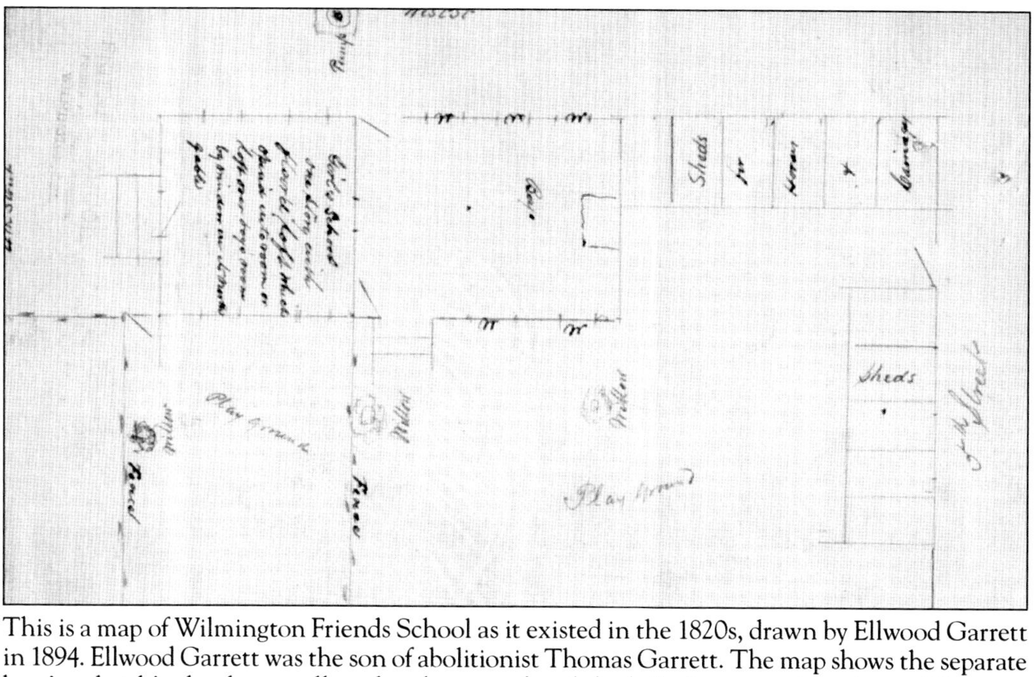

This is a map of Wilmington Friends School as it existed in the 1820s, drawn by Ellwood Garrett in 1894. Ellwood Garrett was the son of abolitionist Thomas Garrett. The map shows the separate boys' and girls' schools, as well as the playground and sheds for horses and carriages. (Courtesy of Wilmington Friends School.)

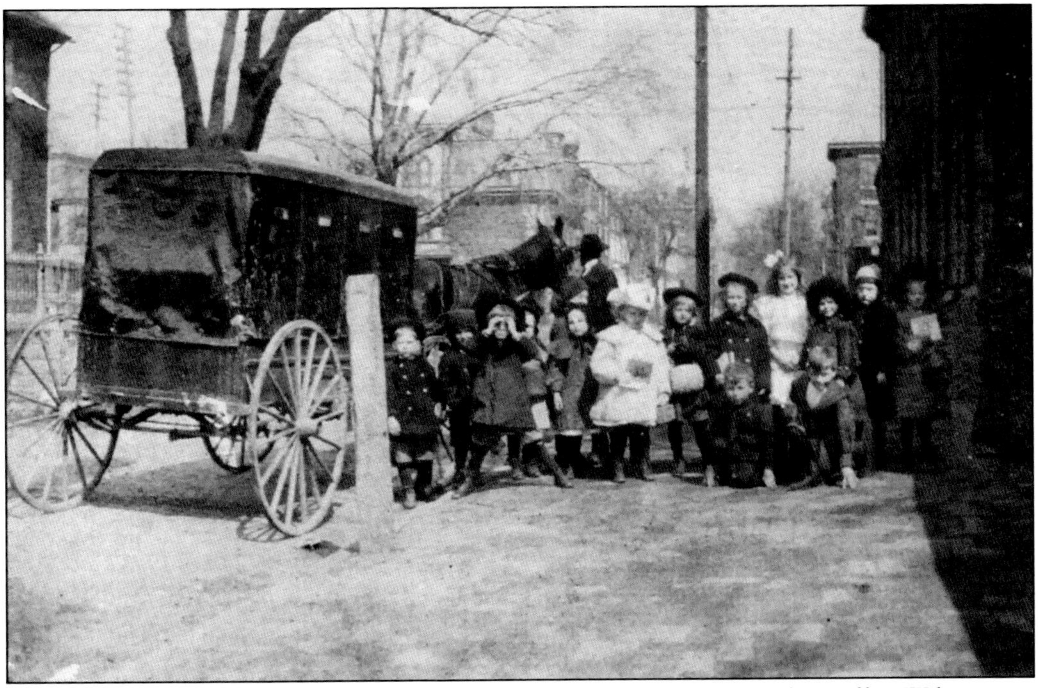

This was the school carriage for Wilmington Friends School in 1905. The staff at Wilmington Friends School believed in transporting its students from an early age. Most of the children riding the school carriage were of primary-school age. (Courtesy of Wilmington Friends School.)

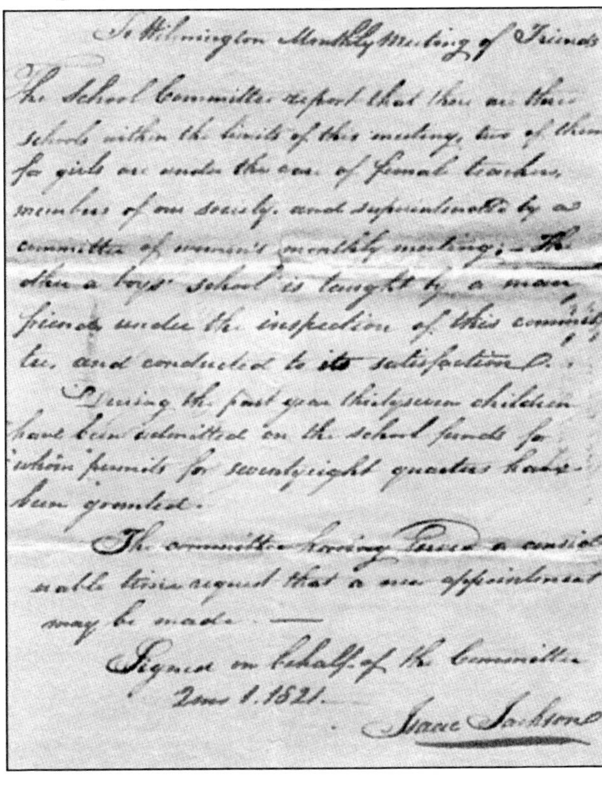

To Wilmington Monthly Meeting of Friends

The School Committee report that there are three schools within the limits of this meeting, two of them for girls are under the care of female teachers, members of our society, and superintended by a committee of women's monthly meeting; — The other a boys' school is taught by a man friend under the inspection of this committee, and conducted to its satisfaction.

During the past year thirtyseven children have been admitted on the school funds for whom permits for seventyeight quarters have been granted.

The committee having served a considerable time request that a new appointment may be made. —

Signed on behalf of the Committee
2mo 1.1821.
Isaac Jackson

This report of the school committee, dated February 1, 1821, states that three schools are under the care of the community and are conducted to its satisfaction. Also, during the past year, 37 children had been admitted on school funds; permits for 78 quarters had been granted. (Courtesy of Wilmington Friends School.)

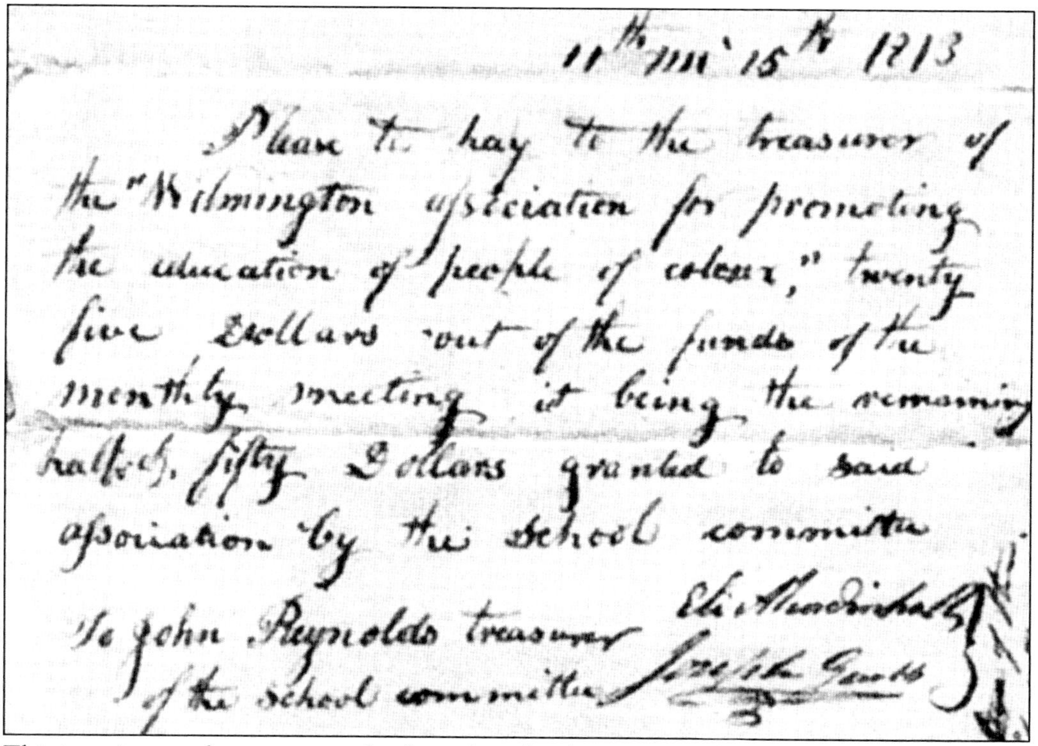

11th mo 15th 1813

Please to pay to the treasurer of the "Wilmington association for promoting the education of people of colour," twenty five Dollars out of the funds of the monthly meeting it being the remaining half of fifty Dollars granted to said association by the school committee

Eli Mendinhall
To John Reynolds treasurer of the school committee
Joseph [illegible]

This is a picture of a payment order from the school committee dated November 15, 1813, for the remaining $25 of $50 pledged in 1813 to the Wilmington Association for the Promoting of Education of People of Color. (Courtesy of Wilmington Friends School.)

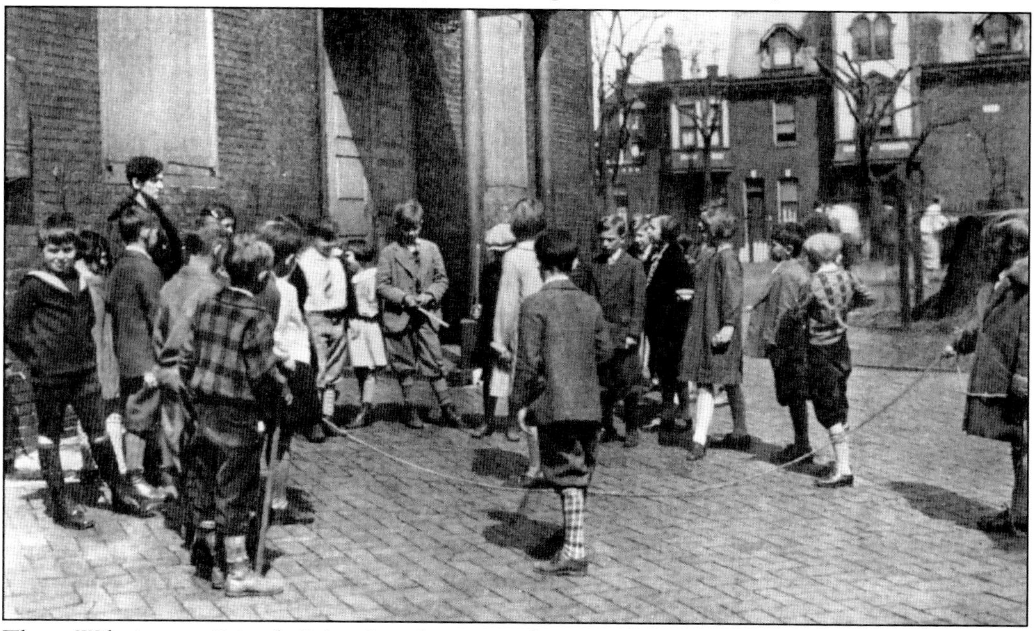

These Wilmington Friends School students are playing in 1927. Note the presence of a teacher supervising their games. Soon the impact of the Great Depression would be felt on the school population. The school relocated in the late 1930s. (Courtesy of Wilmington Friends School.)

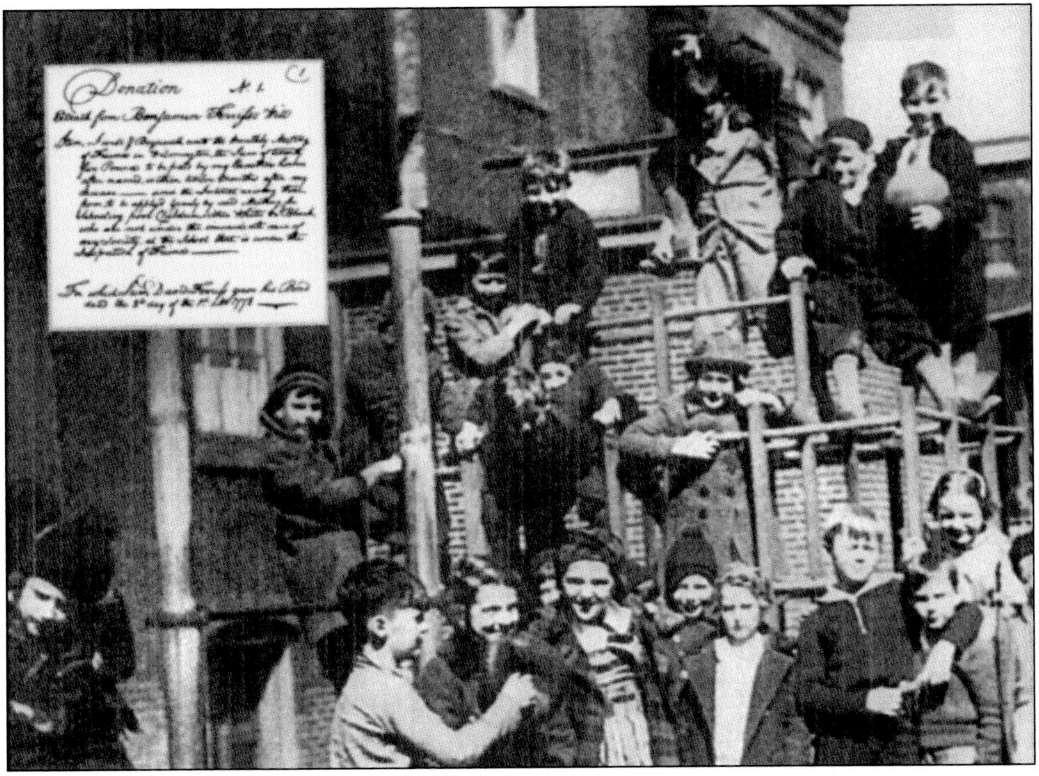

In the upper left corner is a picture of Ferris's 1778 will: "I bequeath unto the monthly meeting of Friends in Wilmington the sum of 25 pounds to be paid by my executrix herein after named and the interest arising there from to be applied yearly by said Meeting for schooling poor children, either white or black, who are not under the immediate care of any society at the school that is under the inspection of Friends." (Courtesy of Wilmington Friends School.)

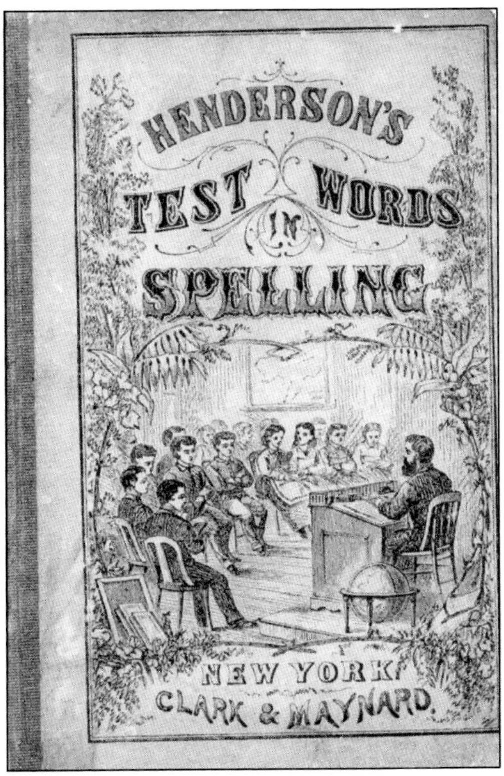

This was the cover of Henderson's Test Words in Spelling. This book was typical of texts used in Wilmington Friends School in the 19th century. Students were regularly given grades in spelling, which was then called orthography, as shown in the students' final reports. (Courtesy of Wilmington Friends School.)

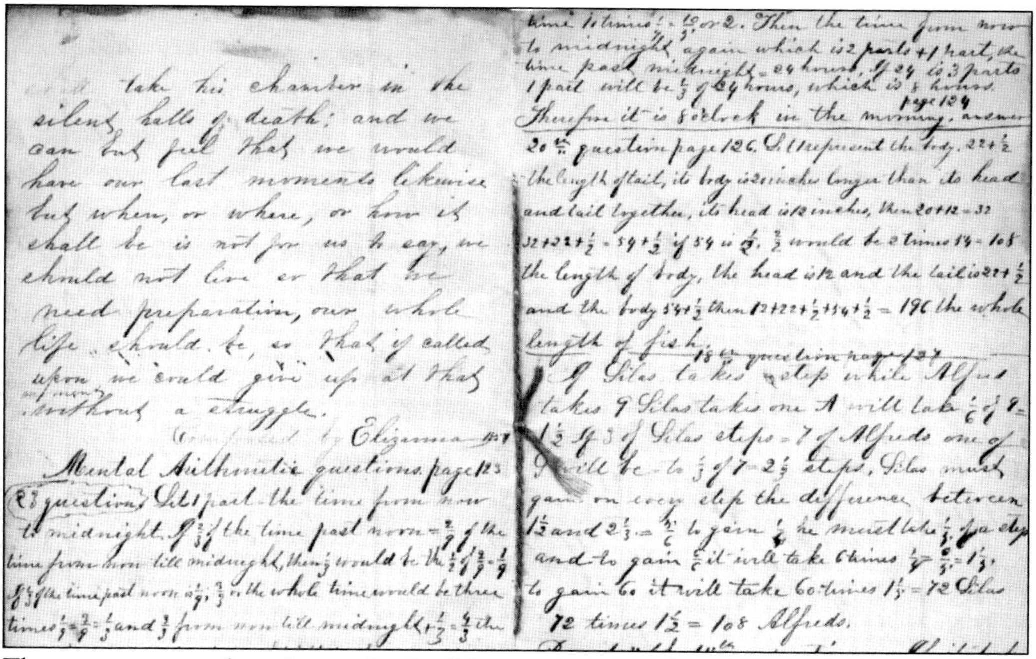

take his chamber in the silent halls of death: and we can but feel that we would have our last moments likewise but when, or where, or how it shall be is not for us to say, we should not live so that we need preparation, our whole life should be, so that if called upon we could give up at that moment without a struggle.

Composed by Elizanna

Mental Arithmetic questions page 123

These are two pages from the copybook of Elizanna Patterson from Wilmington Friends School. They show Mental Arithmetic and the conclusion of a composition of "On Death." The copybook dates from 1858. Such compositions were common during the 19th century. (Courtesy of Wilmington Friends School.)

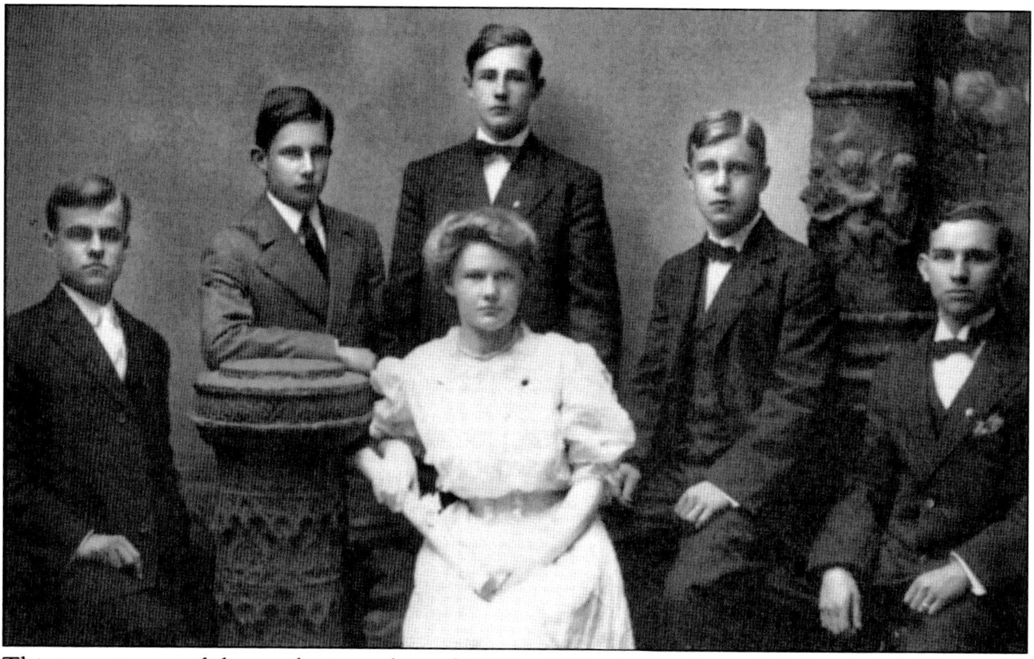

This is a picture of the graduating class of 1907 at Wilmington Friends School. S. Lester Levy, who is pictured here on the far right of this photograph, became the second Rhodes Scholar who graduated from Wilmington Friends School. Note the lone female scholar. (Courtesy of Wilmington Friends School.)

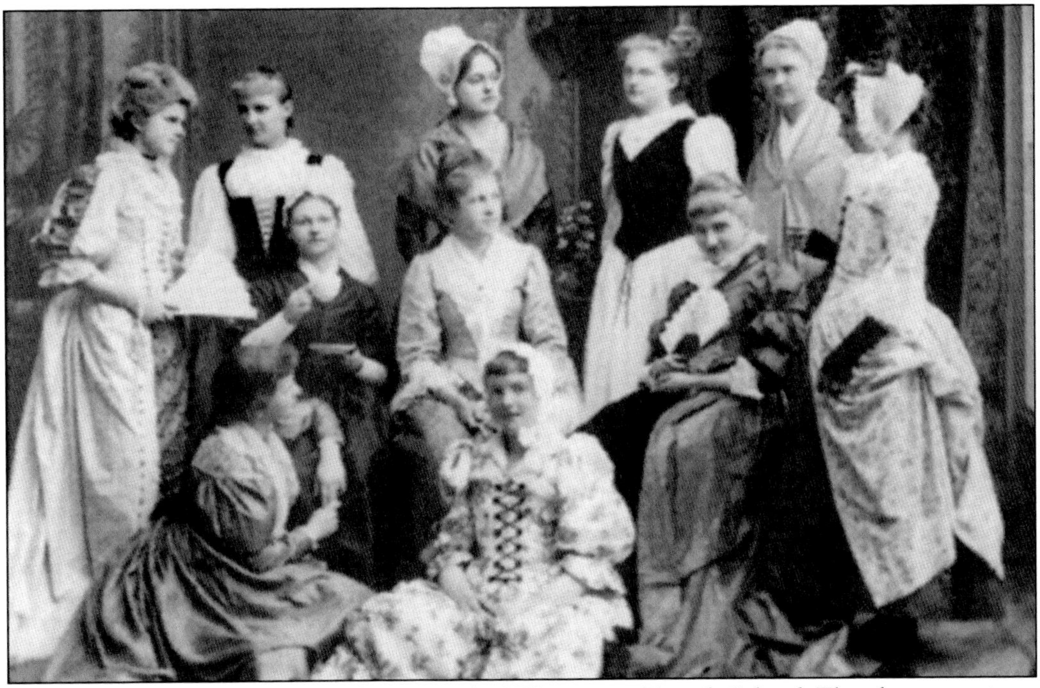

This is a picture of the cast of a play put on by Wilmington Friends School. The play was written by Miss Crew. A teacher of English grammar and of English literature at Wilmington Friends School, Crew wrote the play in 1892. (Courtesy of Wilmington Friends School.)

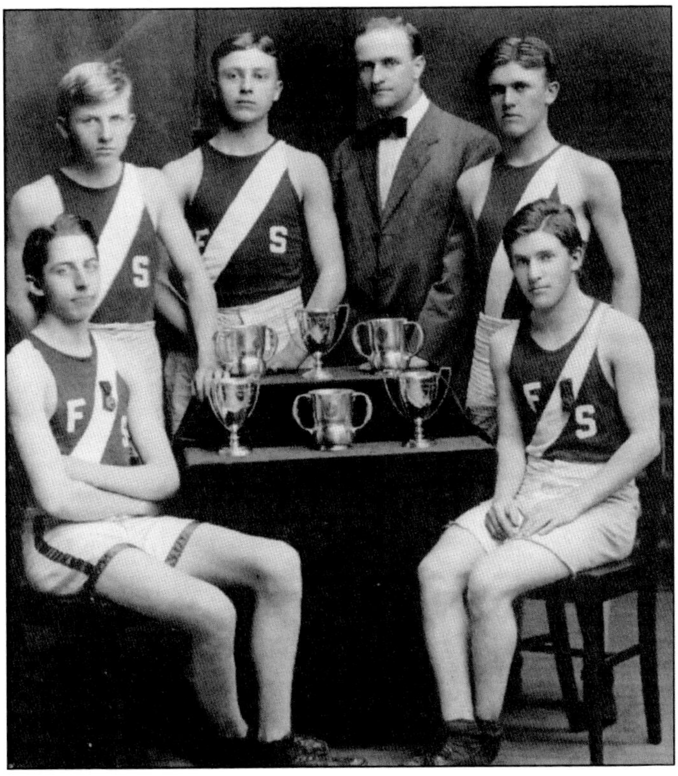

This is the track team at Wilmington Friends School in 1912. The track coach then was Chester Ross (pictured). The track team of 1912 was very successful. It finished second in the Penn Relays. The team also finished first at West Chester. (Courtesy of Wilmington Friends School.)

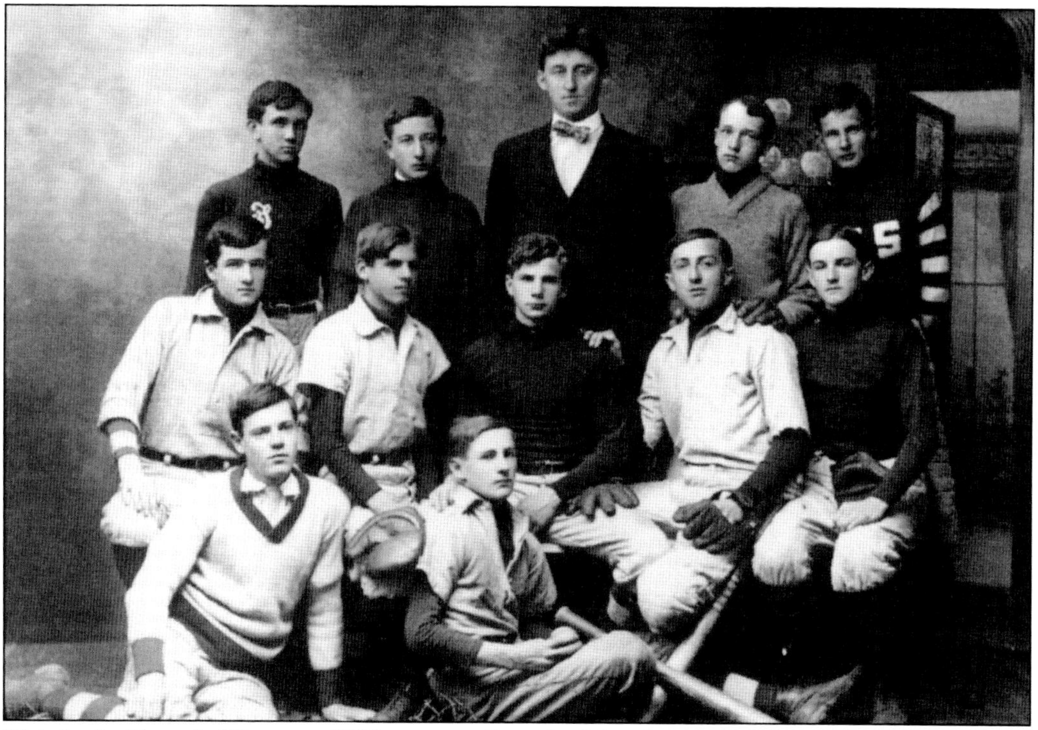

This is the "base ball" team of Wilmington Friends School in 1907. The Wilmington Friends School team had a 0-2 record. The boy pictured on the far left in the middle row is C. D. Buck. He became a successful politician. He even became governor and senator of Delaware. (Courtesy of Wilmington Friends School.)

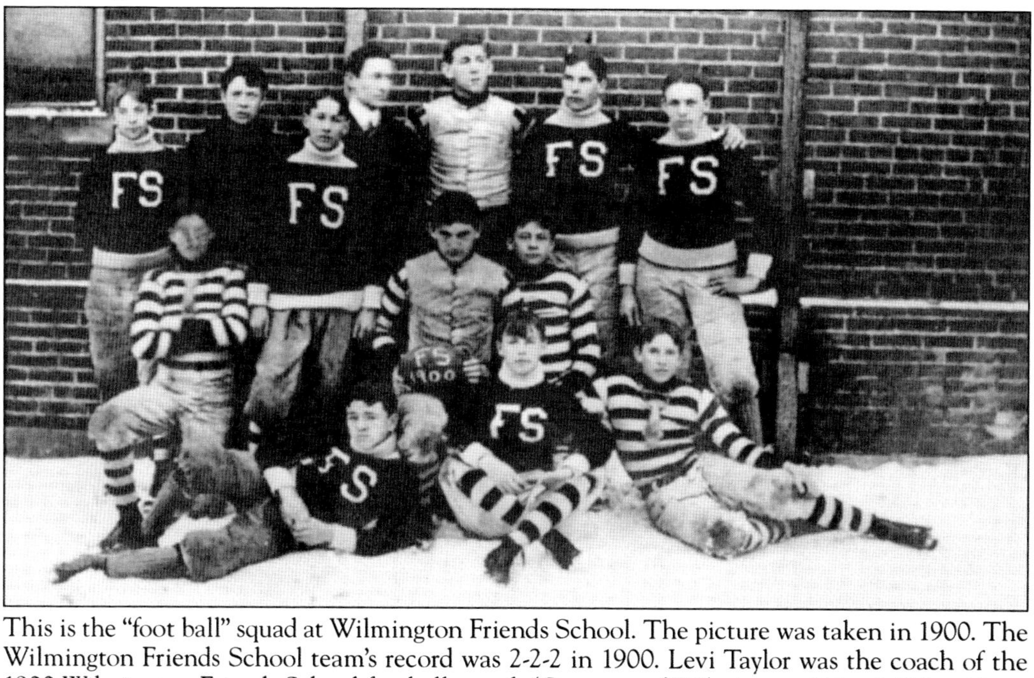

This is the "foot ball" squad at Wilmington Friends School. The picture was taken in 1900. The Wilmington Friends School team's record was 2-2-2 in 1900. Levi Taylor was the coach of the 1900 Wilmington Friends School football squad. (Courtesy of Wilmington Friends School.)

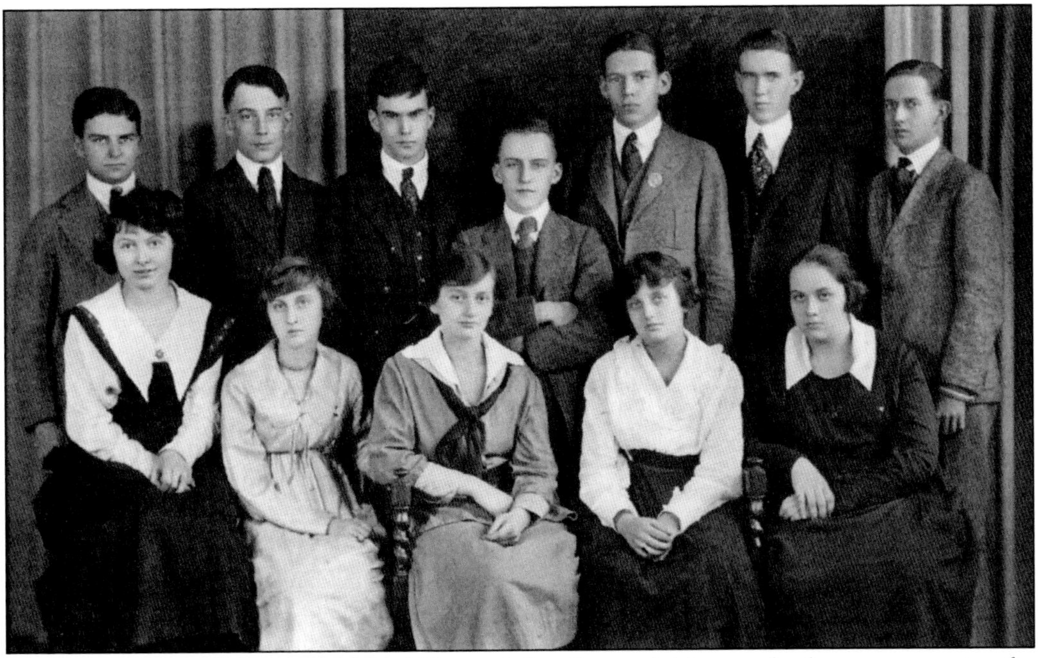

This is a picture of the staff of the *Whittier Miscellany*, which was the literary magazine for Wilmington Friends School. These students from Wilmington Friends School were the staff of the *Whittier Miscellany* from 1917 to 1918. Among those pictured here is editor Richard Cooch, who came from a prominent Wilmington family. (Courtesy of Wilmington Friends School.)

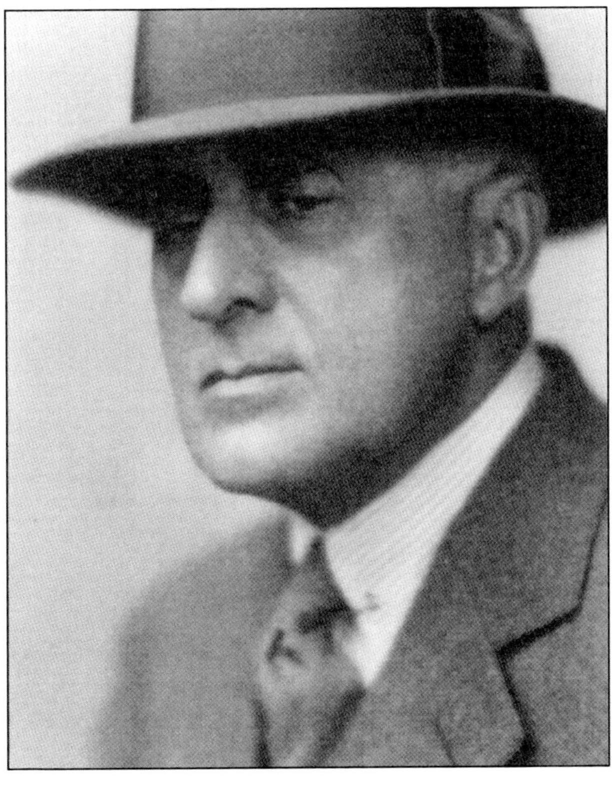

This photograph of Christopher Ward was taken in 1886. He was a historian, a satirist, and a corporate attorney. He was also a member of the first Whittier Society, and he selected the name for the *Whittier Miscellany*. (Courtesy of Historical Society of Delaware.)

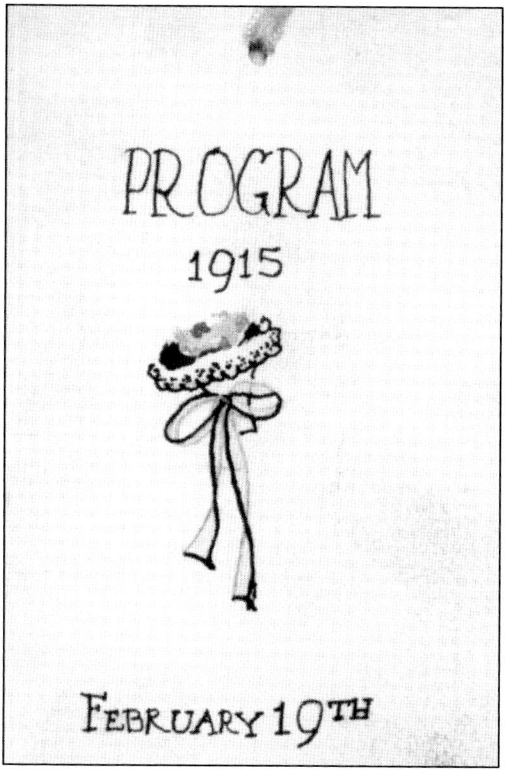

This is a 1915 dance program from the Wilmington Friends School. This was only six years after Wilmington Friends School decided to allow dancing, which was a decision that would probably have shocked early members of the Religious Society of Friends. (Courtesy of Wilmington Friends School.)

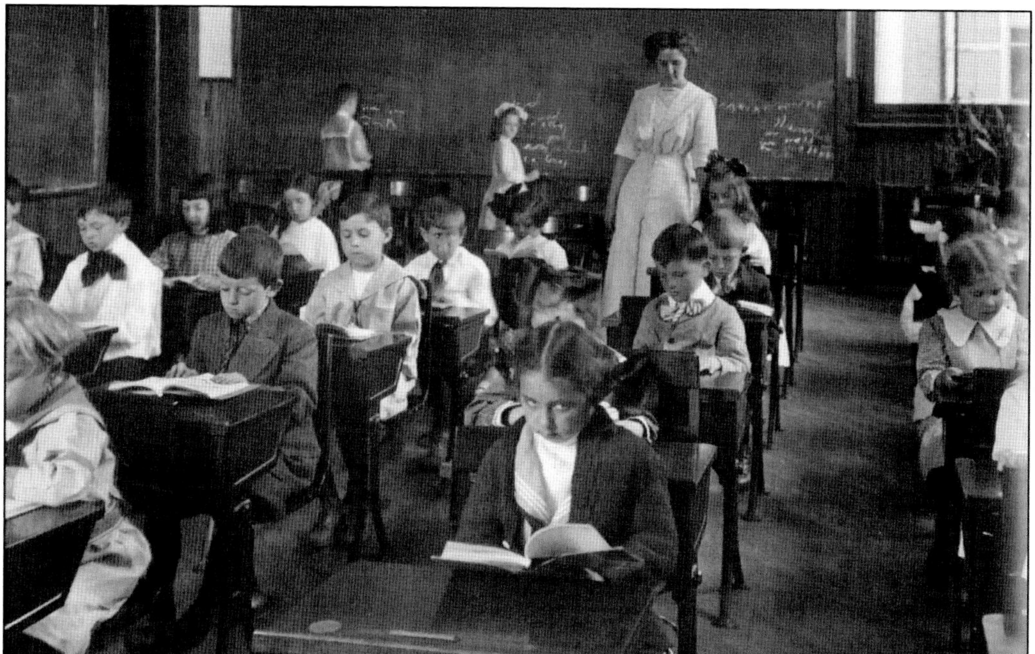

This is a Wilmington Friends School classroom at the turn of the 20th century in Wilmington, Delaware. Most of the children appear to be studying assiduously while the teacher looks on; note the little girl in the front eyeing the photographer. (Courtesy of Wilmington Friends School.)

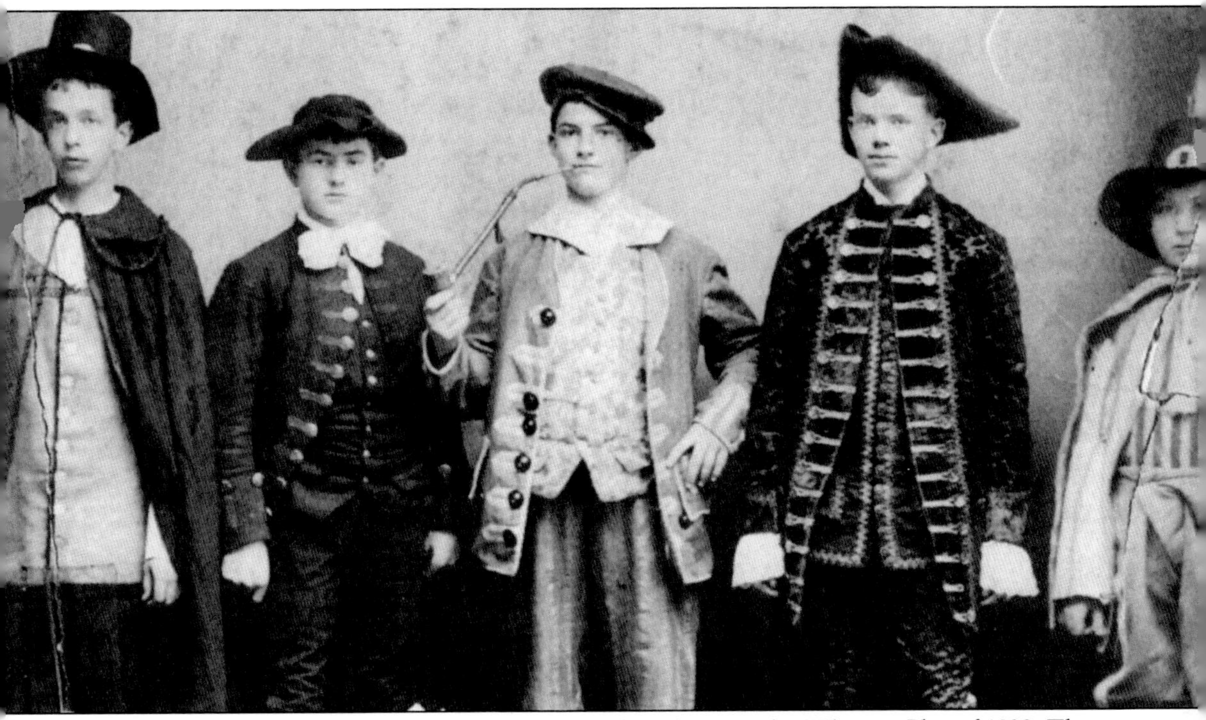

This is a picture of the Wilmington Friends School students in the Whittier Play of 1892. They are dressed up to represent the early American settlers. Eliot Harvey (second from the left) is dressed as a Quaker, Keith Rodney (center) as a Dutch patron, and Warren Haynes (second from the right) as a Virginia Cavalier. (Courtesy of Wilmington Friends School.)

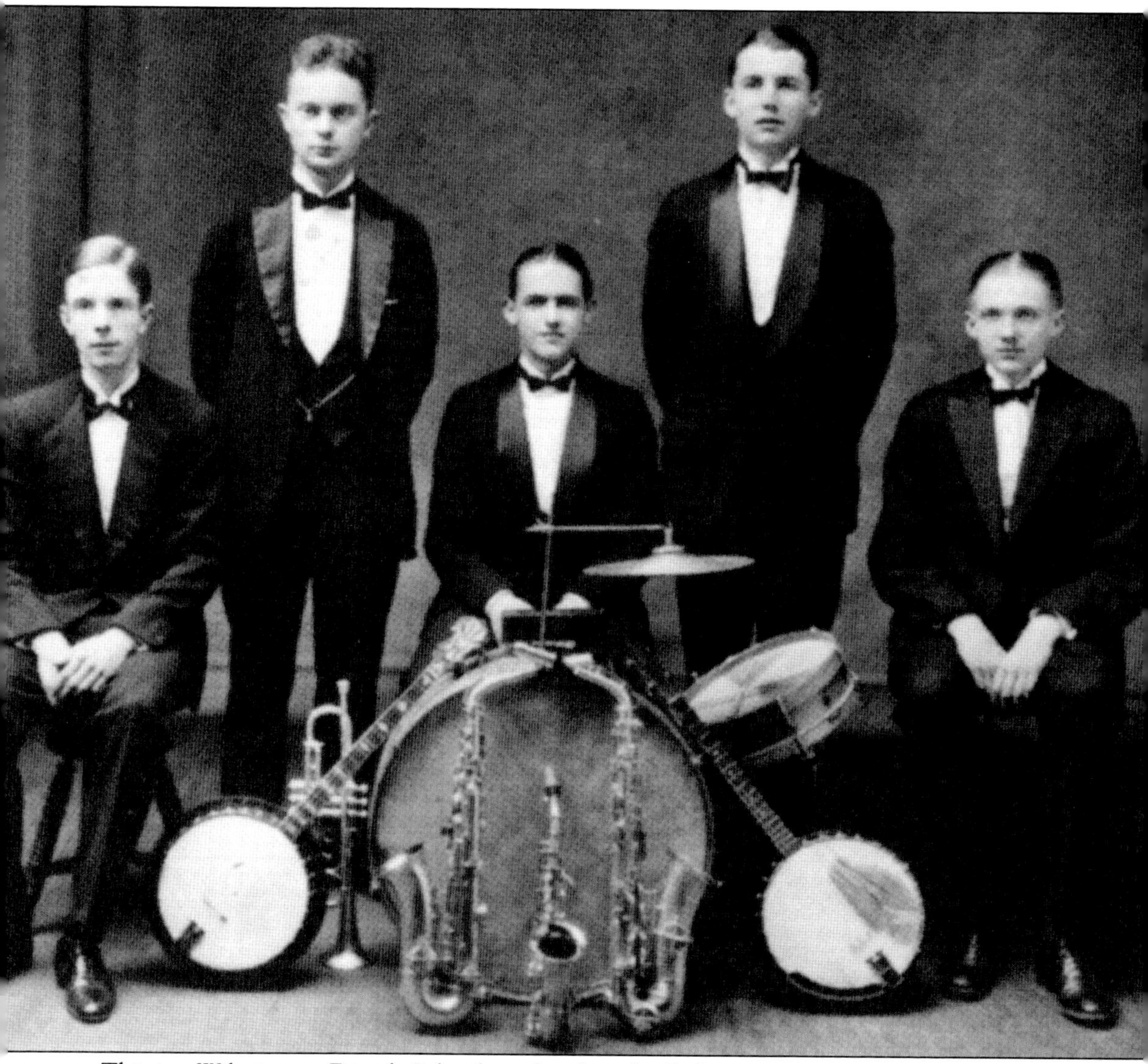

This is a Wilmington Friends School jazz band, with all their instruments, in the midst of the Jazz Age in 1925. Pictured here from left to right are the following: Rob Robinson, Julian Booker, Ross Ford, Henry Sheward, and William Candee. (Courtesy of Wilmington Friends School.)

Four

Cathedral of St. Peter

The Cathedral of St. Peter is known for its splendid architecture and is the seat of the Bishop of Wilmington.

In the mid-1700s, itinerant priests from the Jesuit, Franciscan, and Augustine orders traveled the area. Parish baptismal records date back to 1796 and are written in French, since many Catholics were French refugees who fled a revolution in the Dominican Republic in 1775. Also, many parishioners were Irish workers who worked for the duPonts in the farms and powder mills along the Brandywine.

In 1804, Fr. Patrick Kenney began a 36-year ministry in the area for a congregation that included Mrs. Victor DuPont (Gabrielle). Father Kenney began plans for a church at the present-day site at Sixth and West Streets. He employed the services of Pierre Bauduy, a French refugee who also designed the Wilmington town hall. The first 30-foot-by-40-foot brick, tin-roofed Romanesque church was dedicated to St. Peter in 1816. Extensions to the church were overseen by Father Carrell (who installed the bell tower), Father Reilly, and later pastors. Extensive renovations were made in the 1870s through 1908; these included the additions of frescoes, marble altar and baptistery, chancel railing, bishop's throne, and three stained glass windows including work by the craftsman who worked for the Bavarian royal court.

The Daughters of Charity, the seventh mission of the Mother Elizabeth Ann Seton's community in the United States, opened St. Peter's Female Orphanage at Third and West Streets, then Sixth and West Streets, and in 1840, the sisters opened a boarding school, which became a free academy for girls in 1841. Father Reilly opened a boys' school at Fifth and West Streets and opened St. Mary's College on Delaware Avenue between Jefferson and Madison Streets in 1842. The college closed in 1866 but was reopened in 1868 as a girls' academy. In 1852, a new school and rectory were built on either side of the church.

In 1926, a parochial school for boys and girls was built at Sixth and Tatnall Streets and the church became a cathedral.

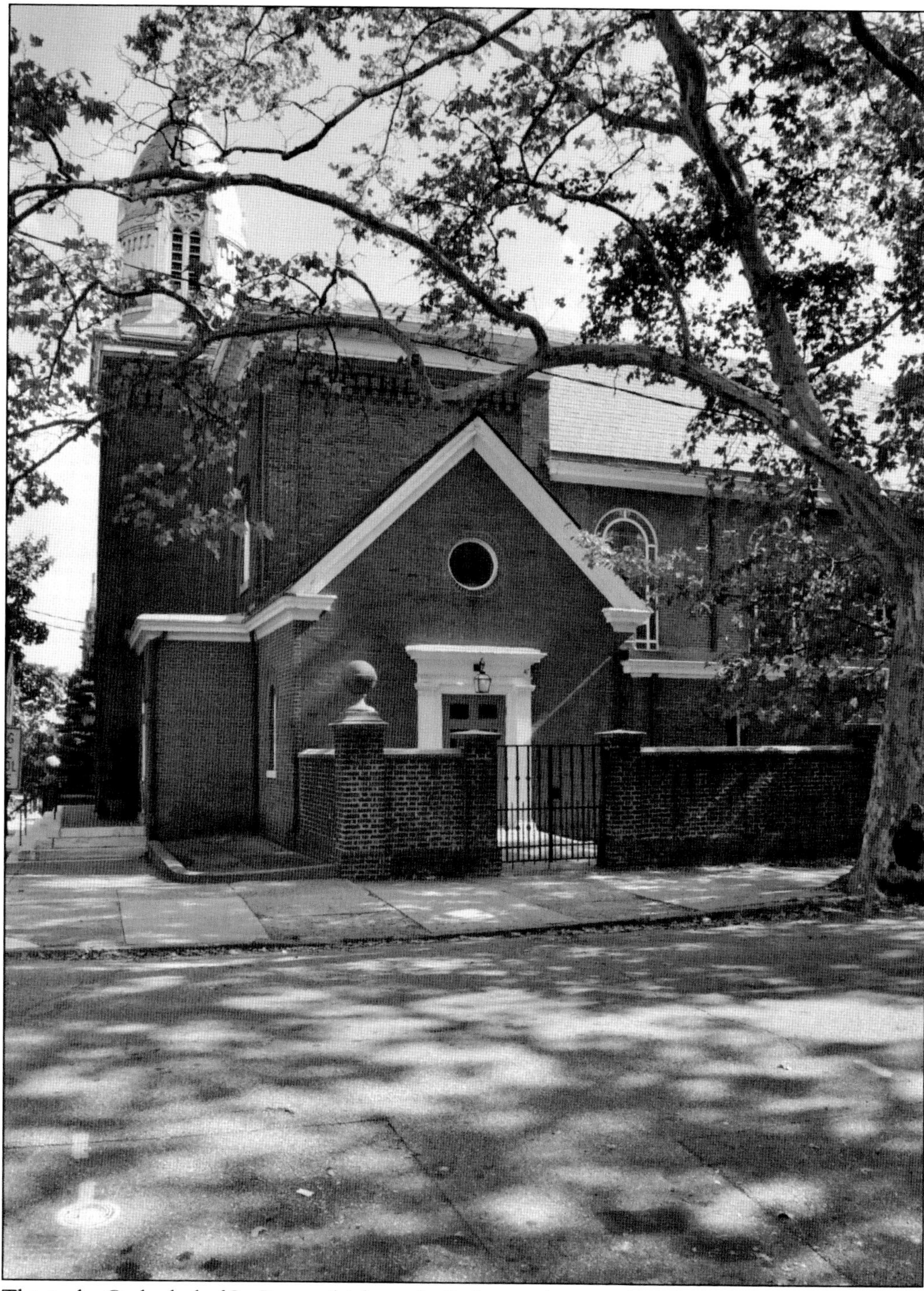

This is the Cathedral of St. Peter, which was built during the period of 1816 to 1818. The cathedral was the first Catholic church in the city of Wilmington, Delaware, and was probably designed by Pierre Bauduy, who designed Wilmington's town hall. (Photograph by Thomas F. Bayard IV.)

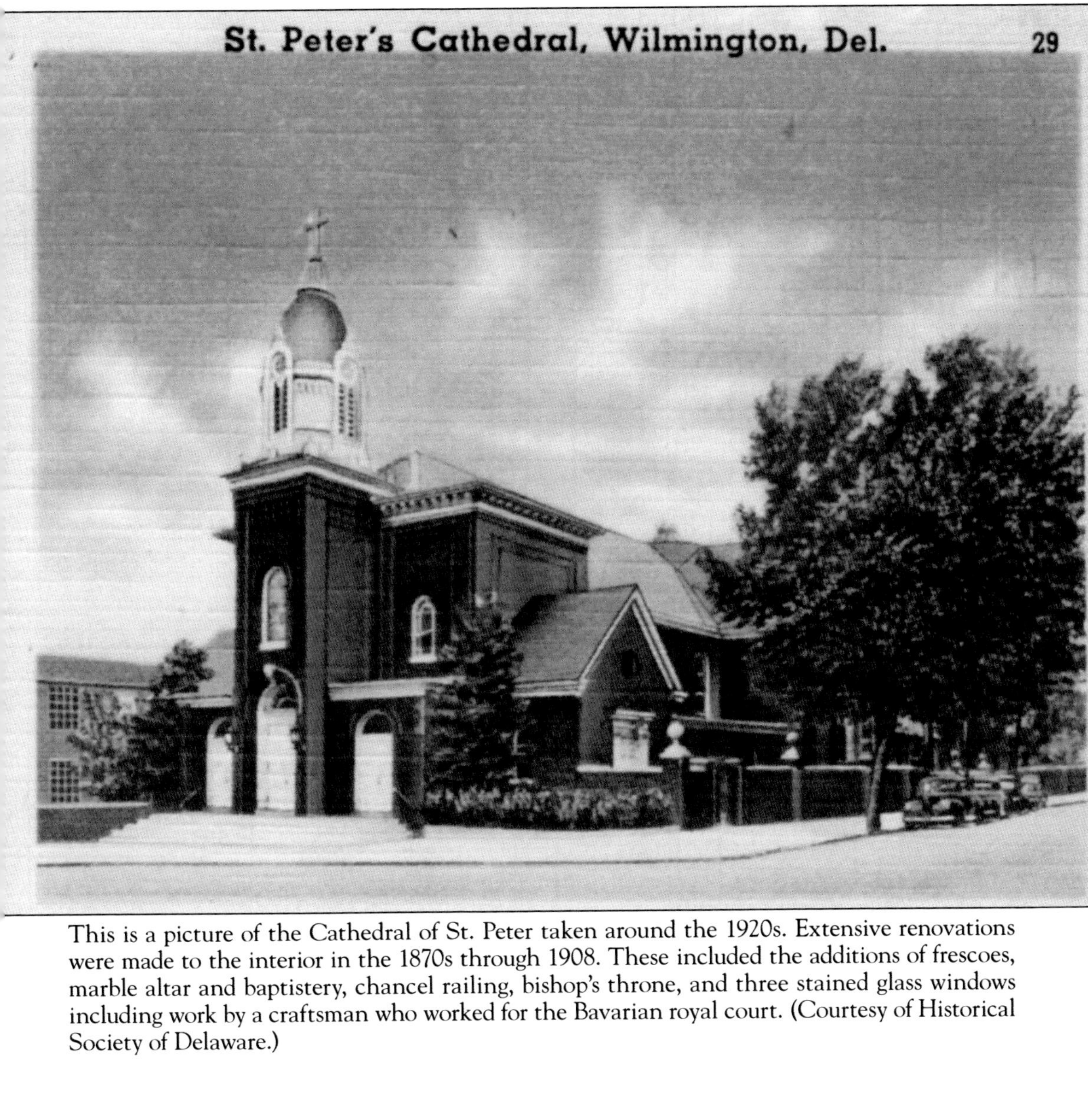

This is a picture of the Cathedral of St. Peter taken around the 1920s. Extensive renovations were made to the interior in the 1870s through 1908. These included the additions of frescoes, marble altar and baptistery, chancel railing, bishop's throne, and three stained glass windows including work by a craftsman who worked for the Bavarian royal court. (Courtesy of Historical Society of Delaware.)

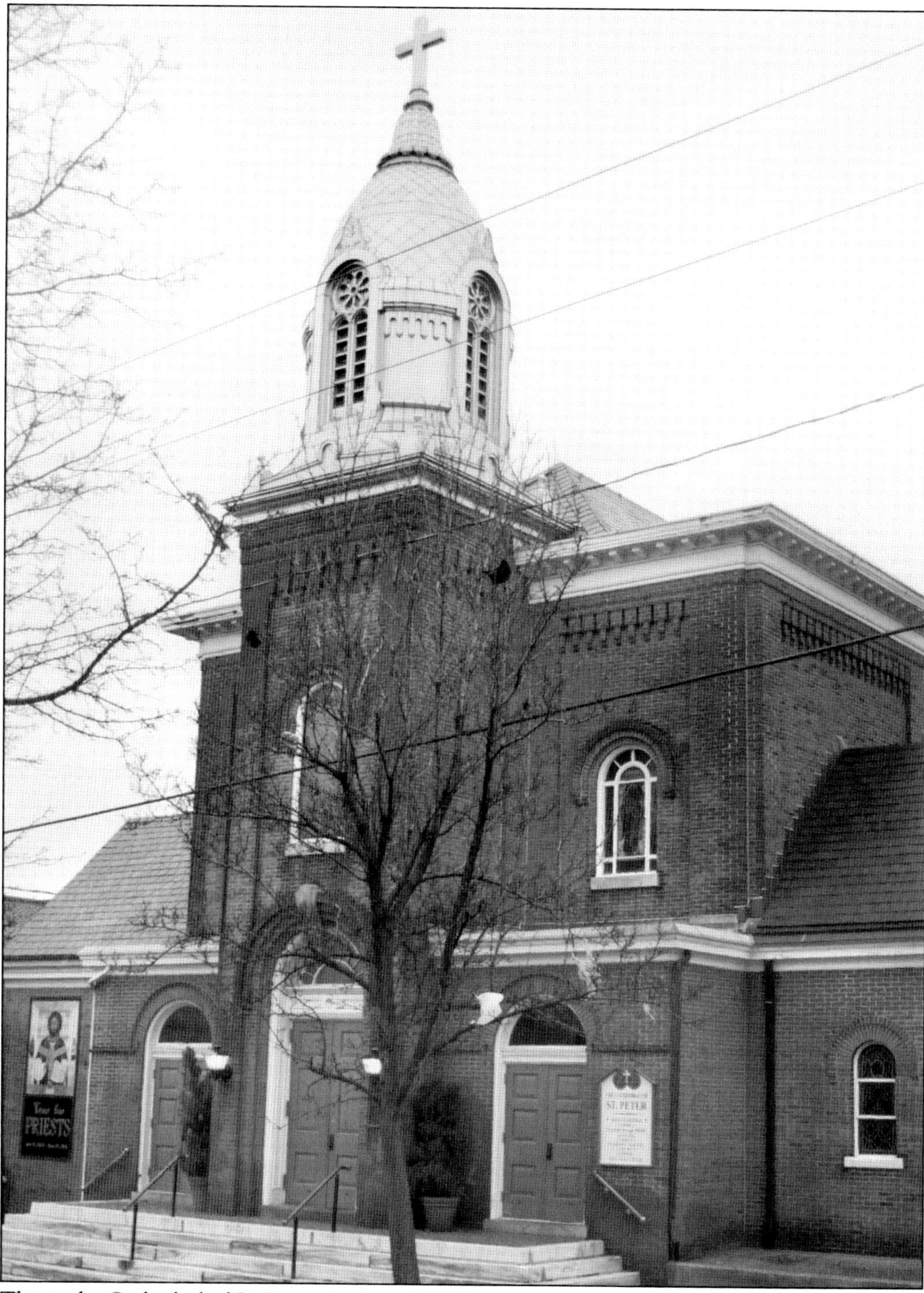

This is the Cathedral of St. Peter. In the mid-1700s, itinerant priests from the Jesuit, Franciscan, and Augustine orders traveled the area. In 1804, Fr. Patrick Kenney began a 36-year ministry in the area that culminated in plans for a church at the present-day site at Sixth and West Streets. (Photograph by James Bierbaum.)

Five

Mission and Geography of Quaker Hill

The Quaker Hill Historic Preservation Foundation is an organization dedicated to preserving, restoring, and promoting the history, social life, and architecture of the Quaker Hill area using a multifaceted outreach effort. This effort includes historical research; educational presentations drawing upon academic, civic, and community resources; guided tours; and social events showcasing the area's cultural amenities. The Foundation's public outreach programs are intended to increase awareness of the area's multicultural history, and support and promote viable housing and economic development. The initiatives are designed to preserve and restore the mixed socioeconomic balance that characterized the traditional neighborhood social life in the Quaker Hill area and shaped its architecture.

On the following pages are examples of some of the historic and architectural highlights available on the Quaker Hill Historic Preservation Foundation walking tour.

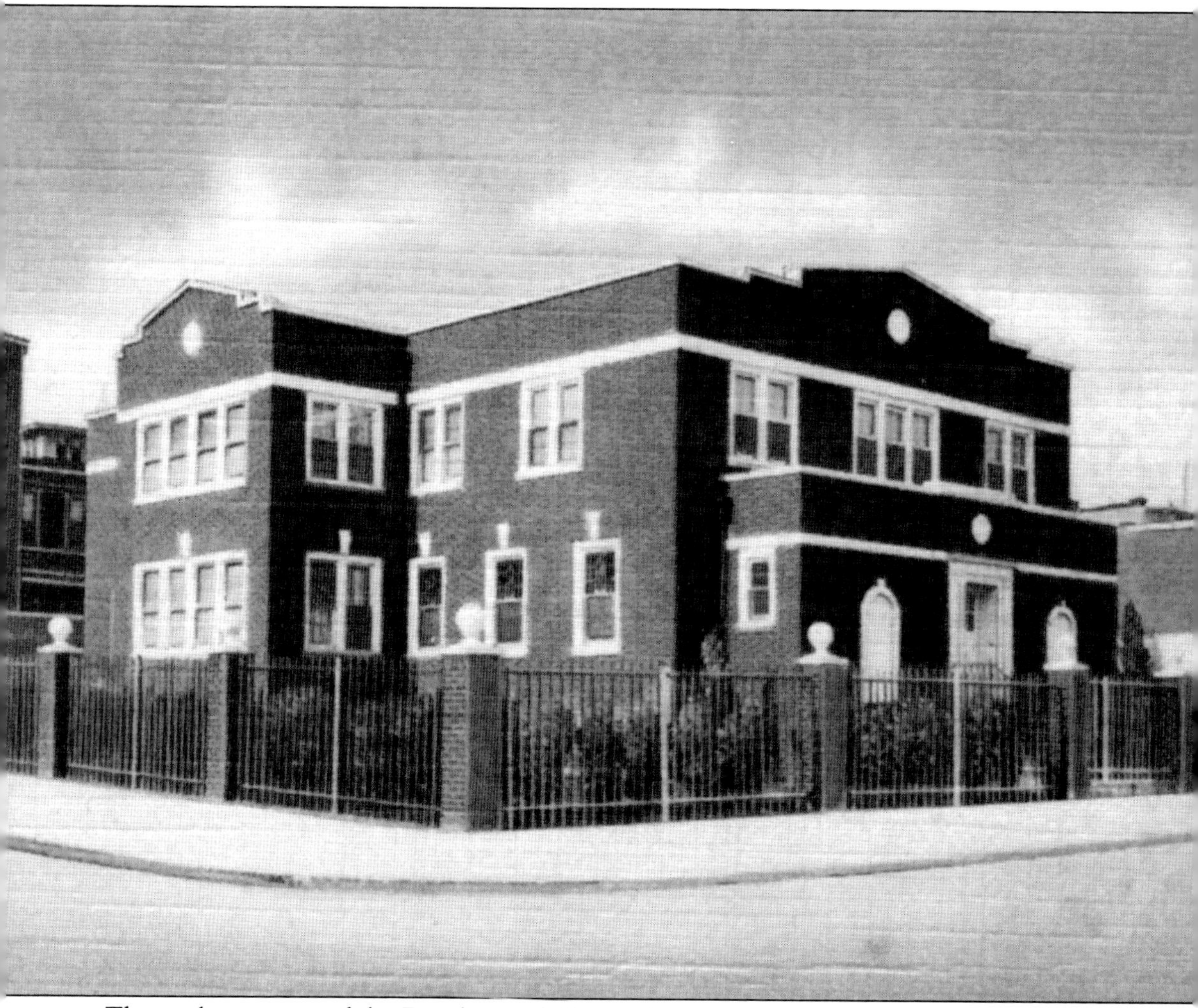

This is the convent of the Daughters of Charity. The Daughters of Charity was the seventh mission of the Mother Elizabeth Ann Seton's community in the United States. They opened St. Peter's Female Orphanage at Third and West Streets, then at Sixth and West Streets. In 1840, they opened a boarding school that became a free academy for girls in 1842. (Courtesy of Historical Society of Delaware.)

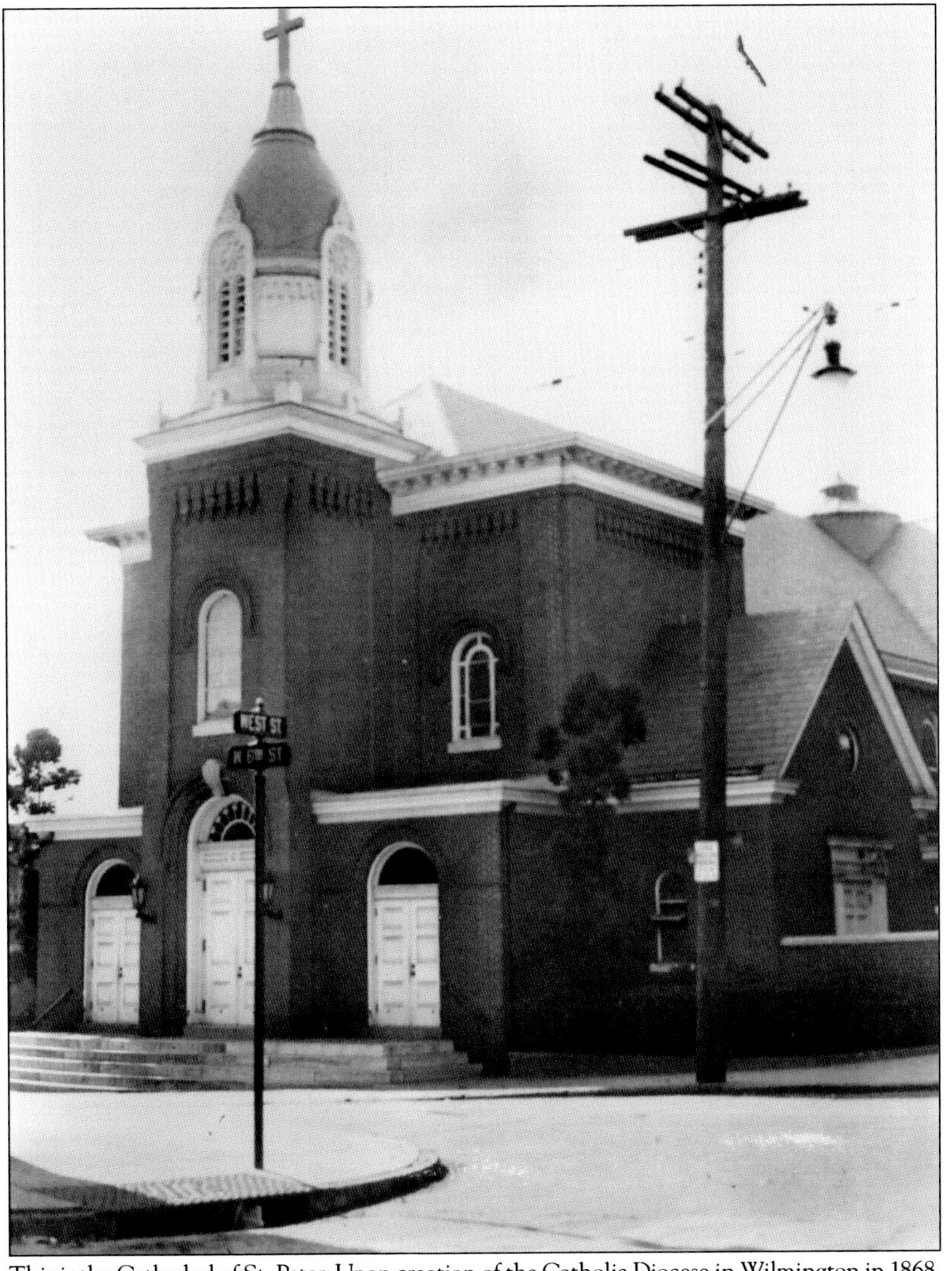

This is the Cathedral of St. Peter. Upon creation of the Catholic Diocese in Wilmington in 1868, Bishop Thomas Becker blessed St. Peter's as the Pro-Cathedral for the newly formed diocese. The church was dedicated as St. Peter's Cathedral in 1905. (Courtesy of Historical Society of Delaware.)

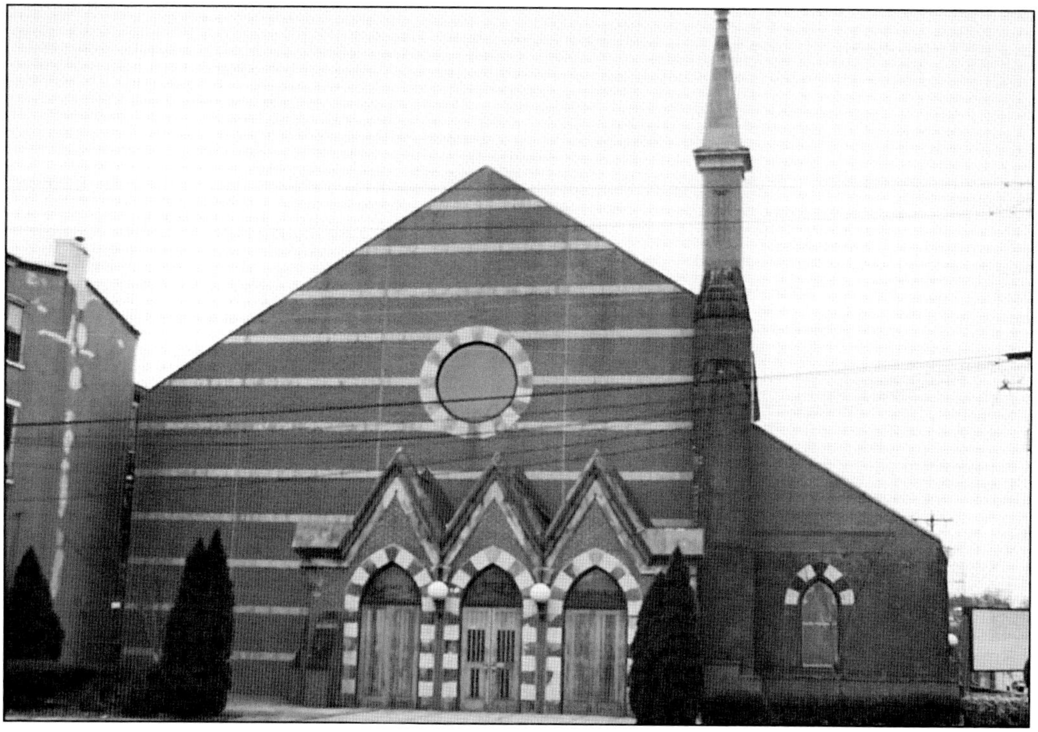

This is the former West Presbyterian Church, built in 1871, which had a face-lift after a fire. The church, composed of brick with brownstone and limestone trim, was built by parishioners from an over-crowded First Presbyterian Church. (Above, photograph by James Bierbaum; below, photograph by Thomas F. Bayard IV.)

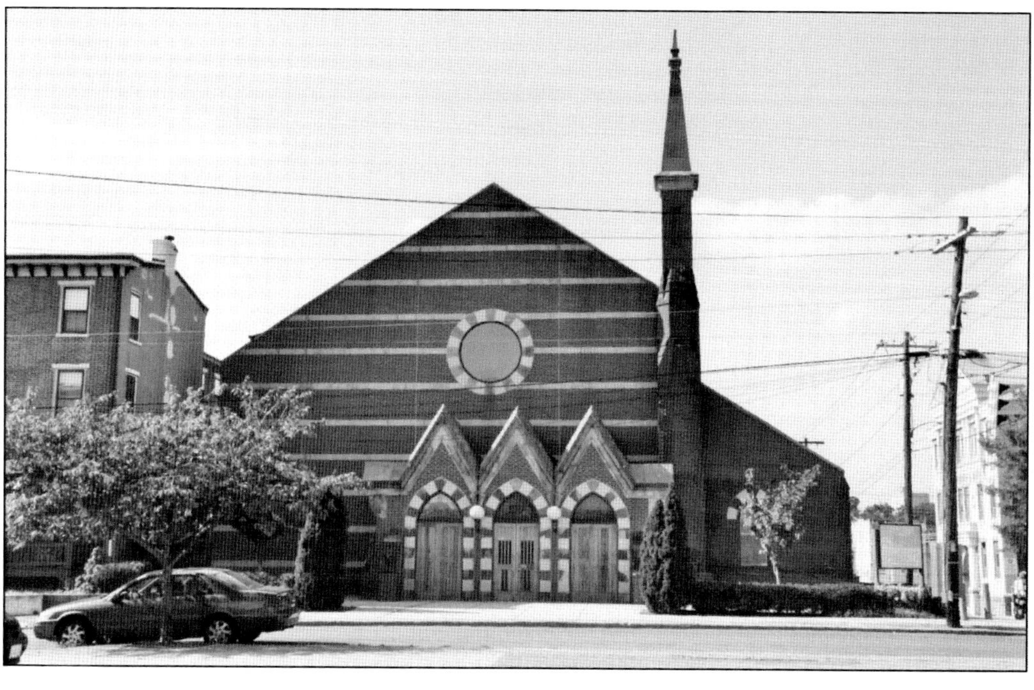

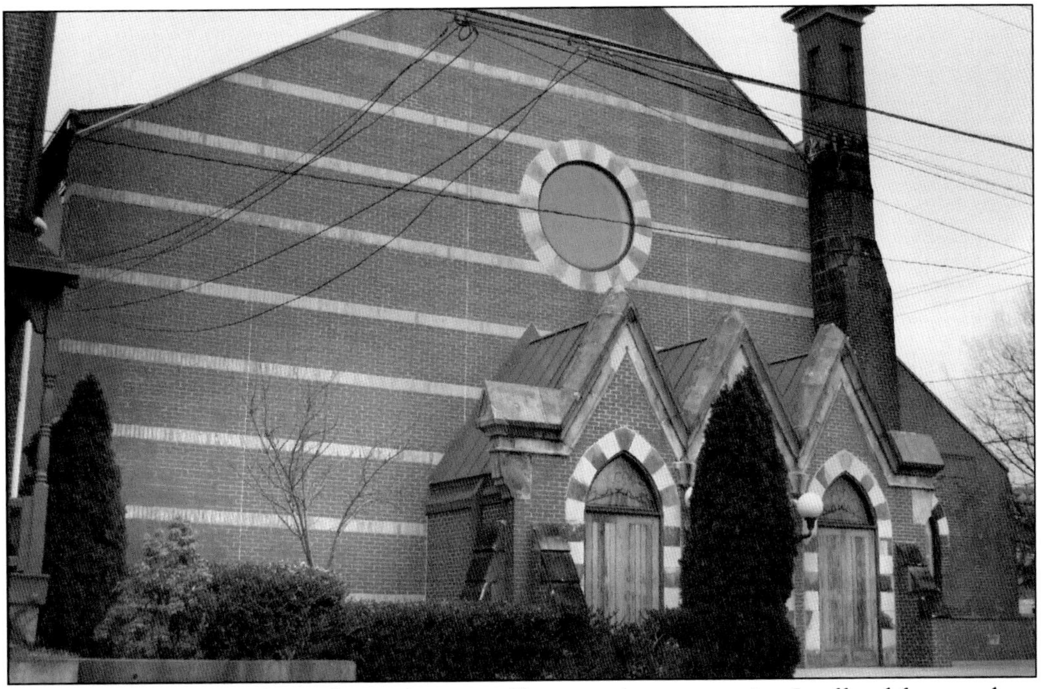

The Presbyterian church was long a beacon of hope to the community. It offered free meals to feed the bodies of the homeless, the Gathering Place played host to performances to lift the spirits of the community, and it also served as a venue for other artists. The church has since closed its doors as a church and is sorely missed by the community. The building has been repurposed as a mental health outpatient facility for Connections. (Photographs by James Bierbaum.)

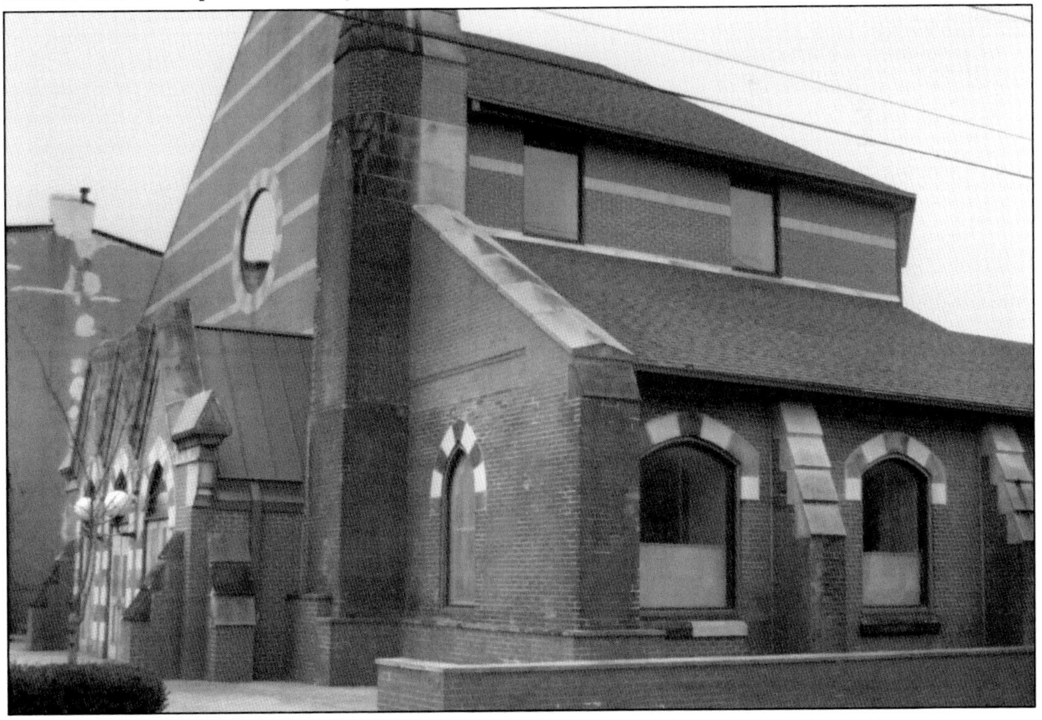

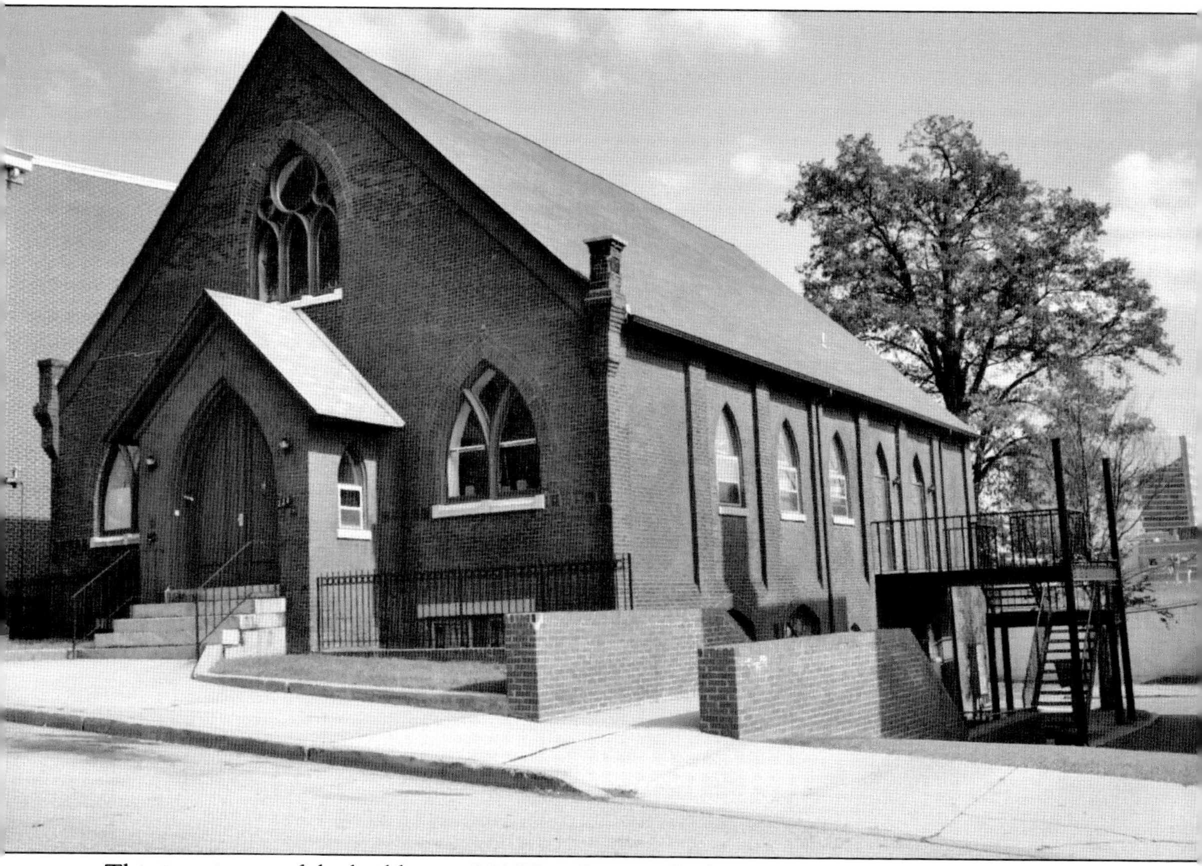

This is a picture of the building at 224 West Street, which was constructed in the period of 1889 to 1890. The building was originally used for the reformed Episcopal Church of the Convent. The structure was subsequently used for four other churches. (Photograph by Thomas F. Bayard IV.)

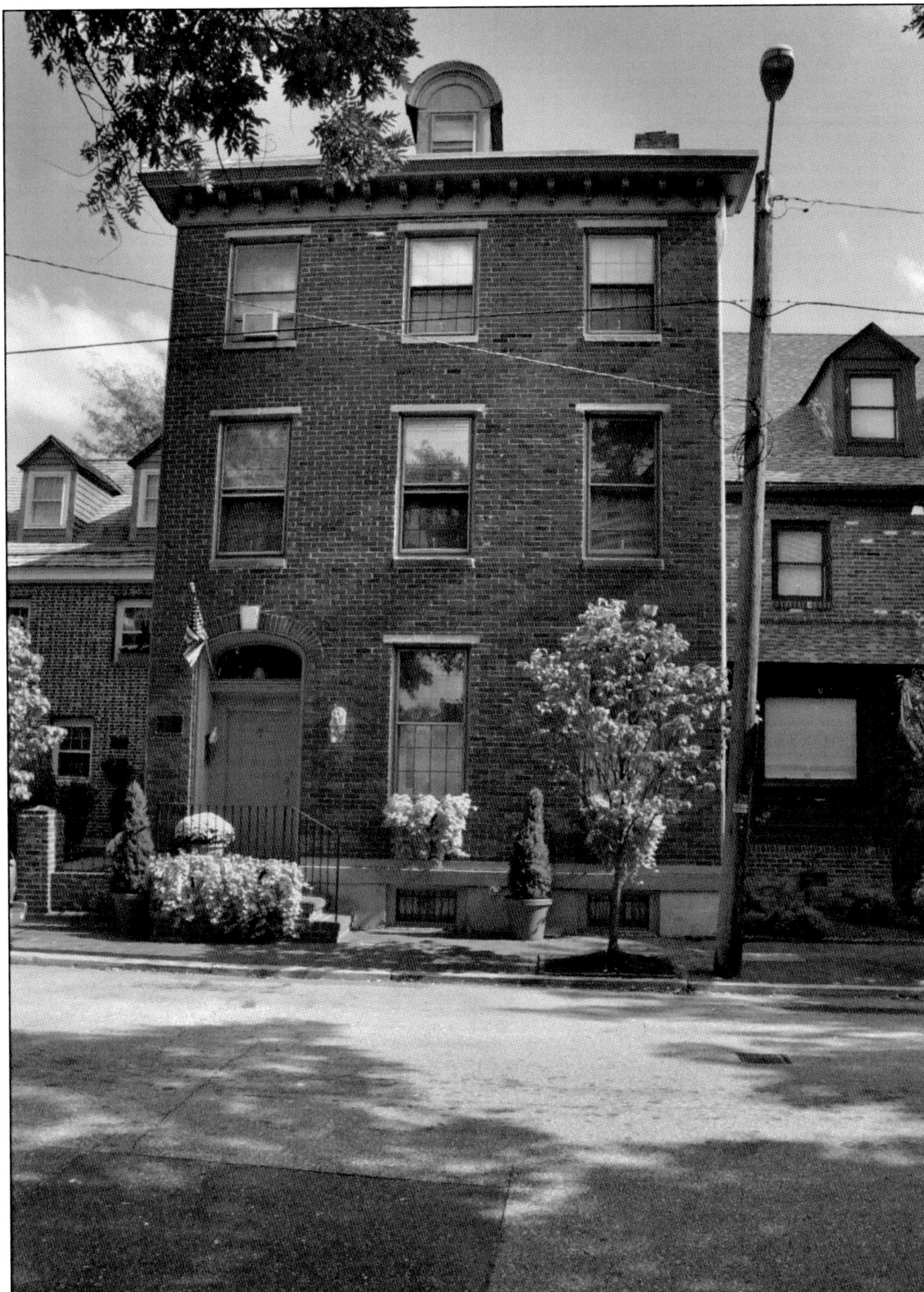

This building at 308 West Street was constructed in 1865. This home was part of lumber merchant Joshua Simmons's family enclave. Joshua Simmons's son George built the home. Bauduy Simmons's home at 304 West Street also survives. (Photograph by Thomas F. Bayard IV.)

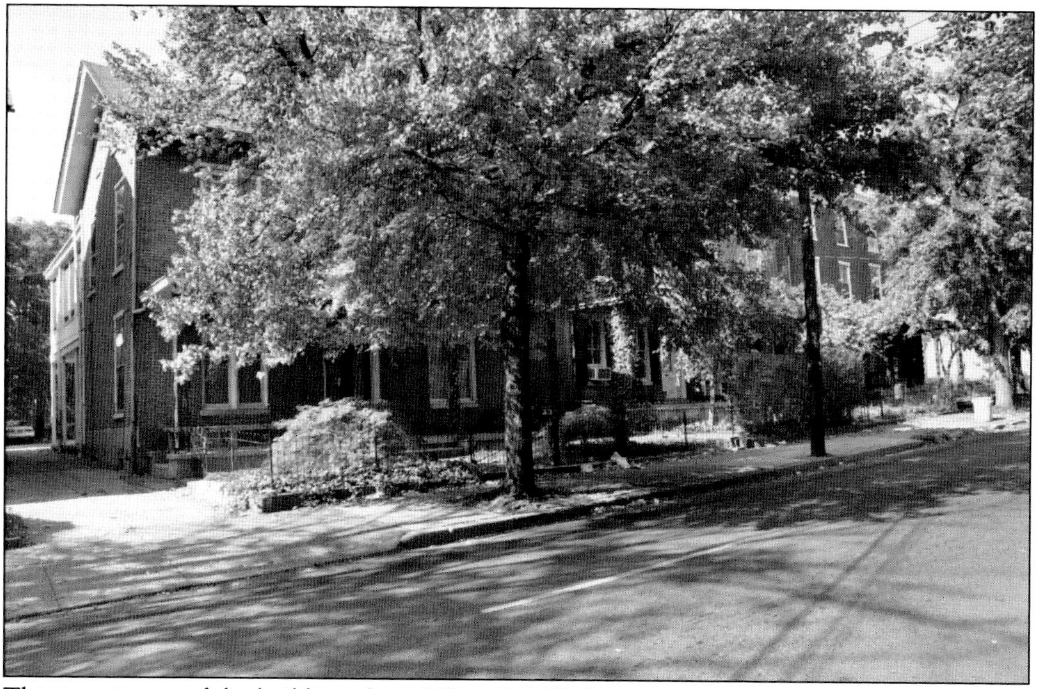

This is a picture of the buildings from 505 to 515 Washington Street, which were built around 1865. The homes were built in the neo-Gothic and Italianate style and they still retain their original ornate wrought iron porch supports. (Photograph by Thomas F. Bayard IV.)

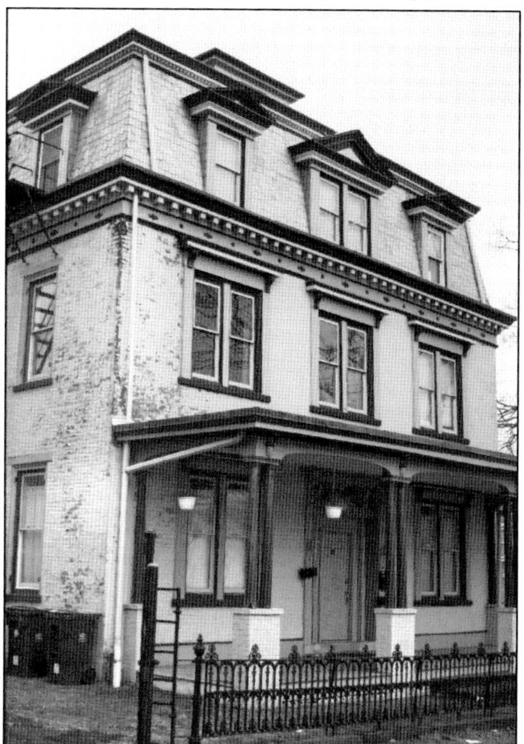

This building stands at 600 Washington Street in Quaker Hill in Wilmington, Delaware. Although the main portion of this fine building was built by Enoch Strotsenburg, a local ironworker, in 1860, the original part of this house was constructed in 1798. (Photograph by James Bierbaum.)

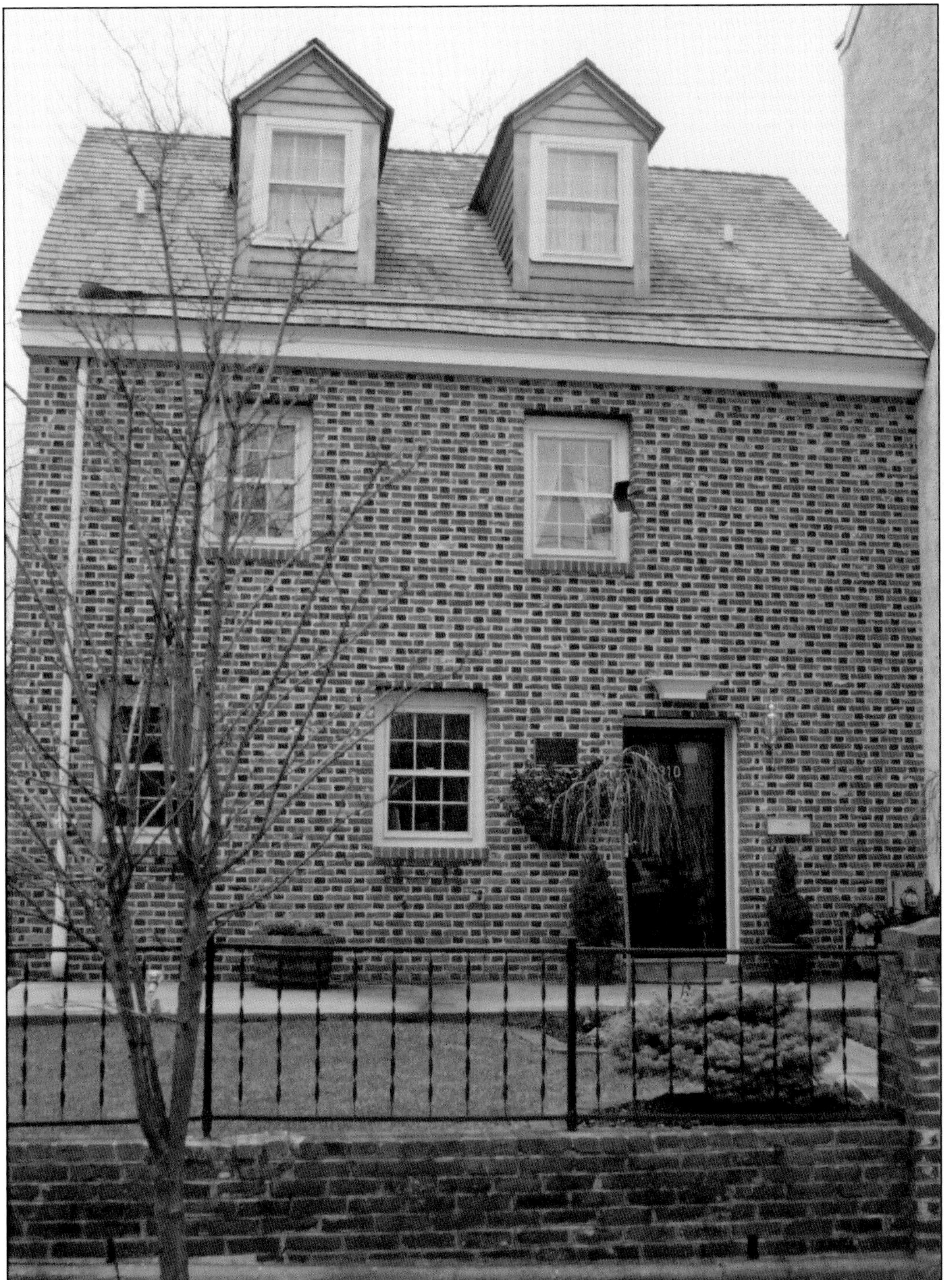

The photograph above shows the house at 310 West Street, which was built around 1750. It is one of the oldest remaining buildings in Quaker Hill. A subbasement in the home is believed to have been an Underground Railroad stop for fugitive slaves in the mid-1800s. (Photograph by James Bierbaum.)

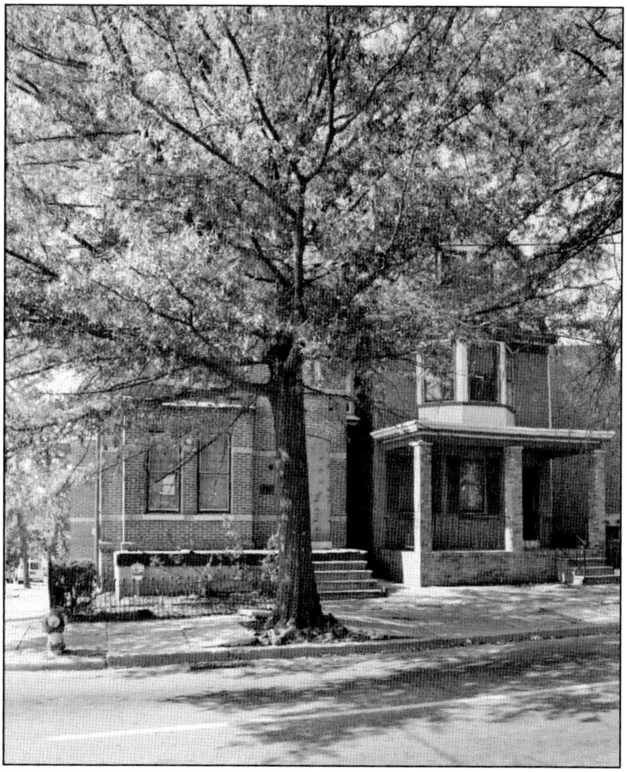

This is the home of architect Edwin Thorne at 401 Washington Street. Various Victorian features are apparent, such as the mansard roof. (Photograph by Thomas F. Bayard IV.)

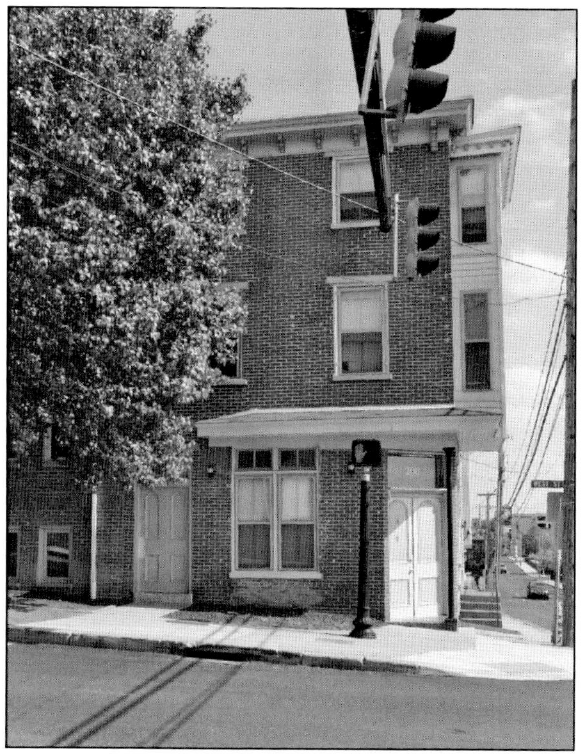

This the corner building at 200 West Second Street, the oldest building in the 200 West Street block still standing. The building originally housed the home of Patrick Taylor as well as his butcher shop. (Photograph by Thomas F. Bayard IV.)

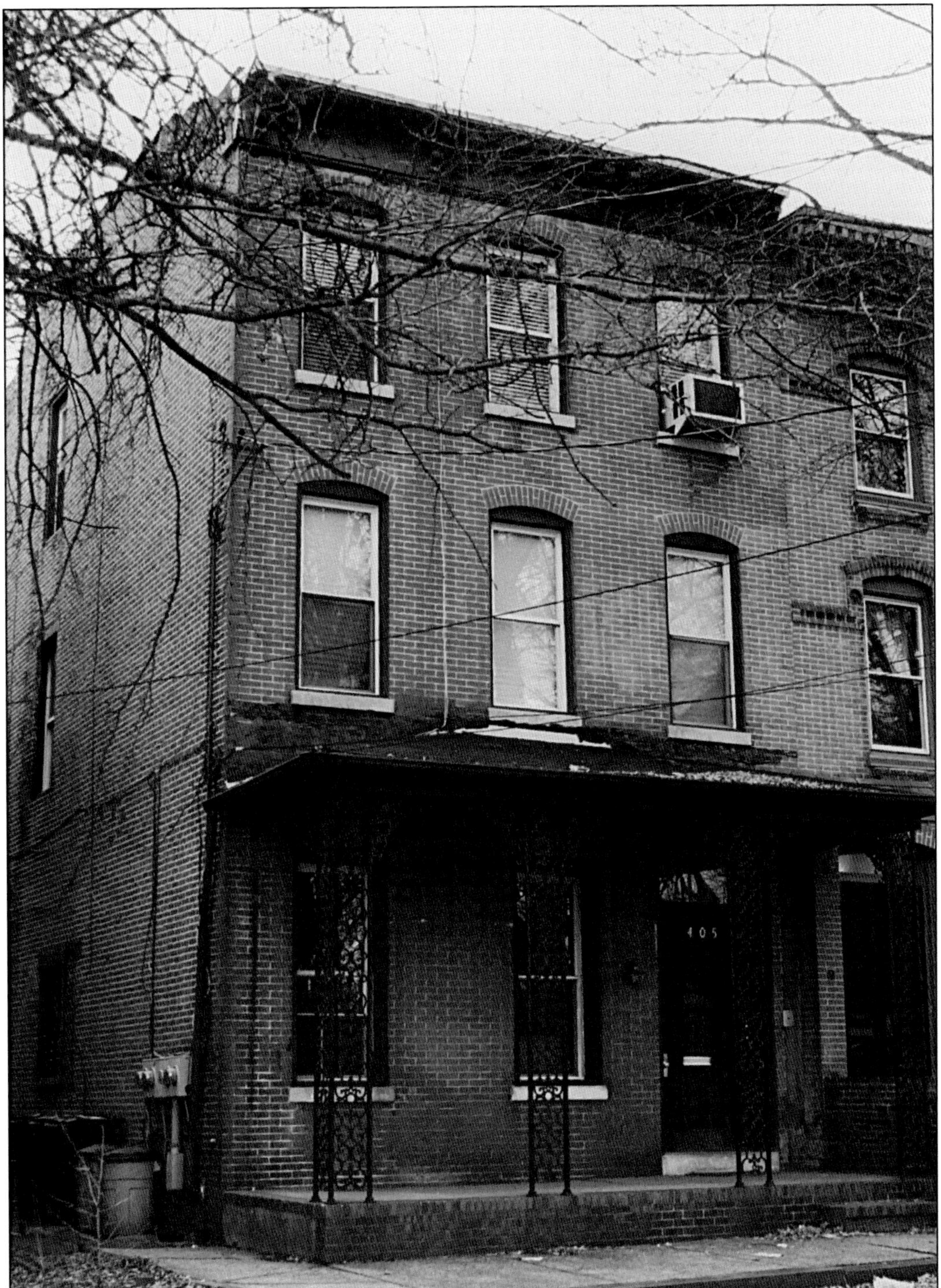

This is a picture of the building at 405 Washington Street. The homes along Washington Street were built around 1865 in the neo-Gothic and Italianate styles. They still retain their original, ornate wrought-iron porch supports, as this one does. (Photograph by James Bierbaum.)

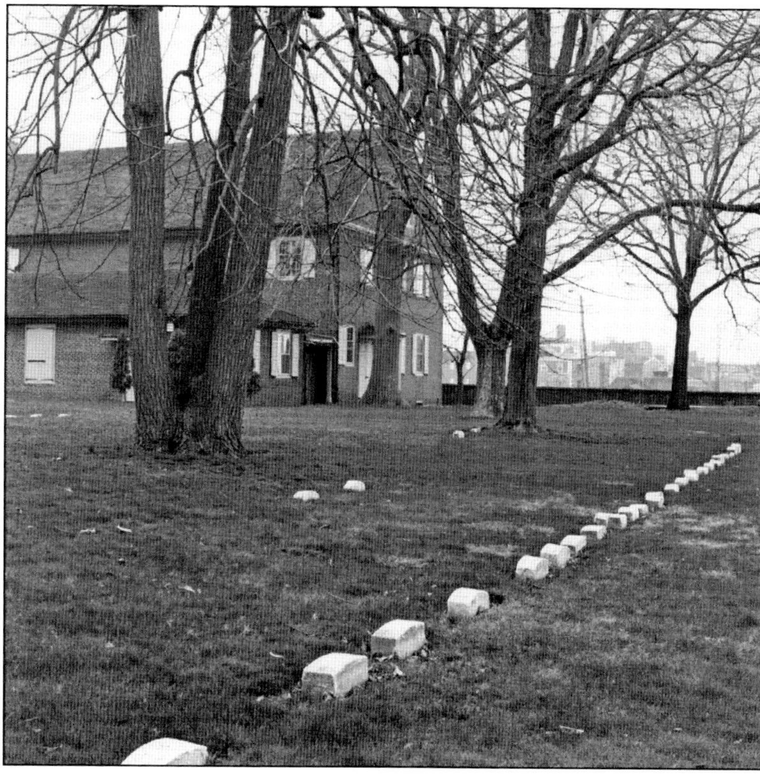

This is Wilmington Friends Meeting as it appeared around 1980. This picture was taken from the Fifth Street side and shows the rows of simple graves in the graveyard. Many distinguished people, such as John Dickinson, are buried here. (Photograph by Thomas F. Bayard IV.)

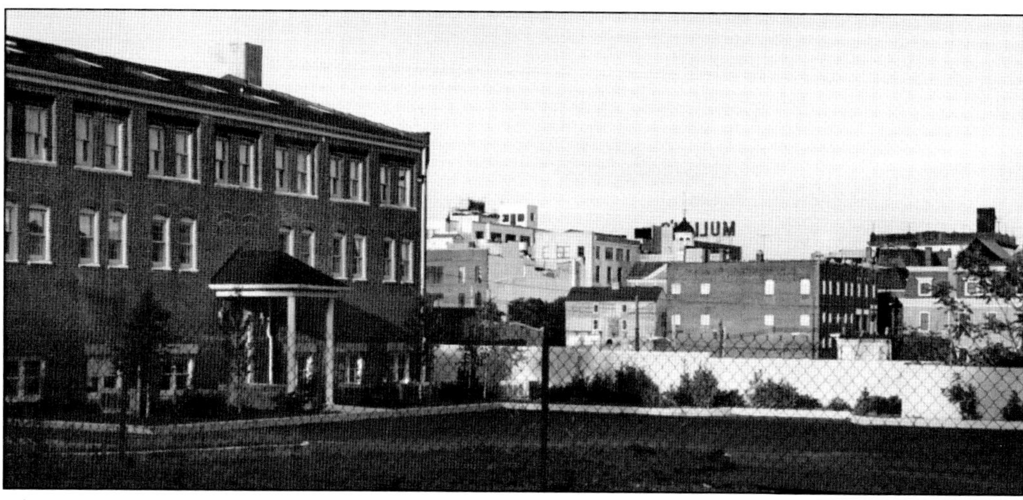

This is what remained of the Wilmington Friends School building in Quaker Hill in 1983. Part of the original building served as apartments in the 1940s and 1950s. Much of the building has been torn down. What remains originally served as a gymnasium. (Photograph by Thomas F. Bayard IV.)

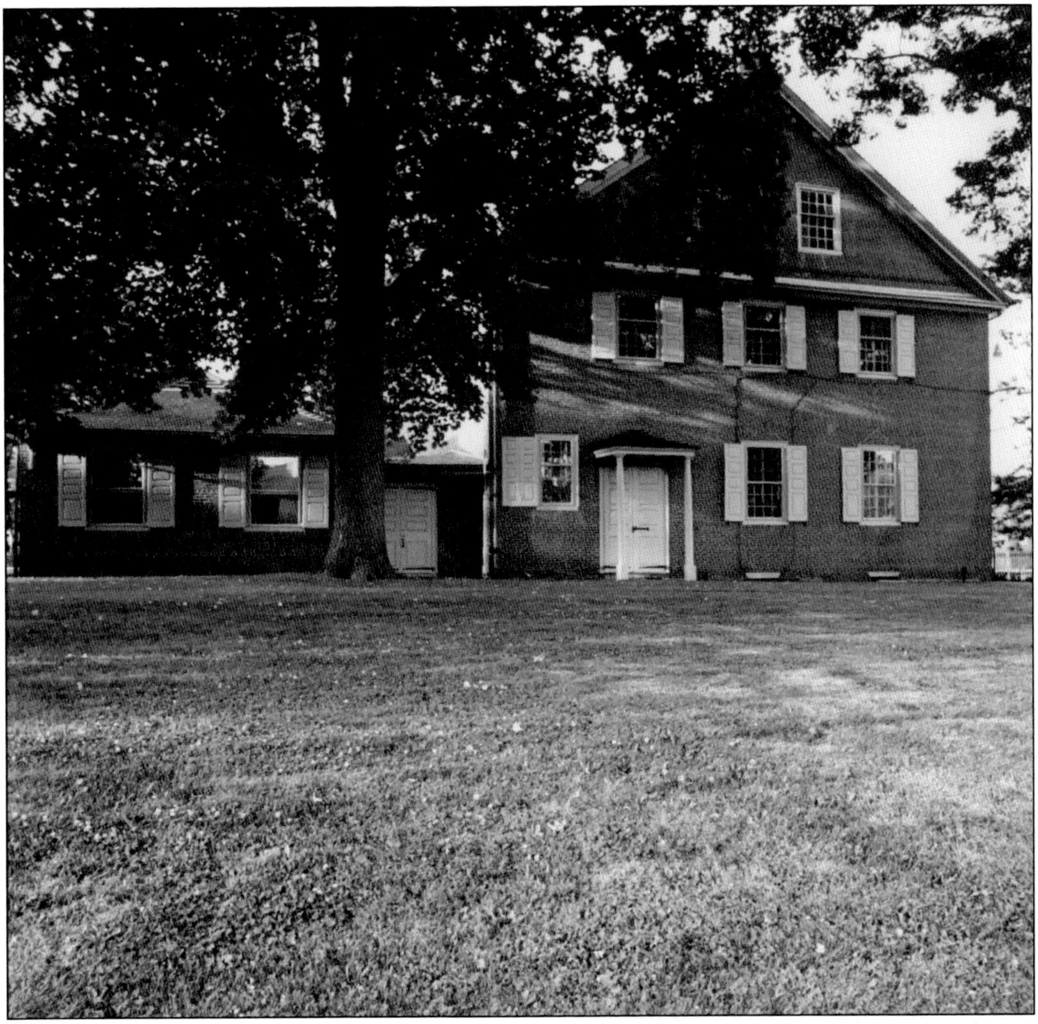

This is the Wilmington Friends Meetinghouse from another angle in 1983. The meetinghouse has several small porches over various entrances, painted gray at that time but now painted cream in accordance with records of its earliest colors. (Photograph by Thomas F. Bayard IV.)

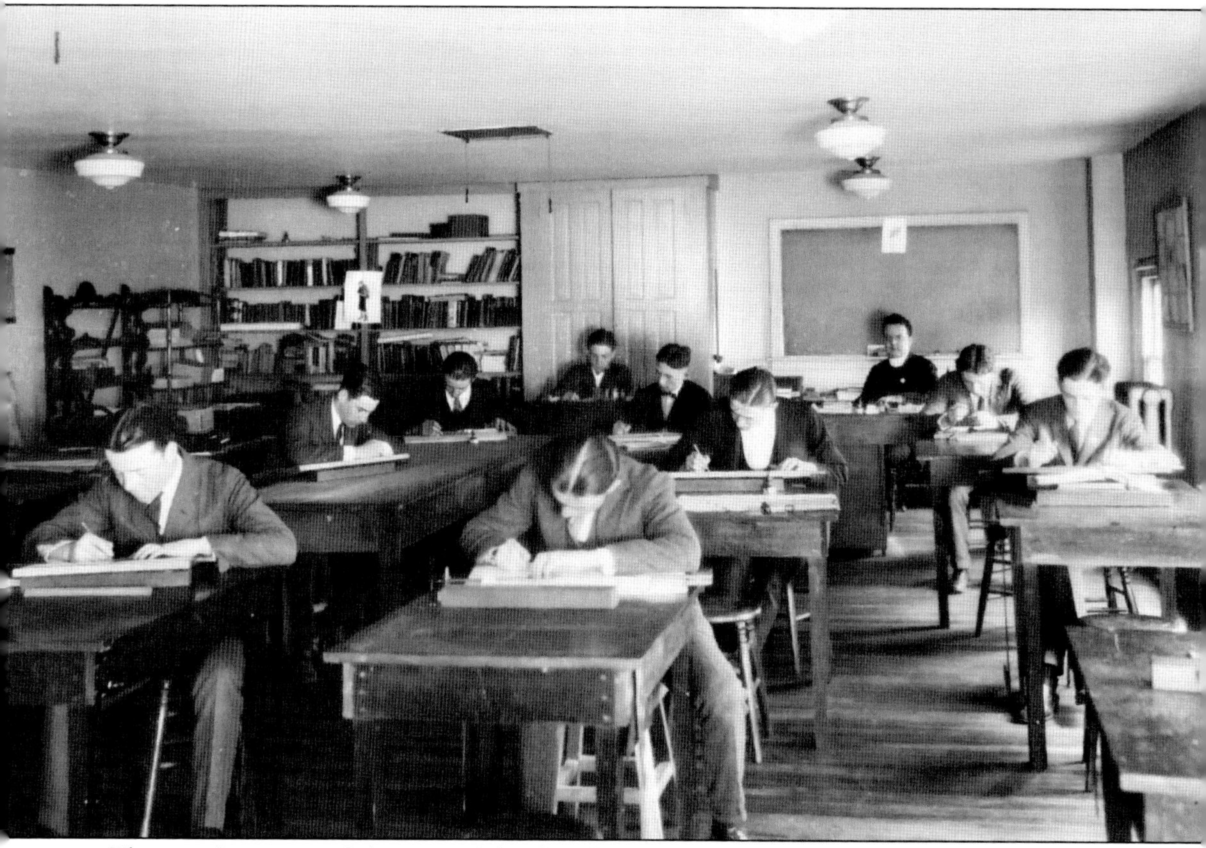

This is a classroom at Salesianum School in the 1920s. The school was founded in 1903 and was operated by the Oblates of St. Frances de Sales. It is an independent Catholic secondary school for boys. It used to be in Quaker Hill. (Courtesy of Historical Society of Delaware.)

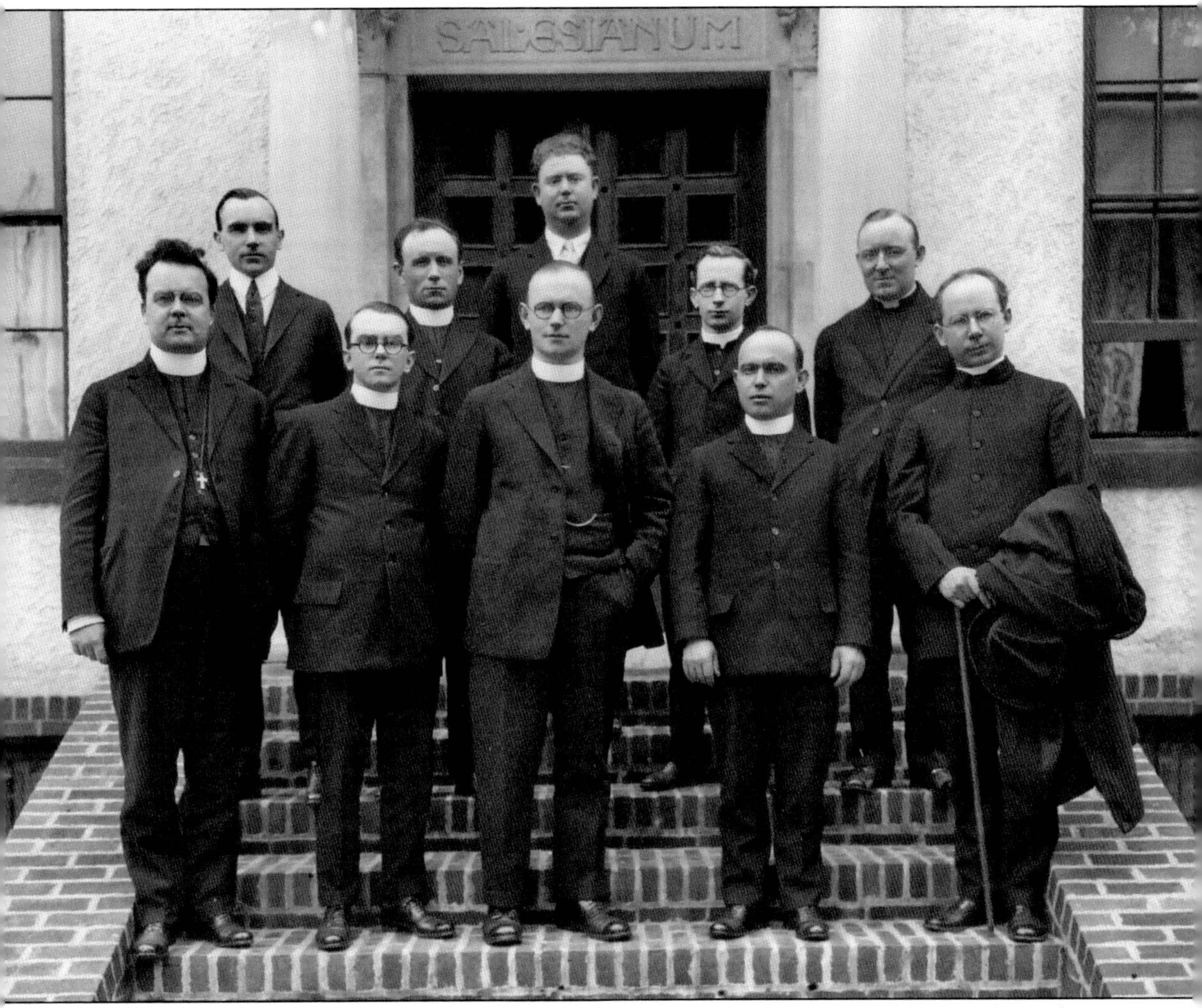

This is a picture of the teaching faculty of Salesianum School. This picture was taken when the school was fairly new, and most of the faculty appear to be priests. (Courtesy of Historical Society of Delaware.)

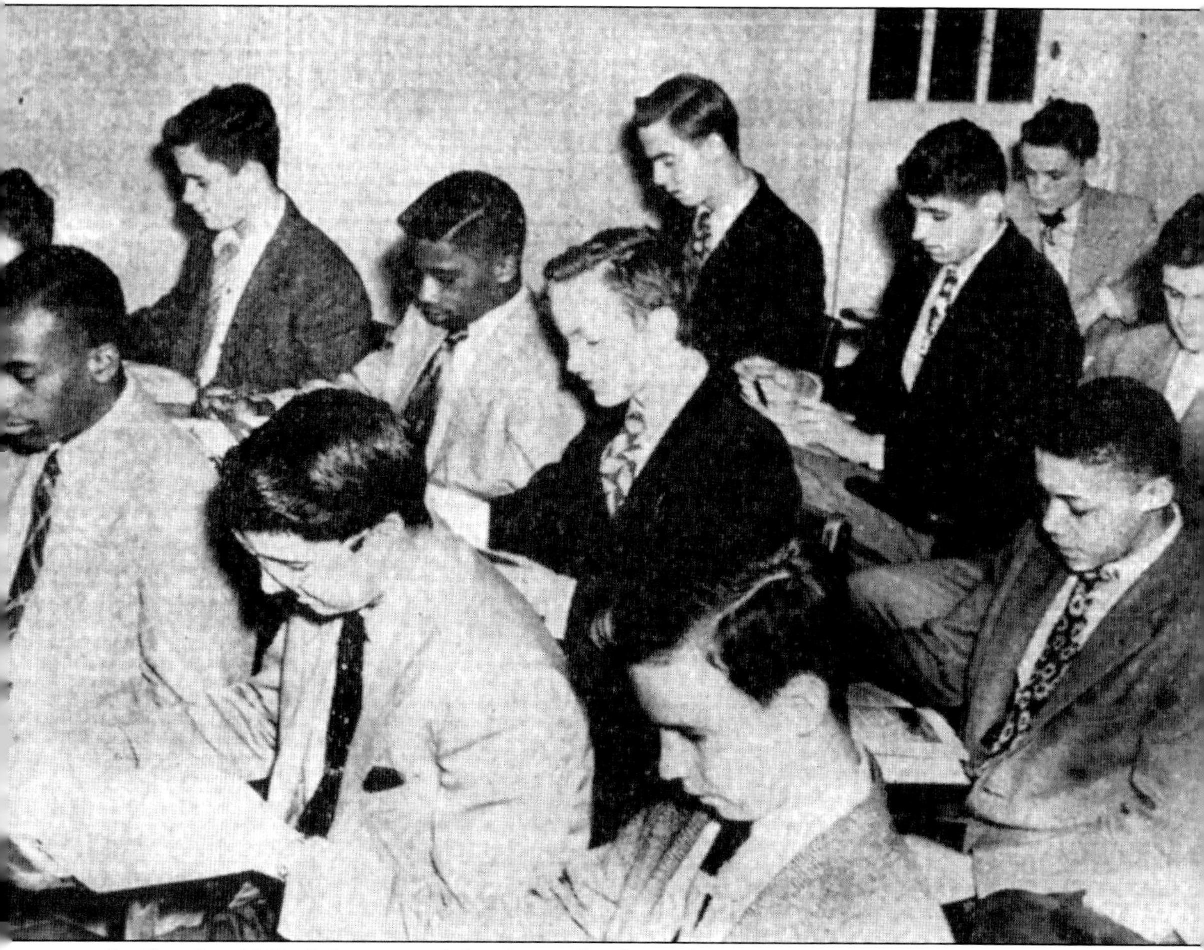

In October 1950, Salesianum School was the first school in Delaware to voluntarily racially integrate its student body. Delaware was later one of four states represented in the landmark case of *Brown v. Topeka Board of Education* integration case before the U.S. Supreme Court. (Courtesy of Historical Society of Delaware.)

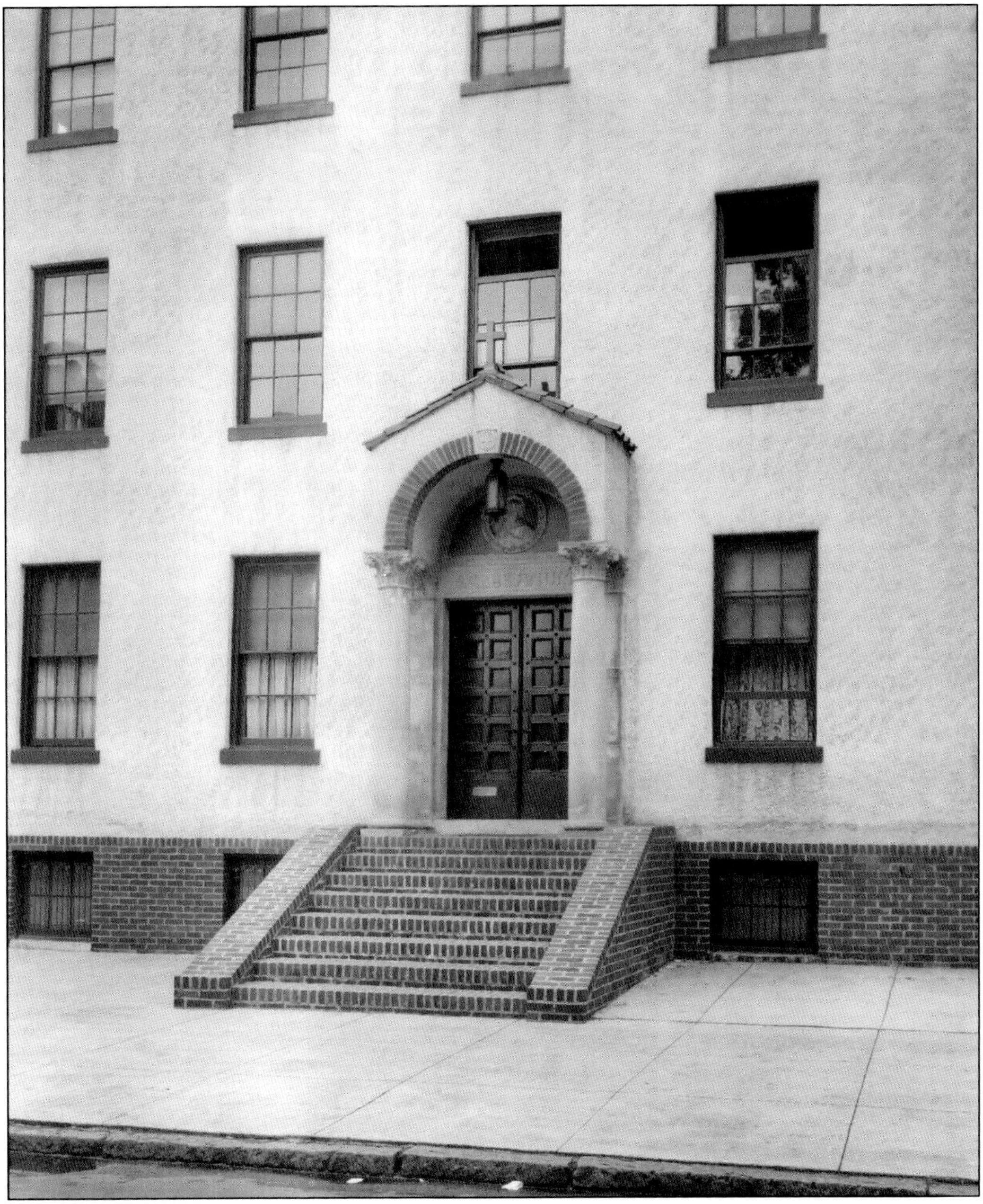

This is a picture of the exterior of Salesianum School taken around 1924. The school was founded in 1903 in Wilmington, Delaware's Quaker Hill but has since moved to another part of town. (Courtesy of Historical Society of Delaware.)

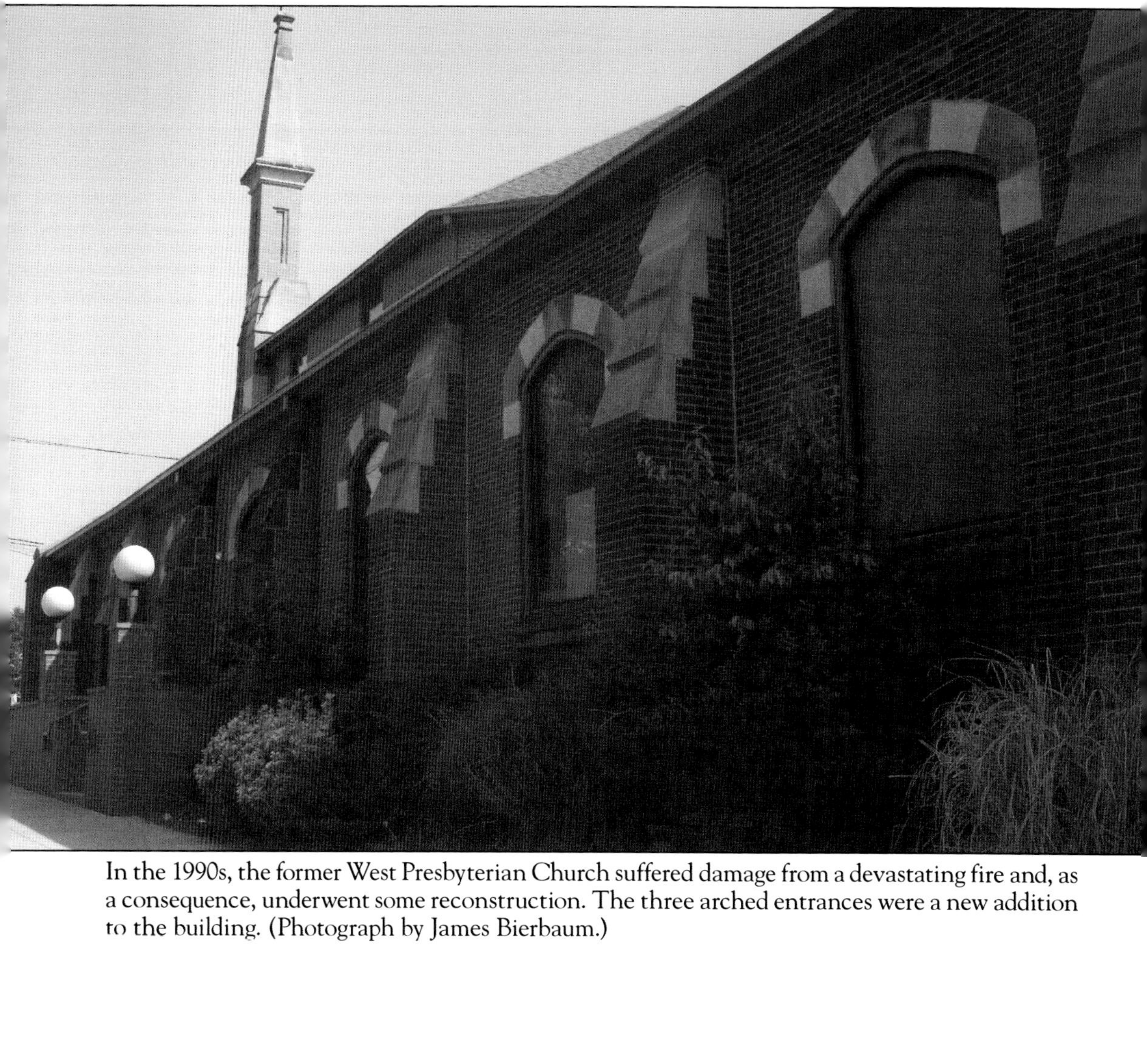

In the 1990s, the former West Presbyterian Church suffered damage from a devastating fire and, as a consequence, underwent some reconstruction. The three arched entrances were a new addition to the building. (Photograph by James Bierbaum.)

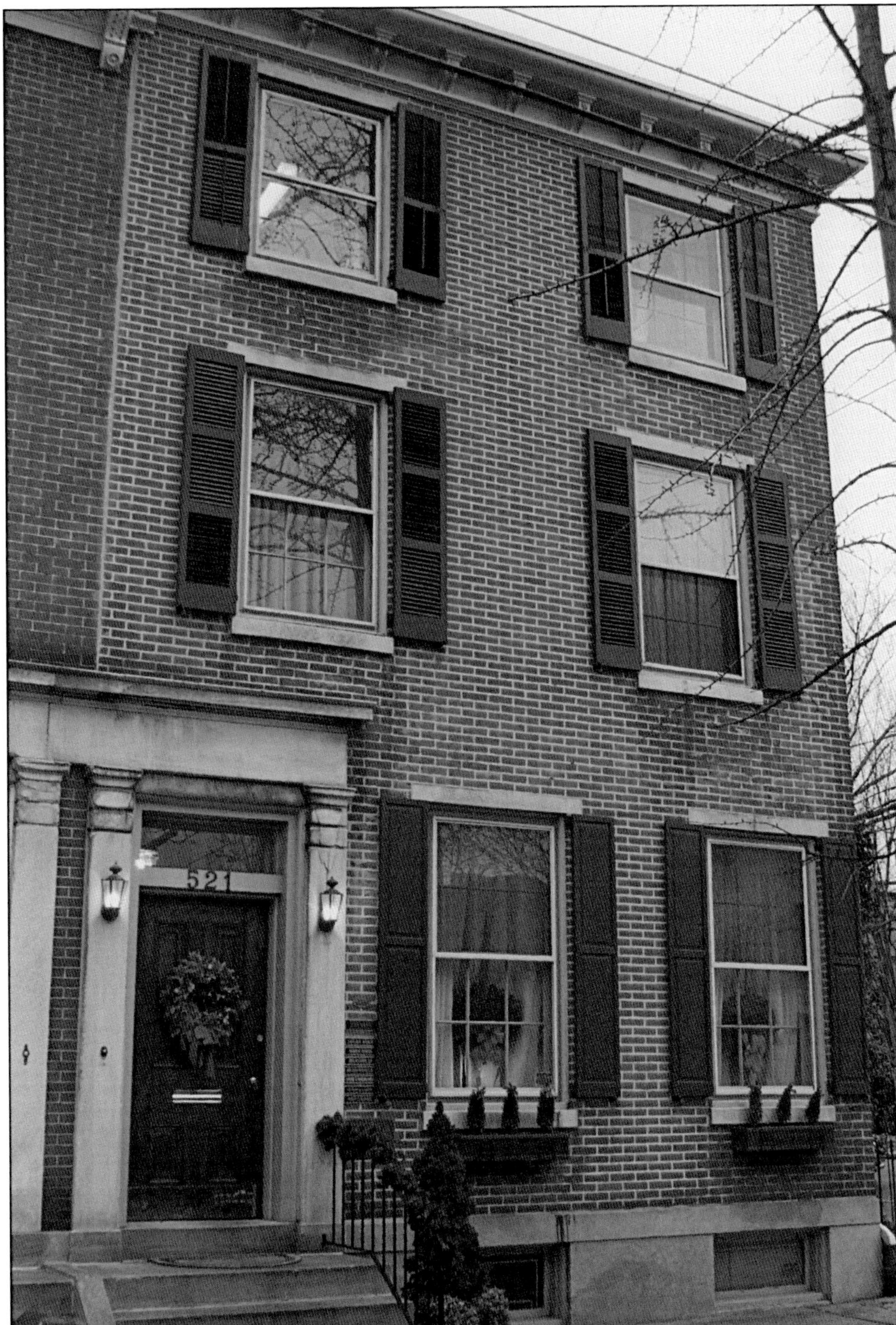

This Law Offices of Bayard Marin and the office of the Quaker Hill Historic Preservation Foundation occupy this historic building at 521 West Street, the interior of which has been restored. The Quaker Hill Historic Preservation Foundation provides educational programs about Quaker Hill history, among other things. (Photograph by James Bierbaum.)

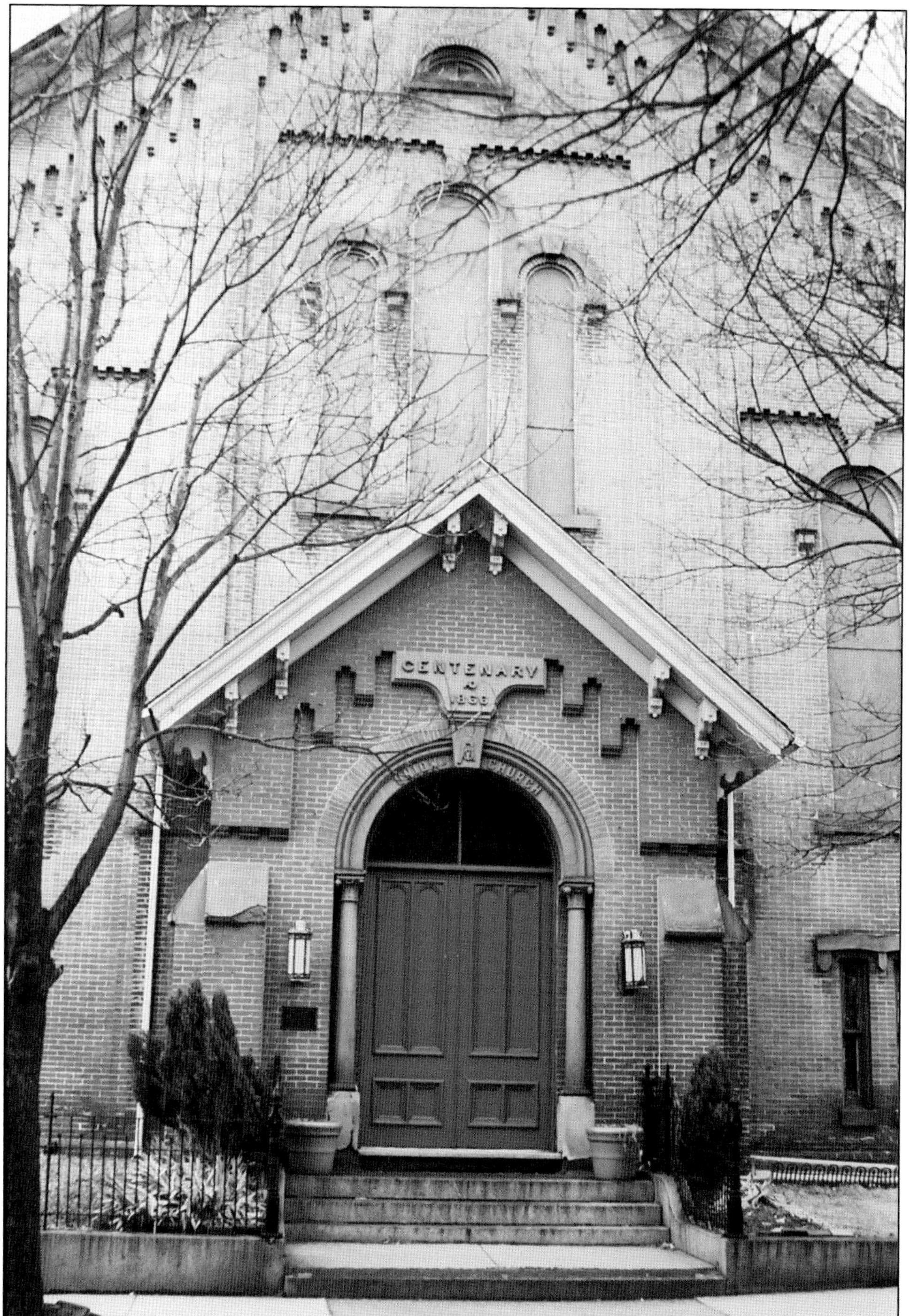

This is the former Union United Methodist Church, which was built in 1868. This church was built by several small neighborhood businessmen, including Cyrus Stern. The building now houses the very vital Tabernacle Full Gospel Baptist Church. (Photograph by James Bierbaum.)

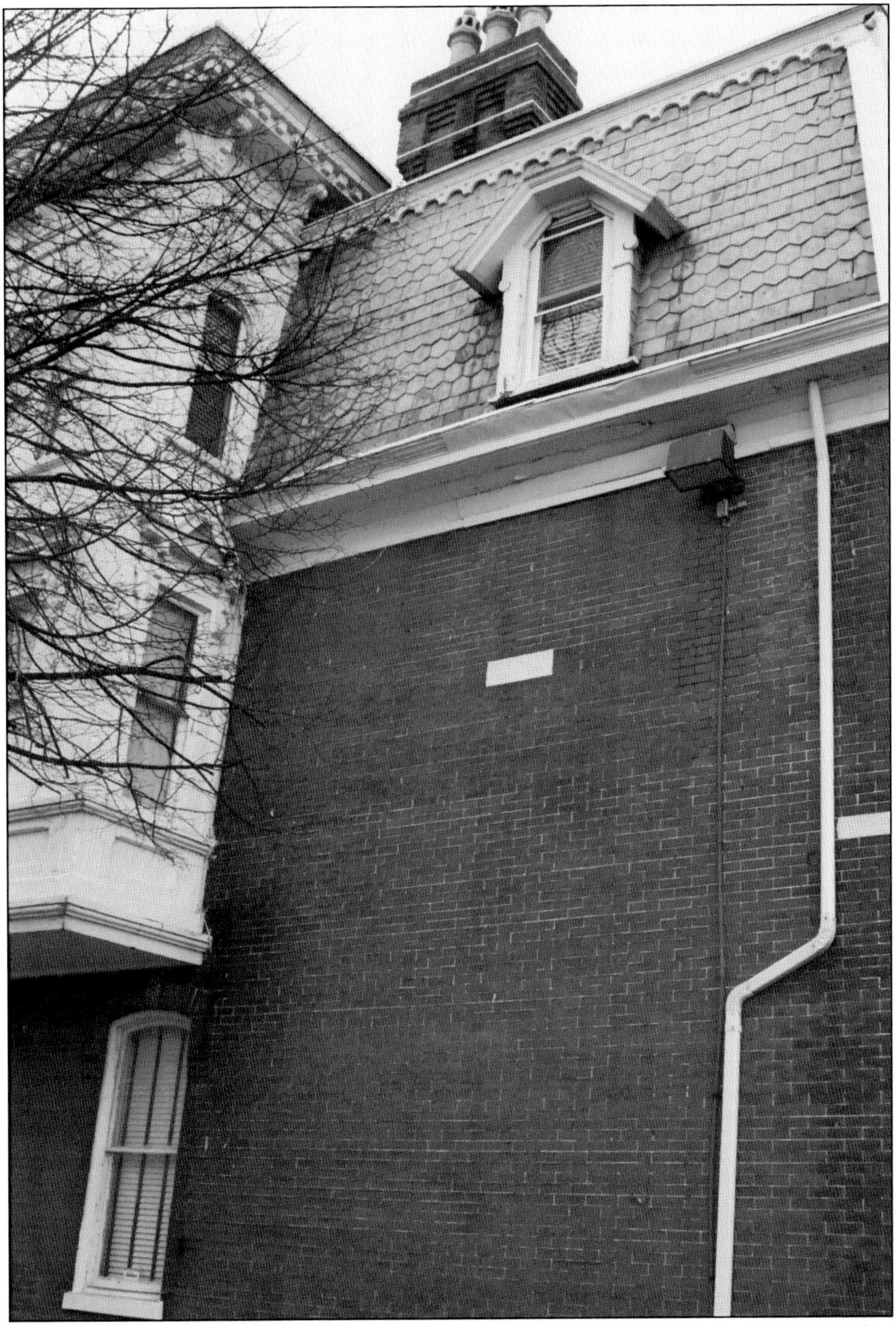

This is the property at 501 West Street, which was erected around 1883. In 1738, this was the site of the first home constructed on Quaker Hill. It was built by Thomas West, who was a relative of Benjamin West, a famous painter at the time of the American Revolution. (Photograph by James Bierbaum.)

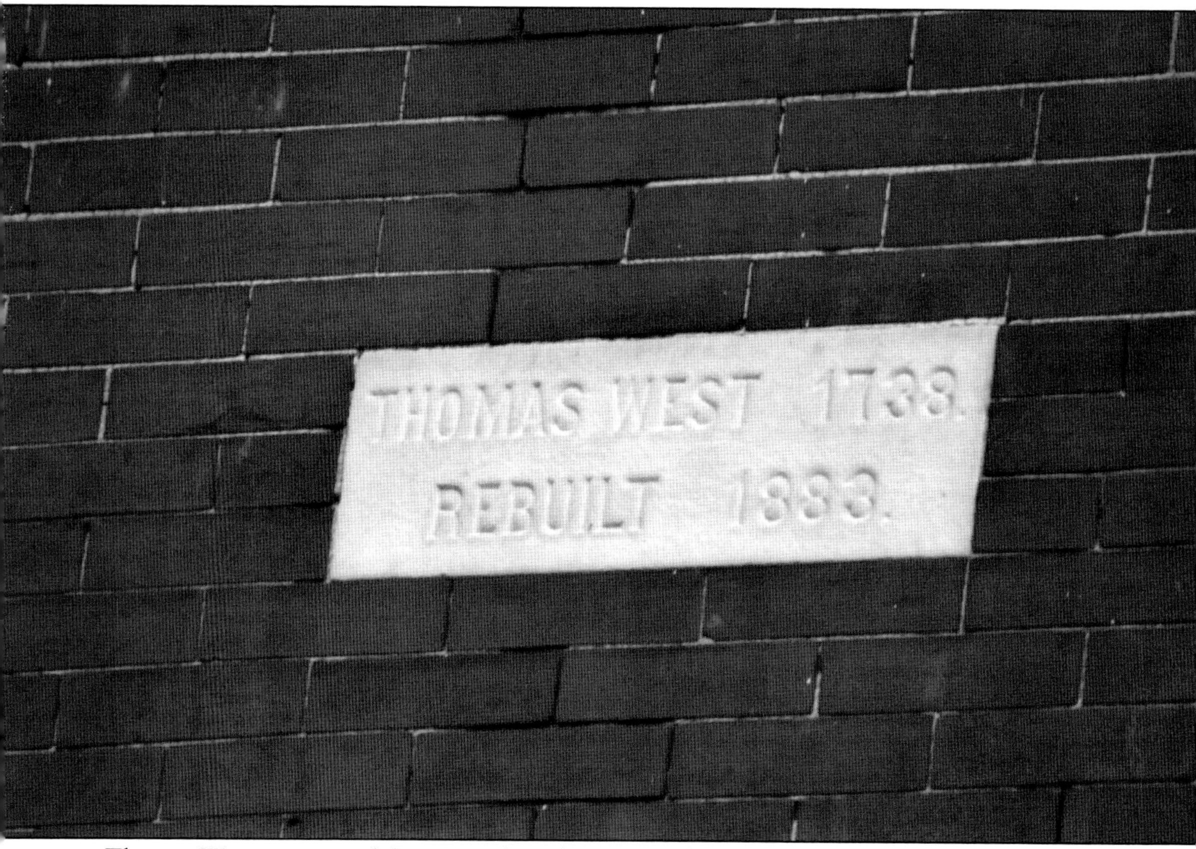

Thomas West was one of the original settlers on Quaker Hill. His great-great grandson, Cyrus Stern, built the home that now exists at 501 West Street. (Photograph by James Bierbaum.)

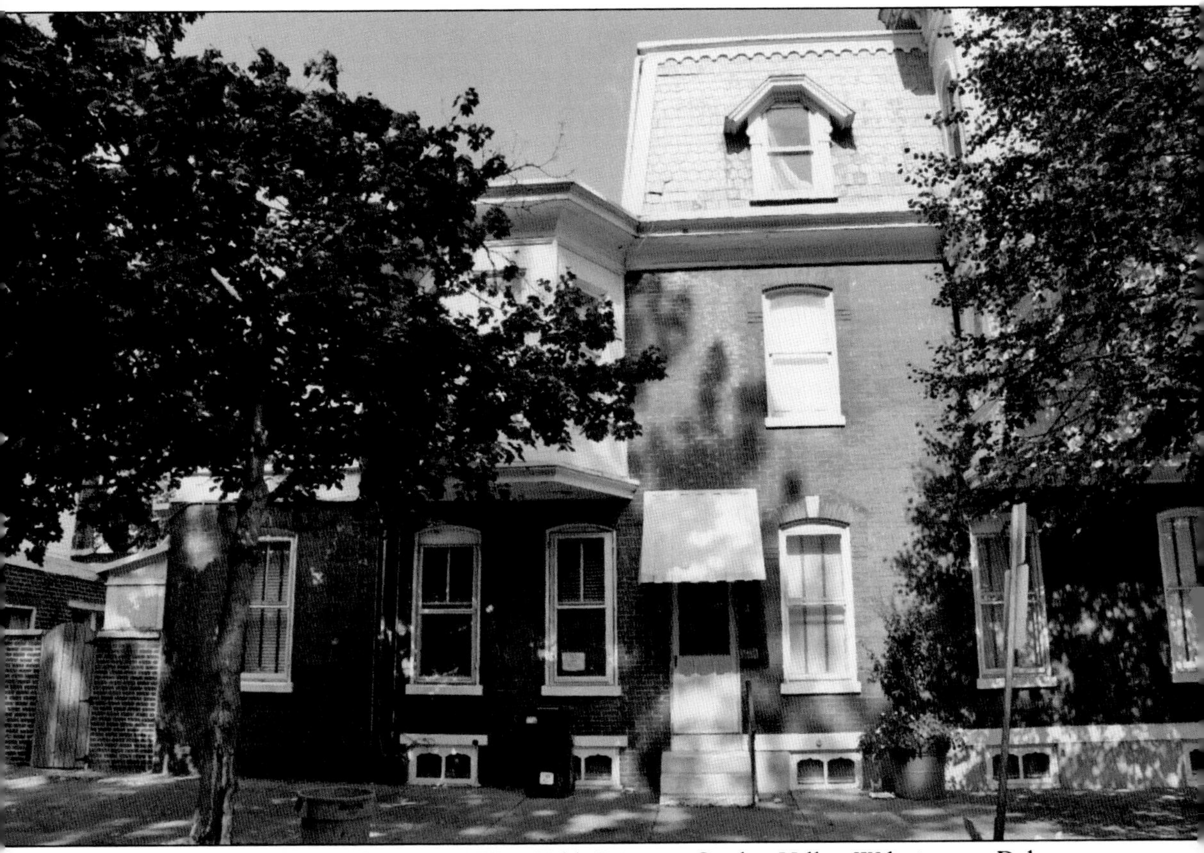

This is a picture of the building at 401 West Fifth Street in Quaker Hill in Wilmington, Delaware. The building is attached to the building built by Cyrus Stern. (Photograph by Earl M. White.)

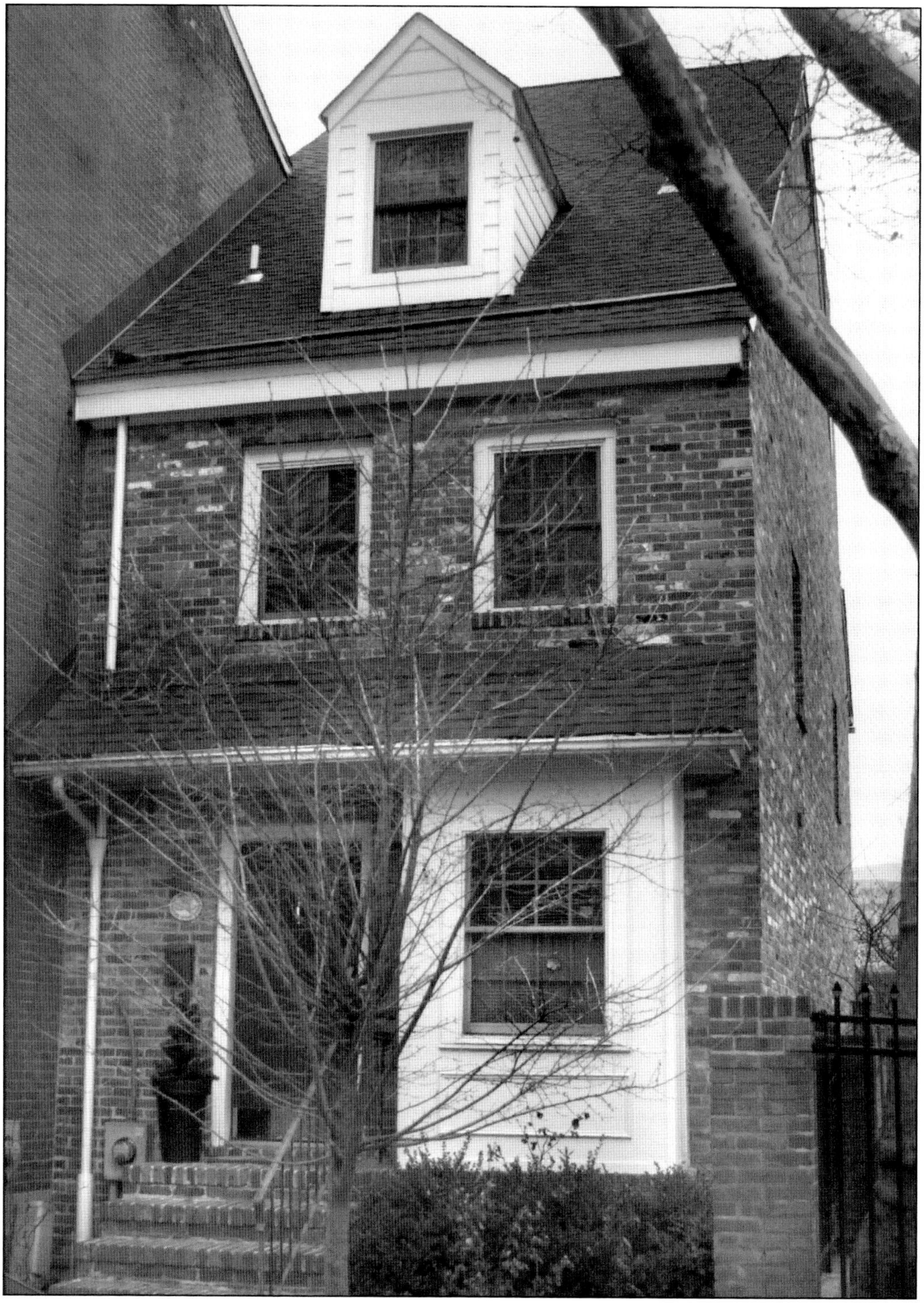

This is a picture of the home located at 302 West Street. This residence was built in the 18th century, and it has been extensively renovated. Twinkling city lights can be viewed from the rear of the house as far as the Delaware Memorial Bridge. (Photograph by James Bierbaum.)

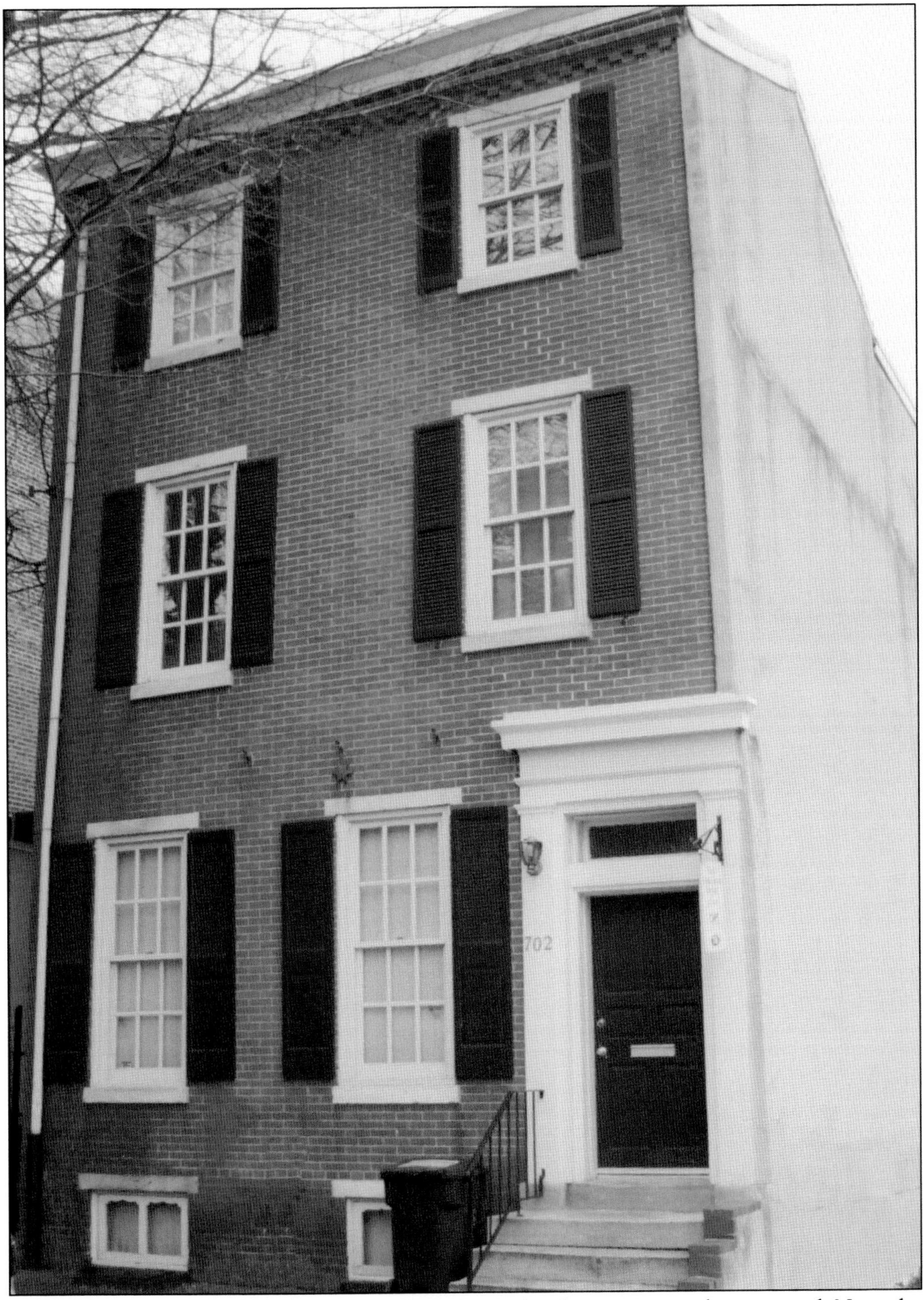

This 18th-century home located at 702 West Street has been extensively renovated. Note the Colonial features of the home, such as the great number of panes in the six windows and the door to one side of the building's front. (Photograph by James Bierbaum.)

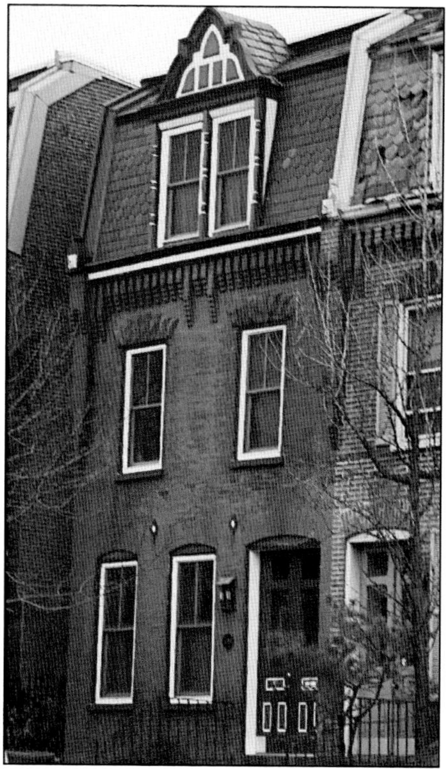

This three-story 1890s-era home at 508 West Fourth Street was completely renovated in 1981. Since that time, numerous enhancements have created an appealing combination of Victorian-era charm and modern convenience. (Photograph by James Bierbaum.)

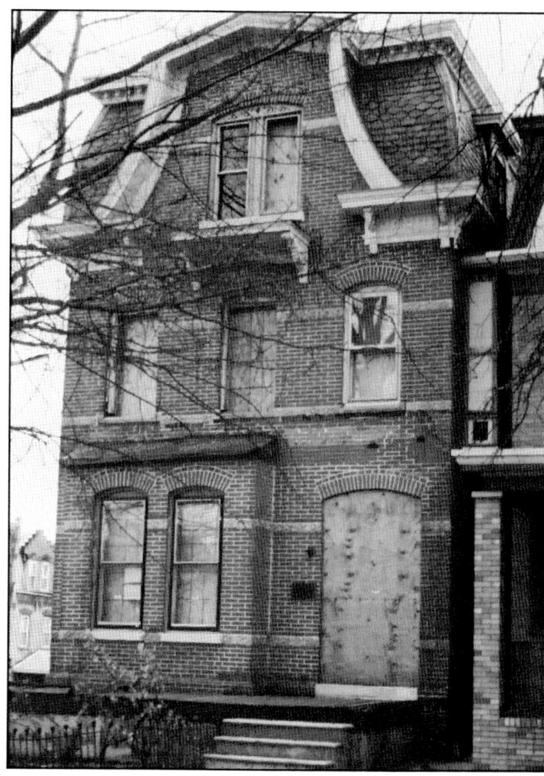

This is the building at 401 Washington Street, which was built in 1881.The house is in the Victorian style. It was built by Edwin Thorne, who was a local architect. It was meant to be an example of his architectural expertise. (Photograph by James Bierbaum.)

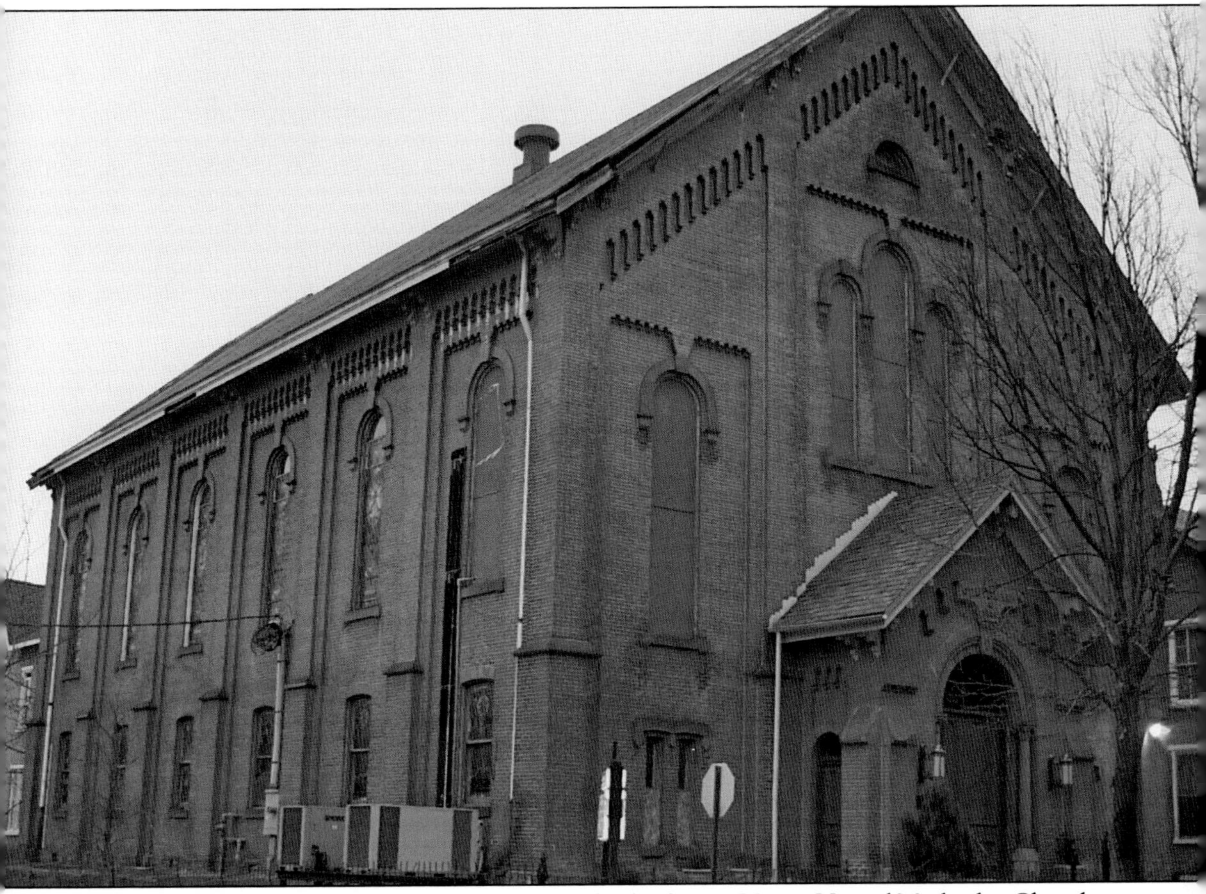

This is the Tabernacle Full Gospel Baptist Church, the former Union United Methodist Church, which was built in 1868. Several small neighborhood businessmen, including Cyrus Stern, helped build the church. The building now houses the very vital Tabernacle Full Gospel Baptist Church. (Photograph by James Bierbaum.)

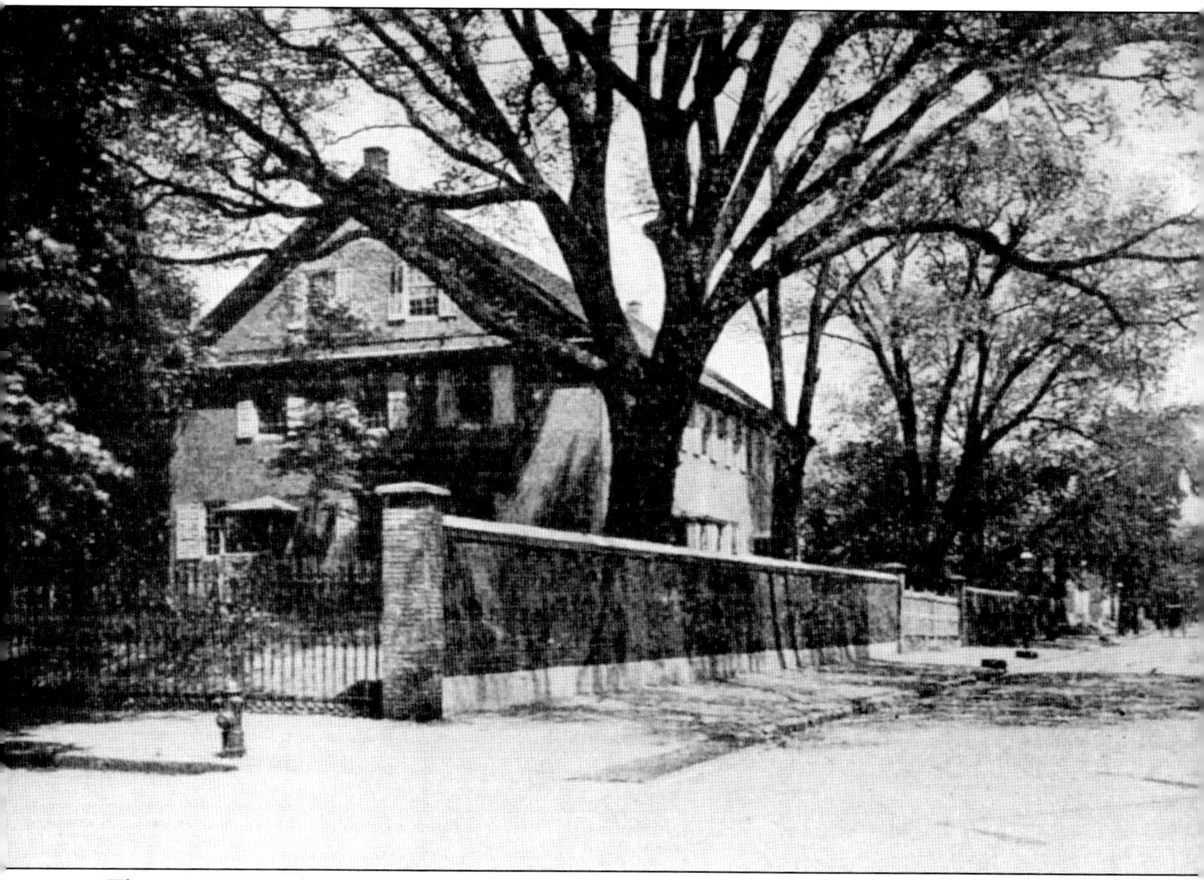

This is a picture of the Wilmington Friends Meetinghouse at Fourth and West Streets in Quaker Hill in Wilmington, Delaware. With its full block of lawn and peaceful history, to many it represents an oasis of calm in the middle of the hectic city. (Courtesy of Wilmington Friends Meeting.)

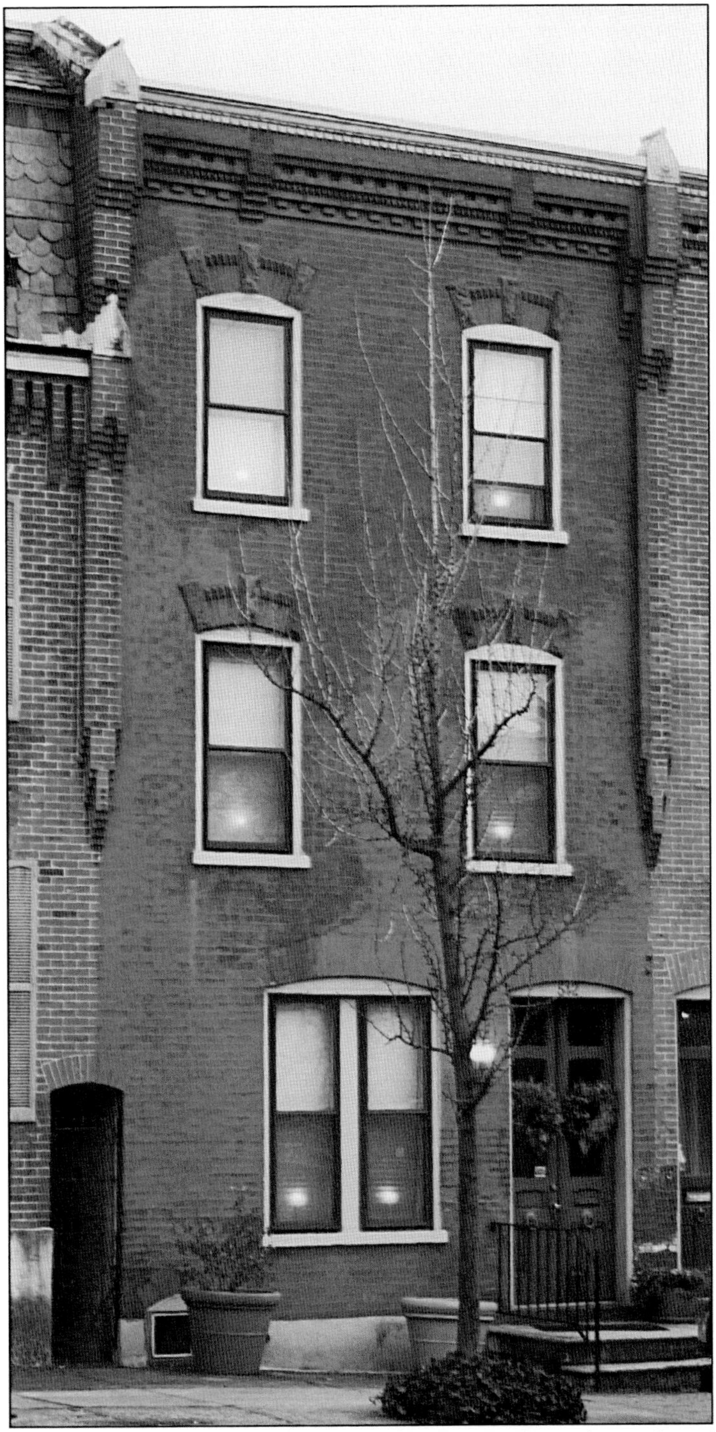

This is a picture of the home at 512 West Fourth Street. Built in the mid- to late 1800s, this house was abandoned until renovated by St. Anthony's parish in the 1980s. (Photograph by James Bierbaum.)

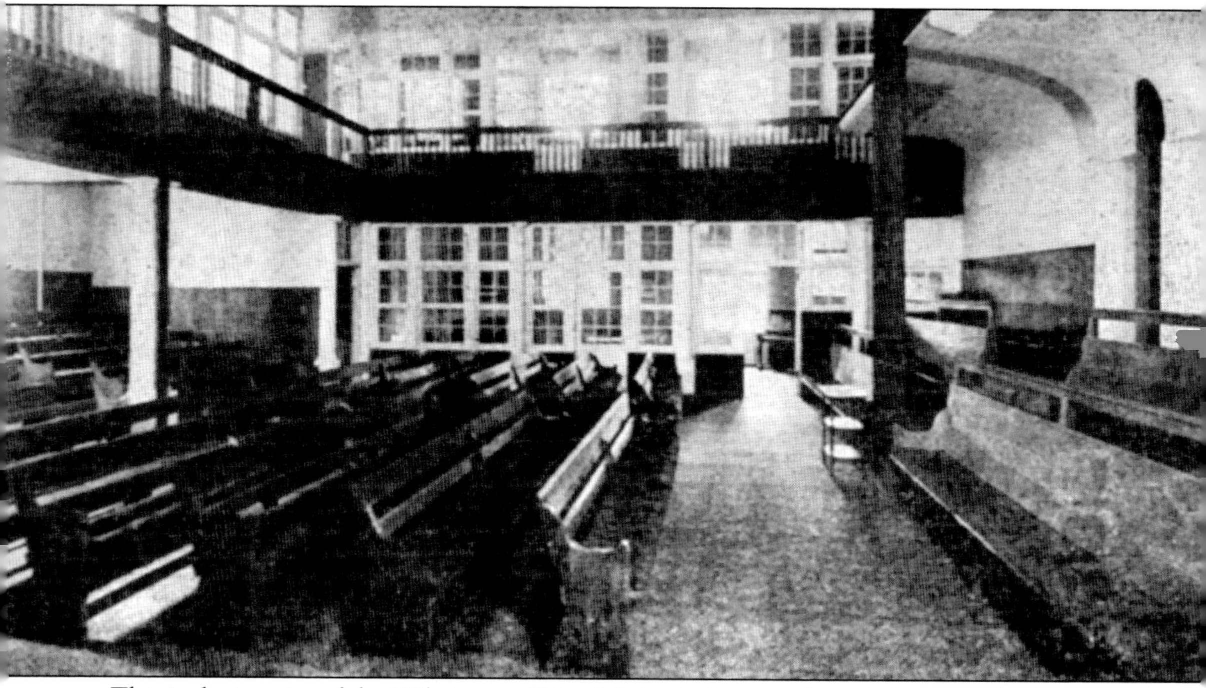

This is the interior of the Wilmington Friends Meetinghouse at Fourth Street and West Street in Wilmington, Delaware. The partition at the far end did not always exist there. (Courtesy of Wilmington Friends Meeting.)

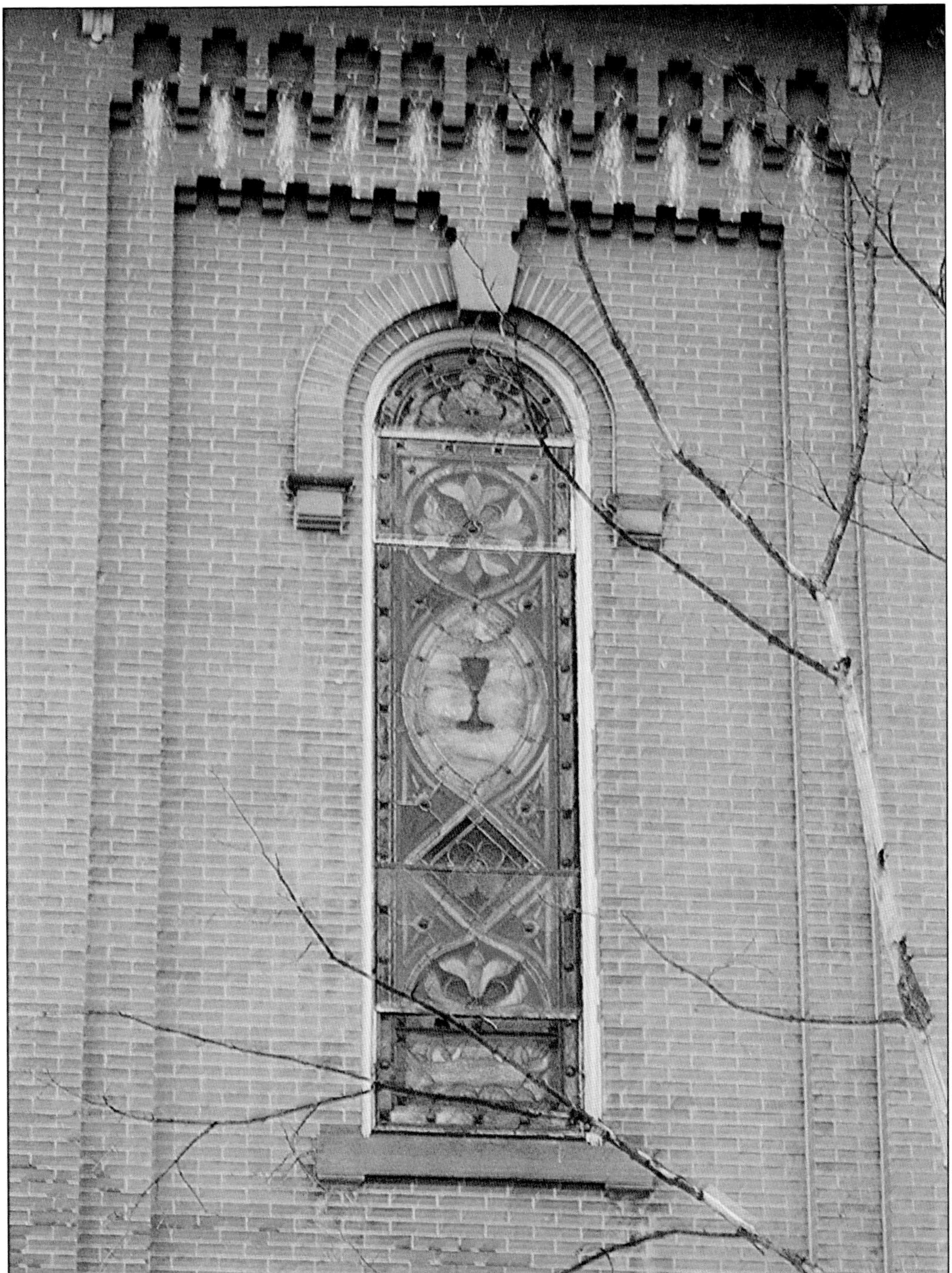

This is another picture of the beautiful stained glass window of the Tabernacle Full Gospel Baptist Church, the former Union United Methodist Church, which was built in 1868. This church was built by several small neighborhood businessmen, including Cyrus Stern. The building now houses the Tabernacle Full Gospel Baptist Church. (Photograph by James Bierbaum.)

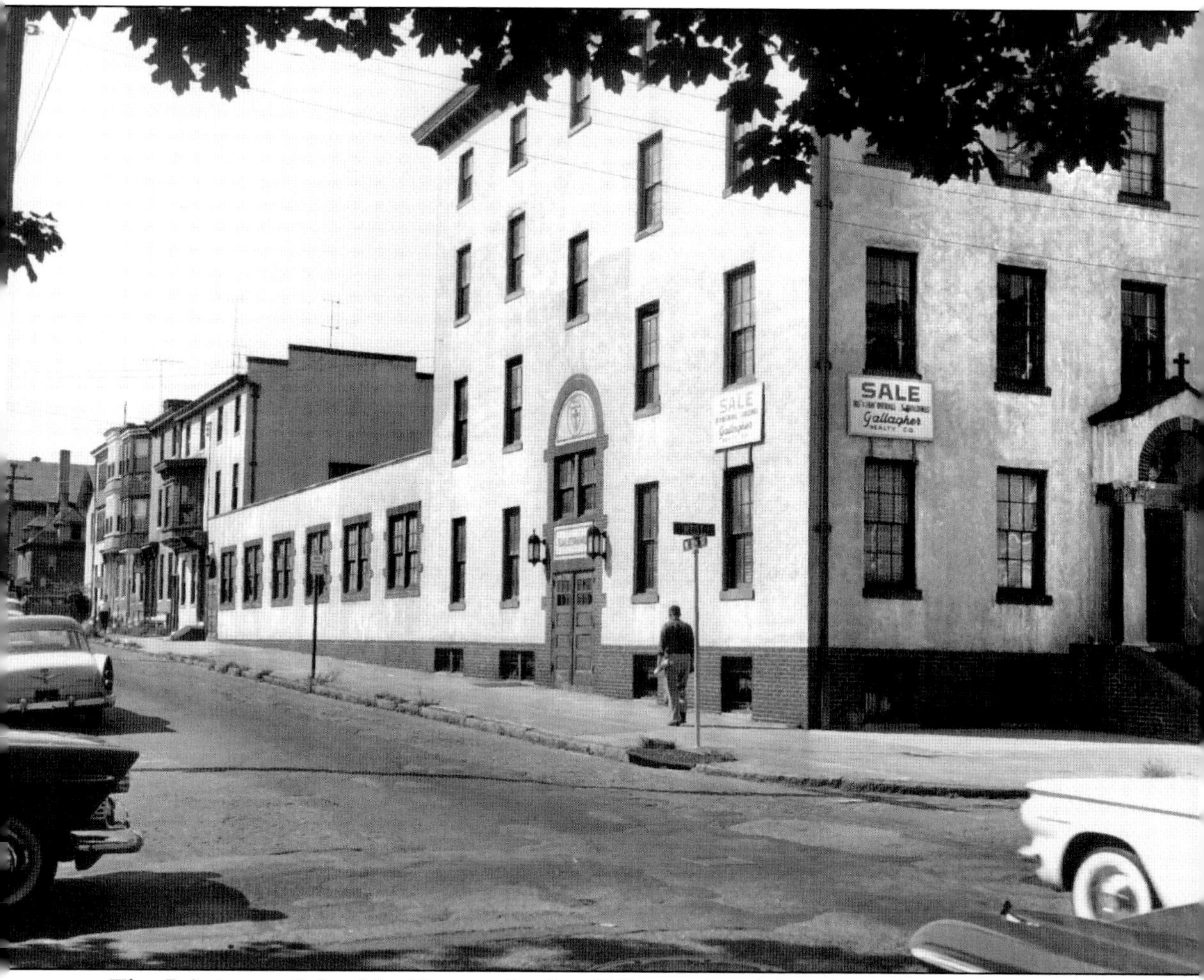

The Salesianum School building in Quaker Hill was placed for sale in the late 1950s and the school relocated to another part of Wilmington, Delaware. Salesianum was a parochial school but was not attached to a parish. (Courtesy of Historical Society of Delaware.)

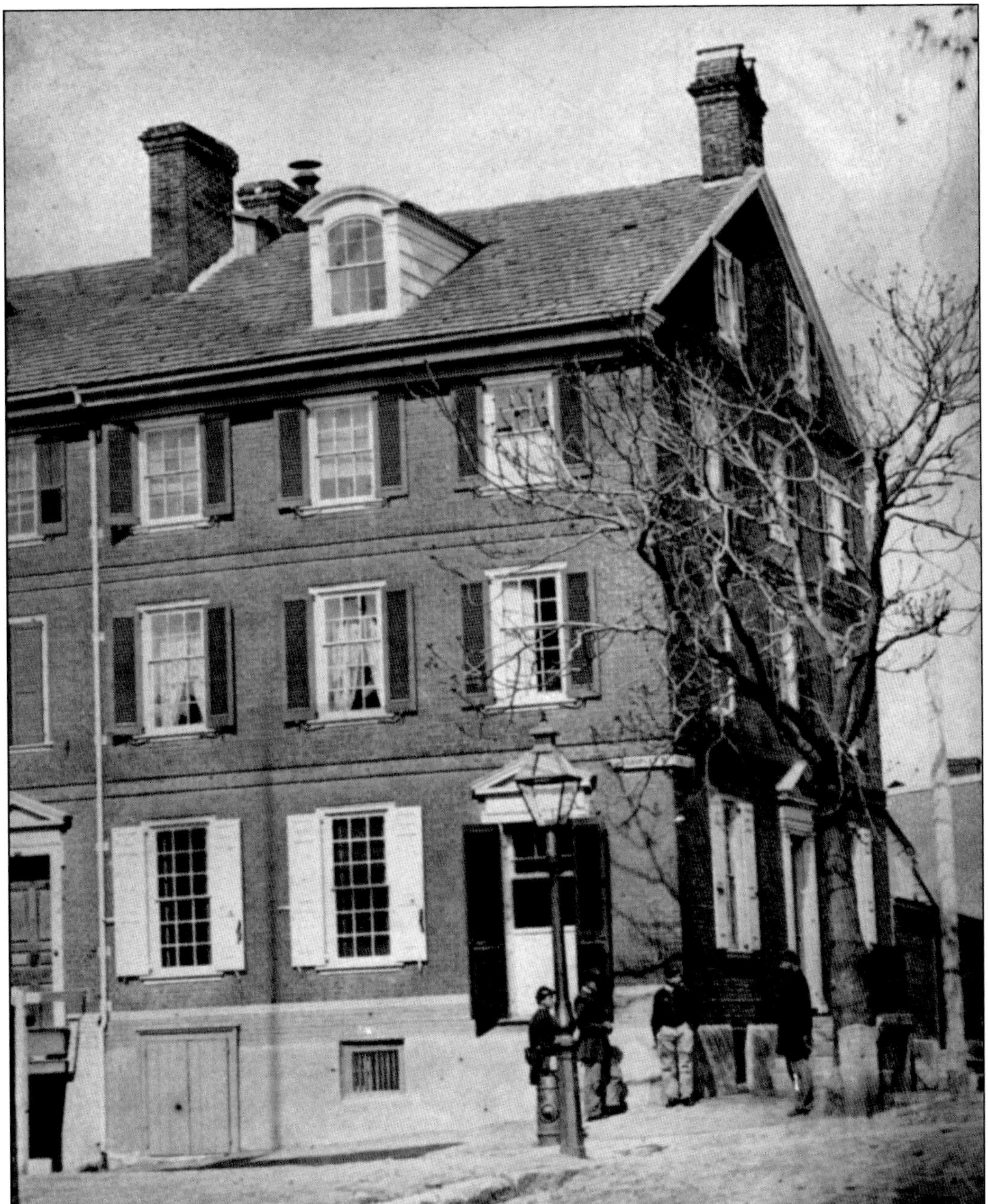

These are Civil War soldiers standing at the corner of Fourth and Shipley Streets in Wilmington, Delaware, in 1860. Delaware was a border state that fought on the Union side in the Civil War, although approximately 2,000 of its more than 20,000 African American residents were enslaved. (Courtesy of Historical Society of Delaware.)

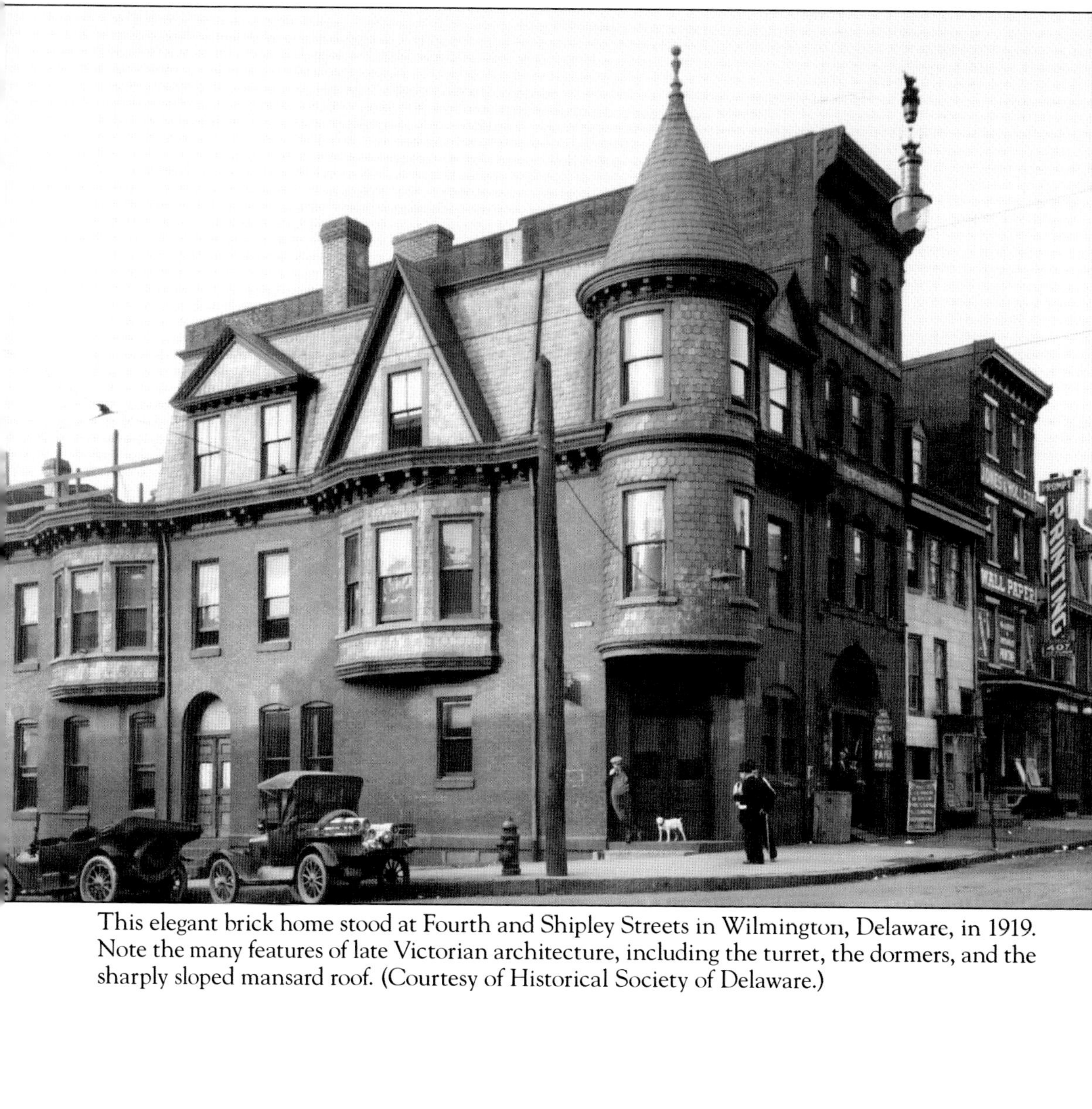

This elegant brick home stood at Fourth and Shipley Streets in Wilmington, Delaware, in 1919. Note the many features of late Victorian architecture, including the turret, the dormers, and the sharply sloped mansard roof. (Courtesy of Historical Society of Delaware.)

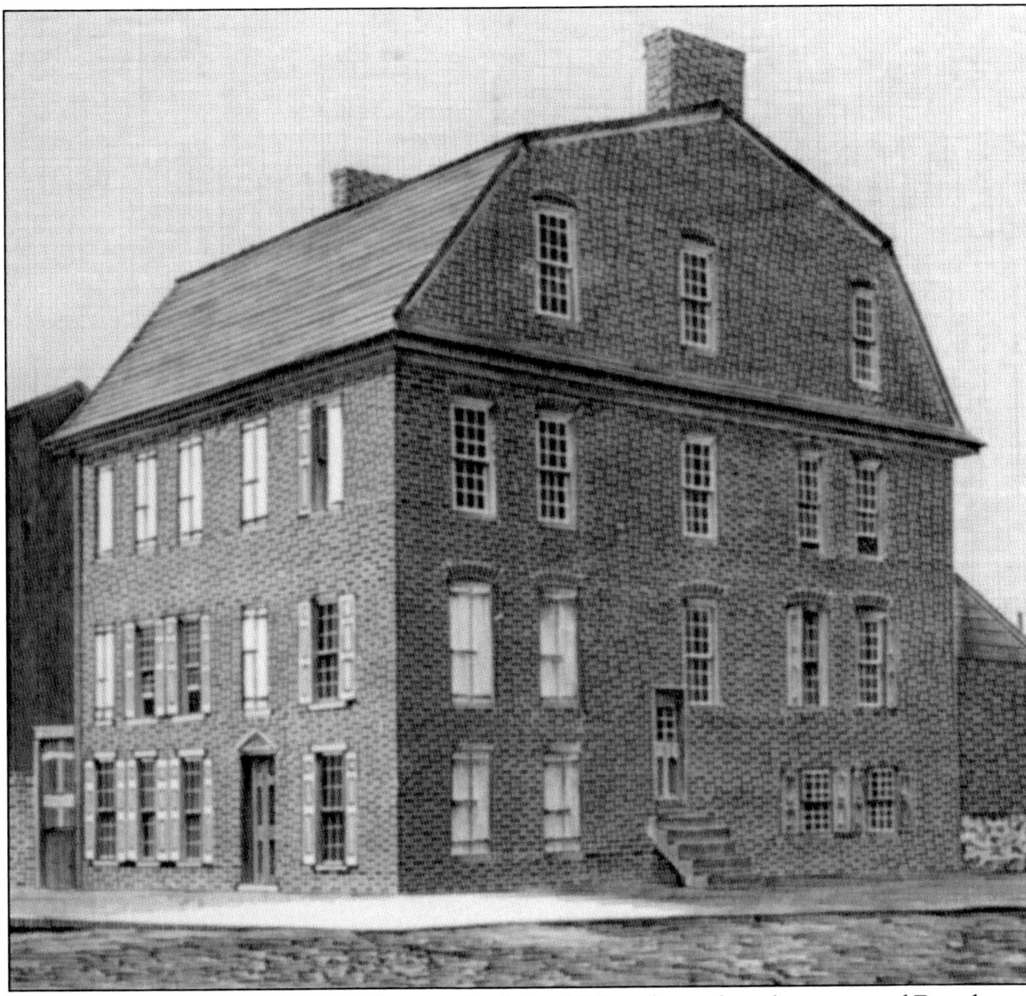

This is an engraving of a house that was built in 1736 and stood at the corner of Fourth and Shipley Streets. It was subsequently taken down in the 1880s. (Courtesy of Historical Society of Delaware.)

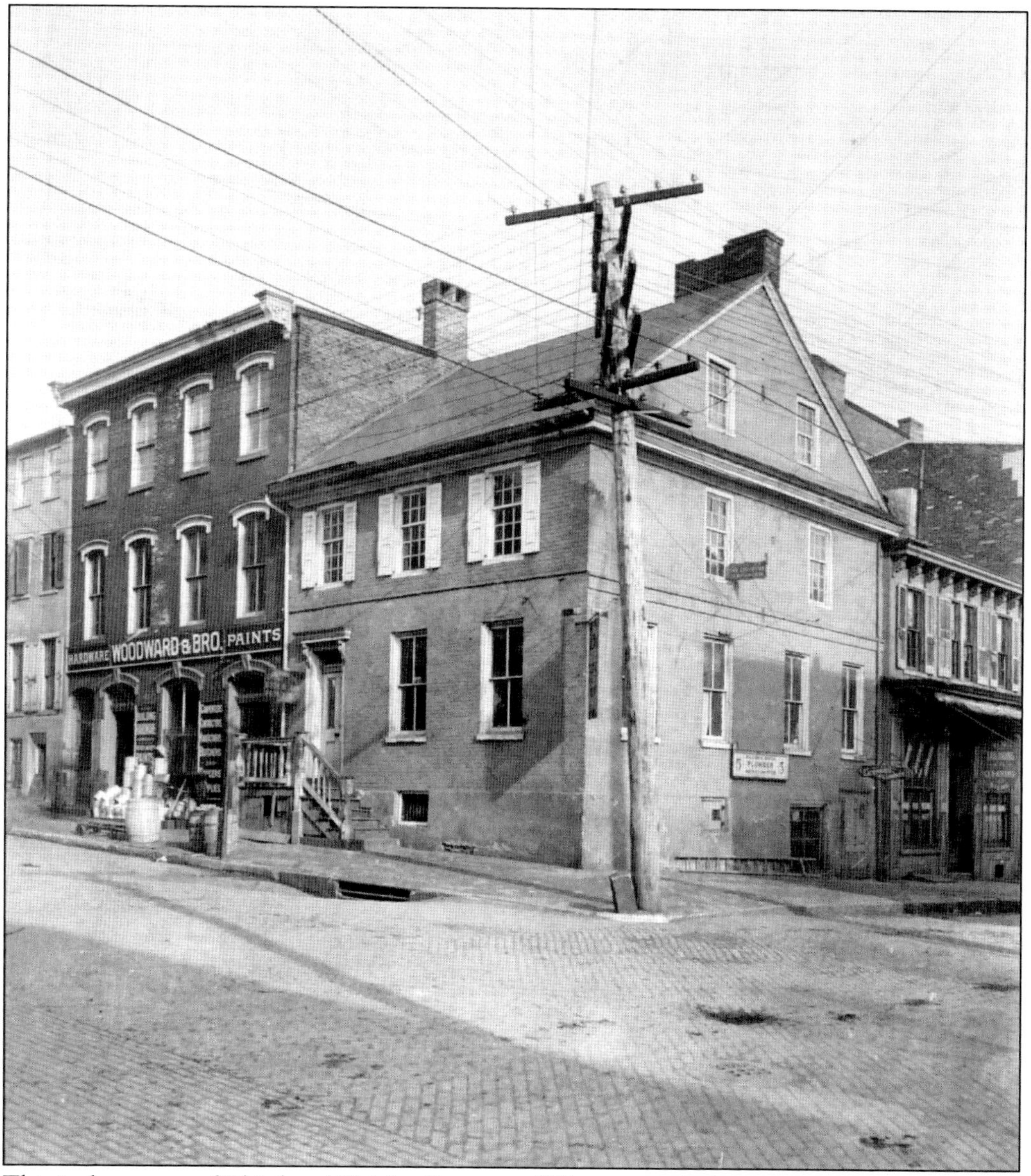

This is the corner of Third and Shipley Streets in Wilmington, Delaware, in 1898. Near here at 227 Shipley Street stood the home of Thomas Garrett, the famous abolitionist who hid fugitive slaves in his home on their way to freedom. (Courtesy of Historical Society of Delaware.)

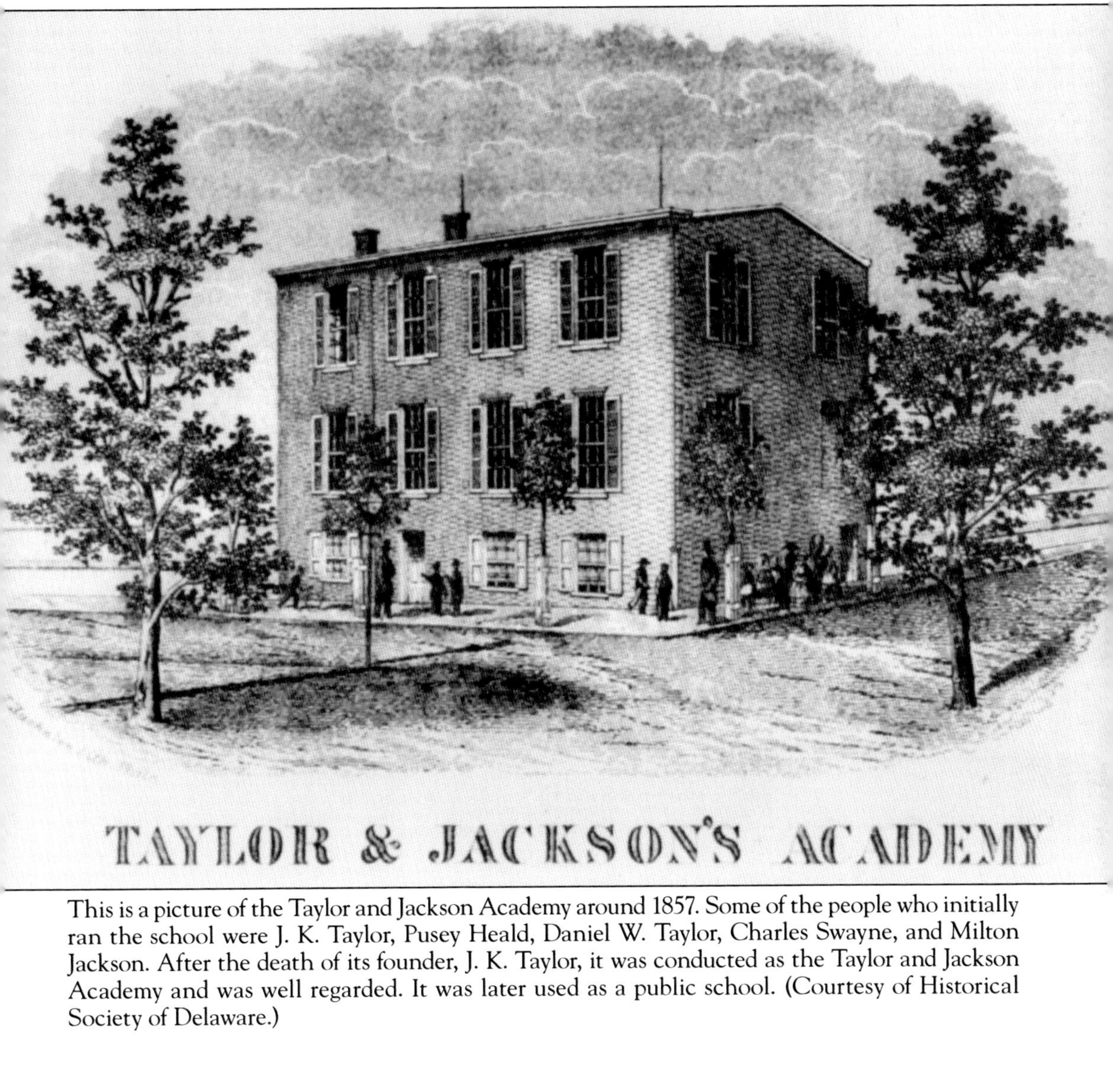

This is a picture of the Taylor and Jackson Academy around 1857. Some of the people who initially ran the school were J. K. Taylor, Pusey Heald, Daniel W. Taylor, Charles Swayne, and Milton Jackson. After the death of its founder, J. K. Taylor, it was conducted as the Taylor and Jackson Academy and was well regarded. It was later used as a public school. (Courtesy of Historical Society of Delaware.)

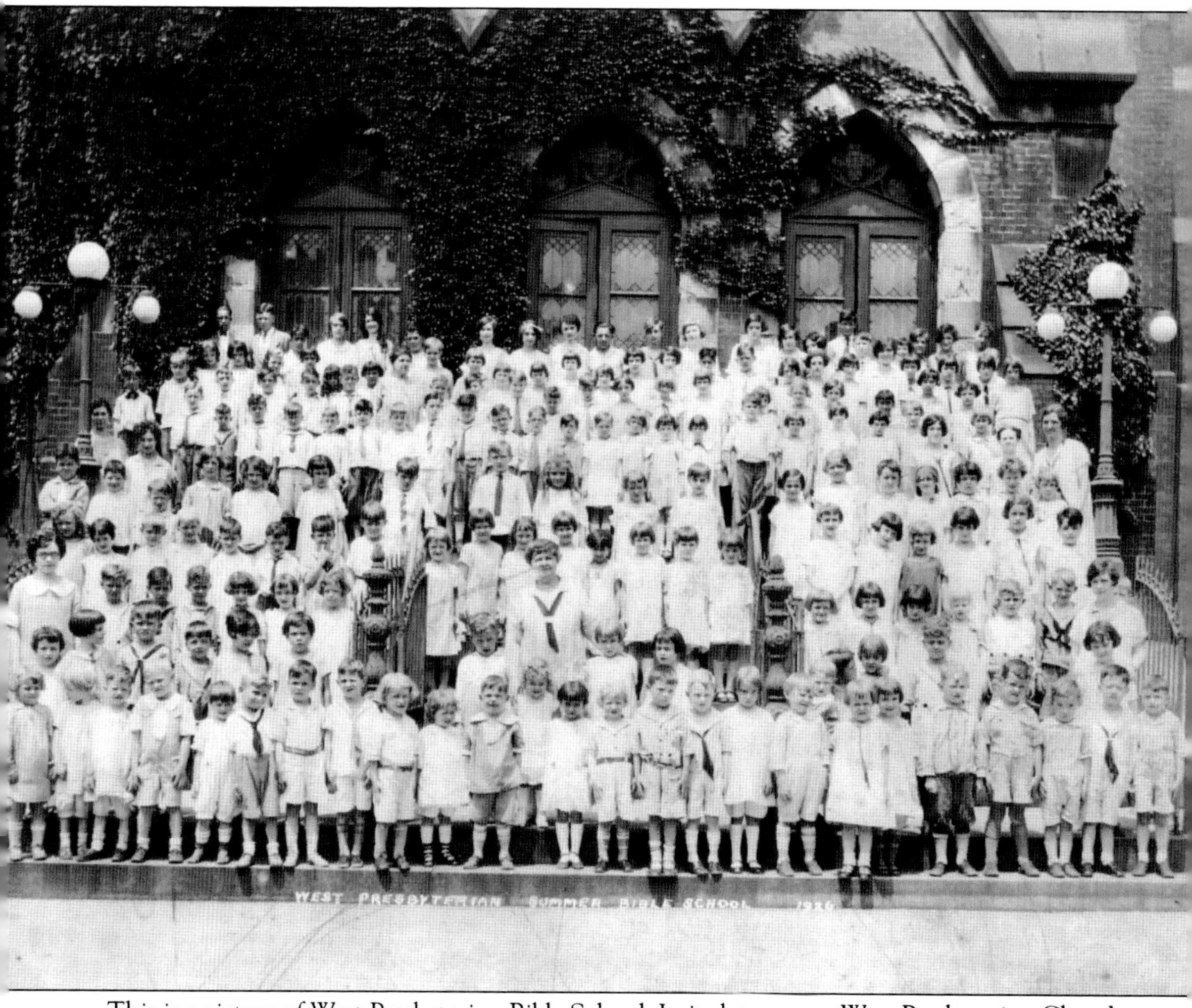

This is a picture of West Presbyterian Bible School. In its later years, West Presbyterian Church was known for social programs, such as its distribution of free breakfasts to the hungry and for artistic programs such as the Gathering Place. The building is now used as a center to treat mentally ill clients. (Courtesy of Historical Society of Delaware.)

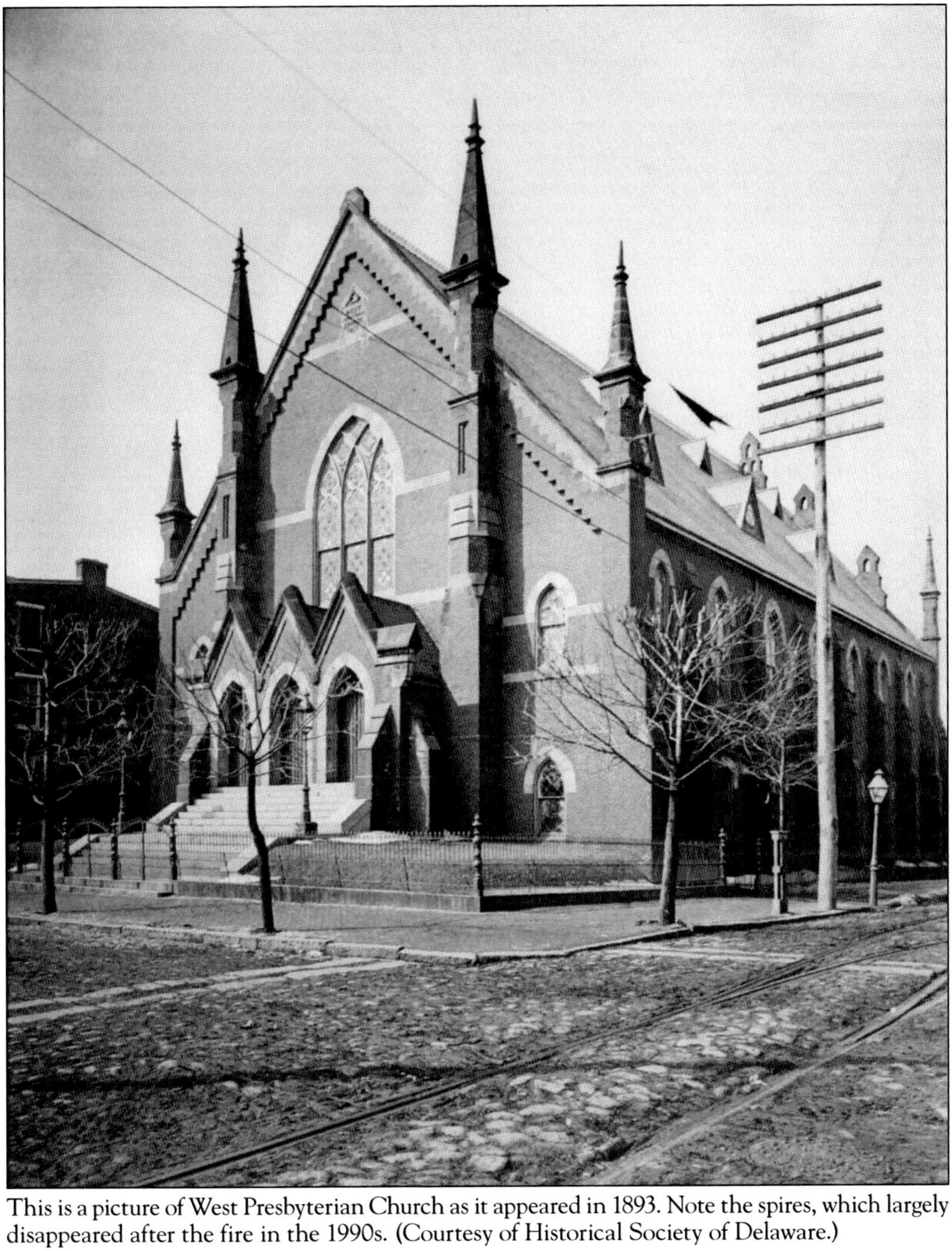

This is a picture of West Presbyterian Church as it appeared in 1893. Note the spires, which largely disappeared after the fire in the 1990s. (Courtesy of Historical Society of Delaware.)

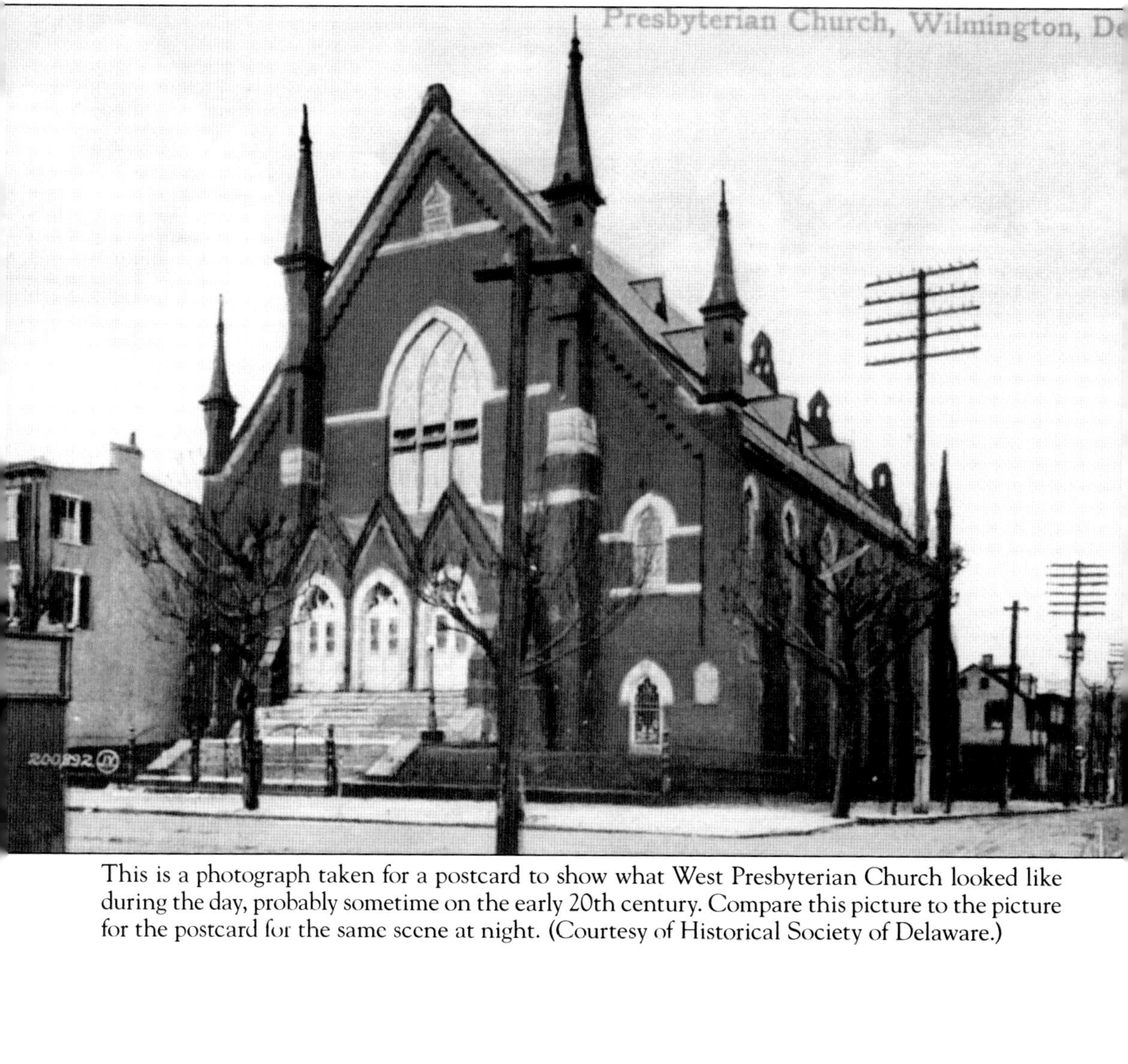

This is a photograph taken for a postcard to show what West Presbyterian Church looked like during the day, probably sometime on the early 20th century. Compare this picture to the picture for the postcard for the same scene at night. (Courtesy of Historical Society of Delaware.)

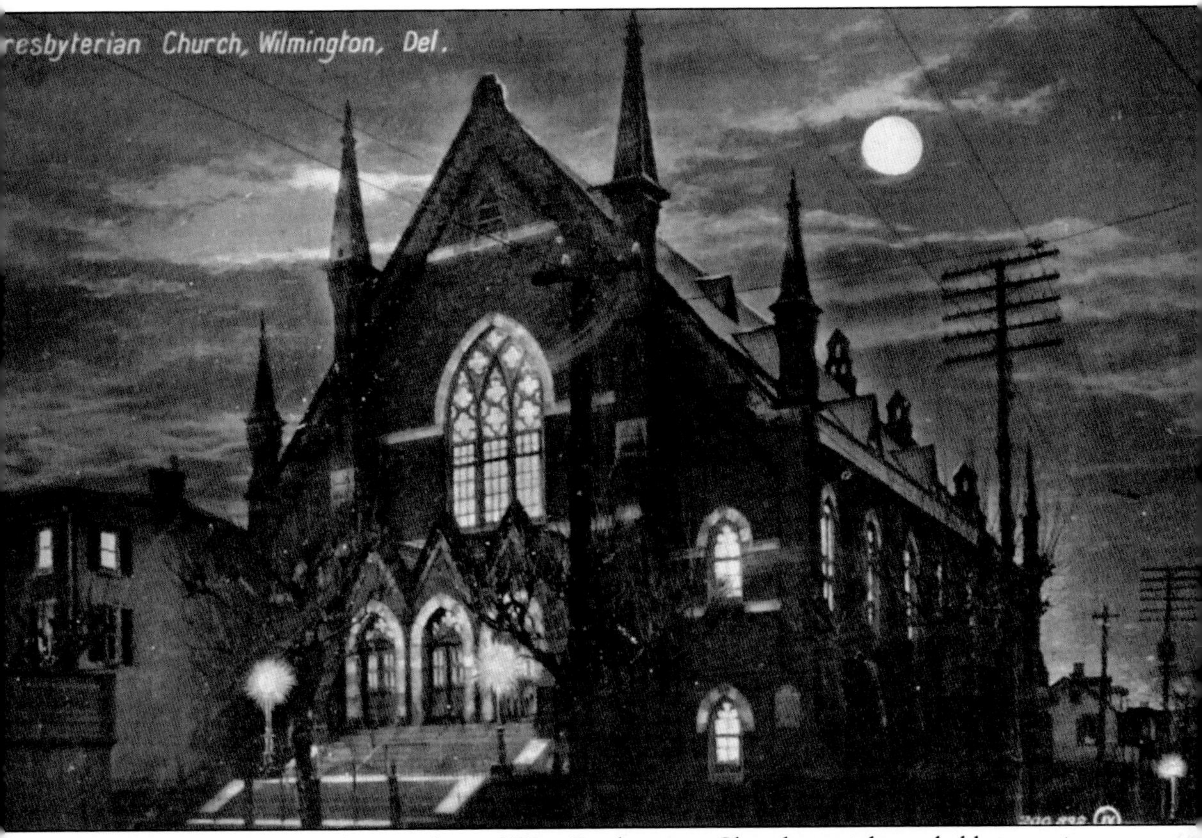

This postcard photograph was taken of West Presbyterian Church at night probably sometime in the early 20th century. Look at how eerie the Gothic lines of the church appear with light flooding from within and the dark clouds moving along without. (Courtesy of Historical Society of Delaware.)

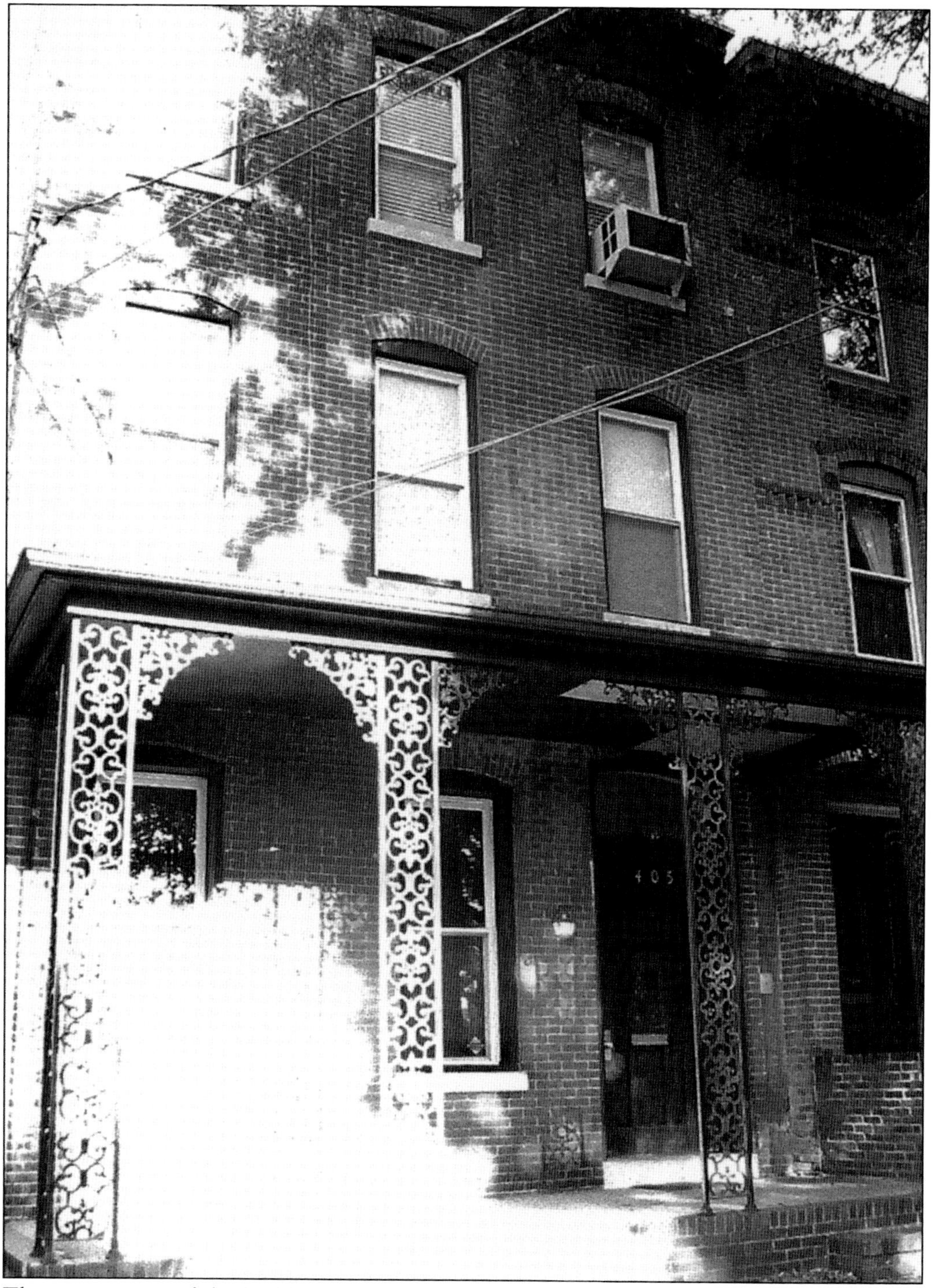

This is a picture of the building at 405 Washington Street. The homes along Washington Street were built around 1865. They were built in the neo-Gothic and Italianate style and they still retain their original ornate wrought iron porch supports, as this one does. (Photograph by Nicole Bright.)

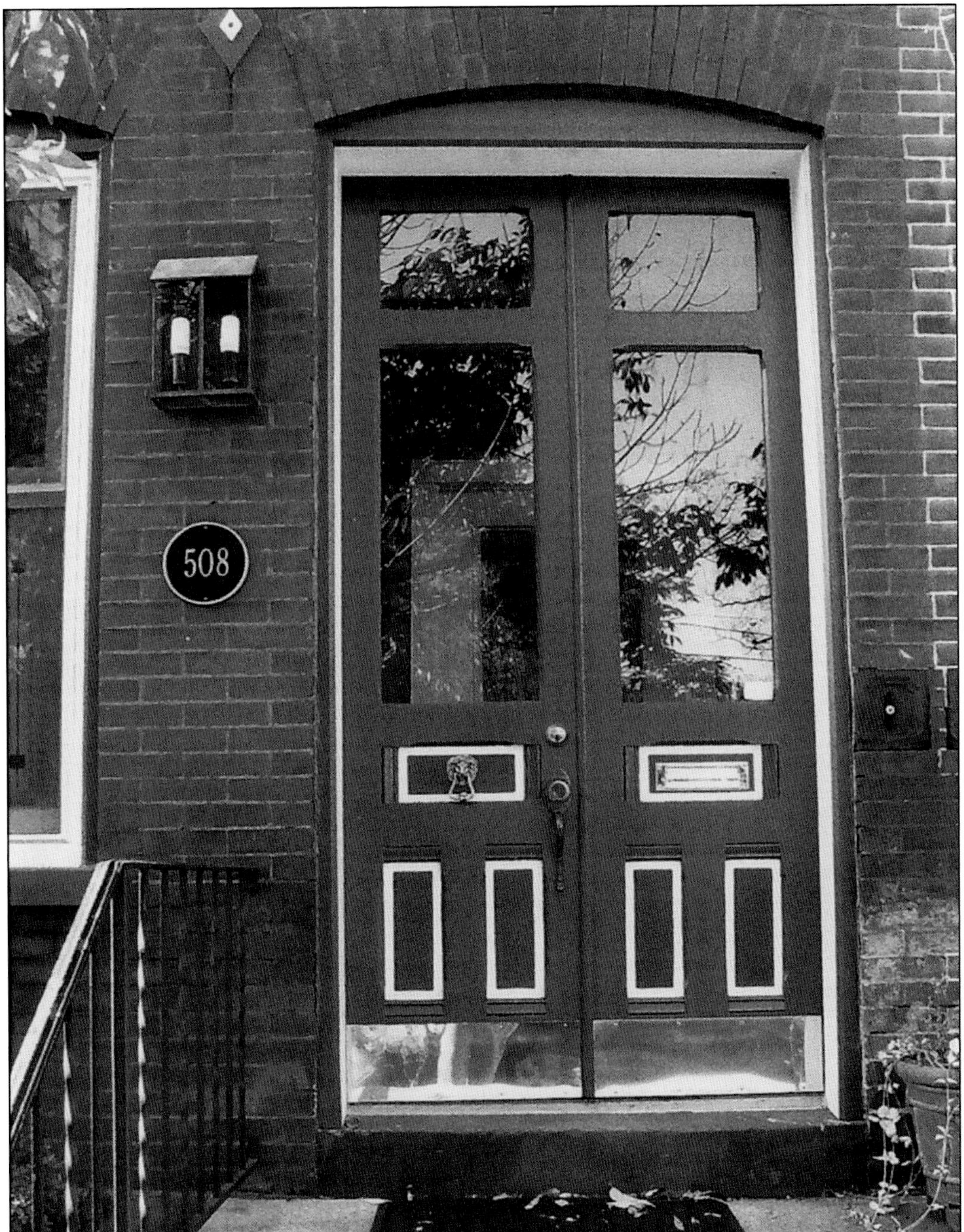

This is a picture of the home at 508 West Fourth Street. A deck off the third floor, which was added during a renovation, offers a panoramic view of the newly developed Wilmington Riverfront. (Photograph by Nicole Bright.)

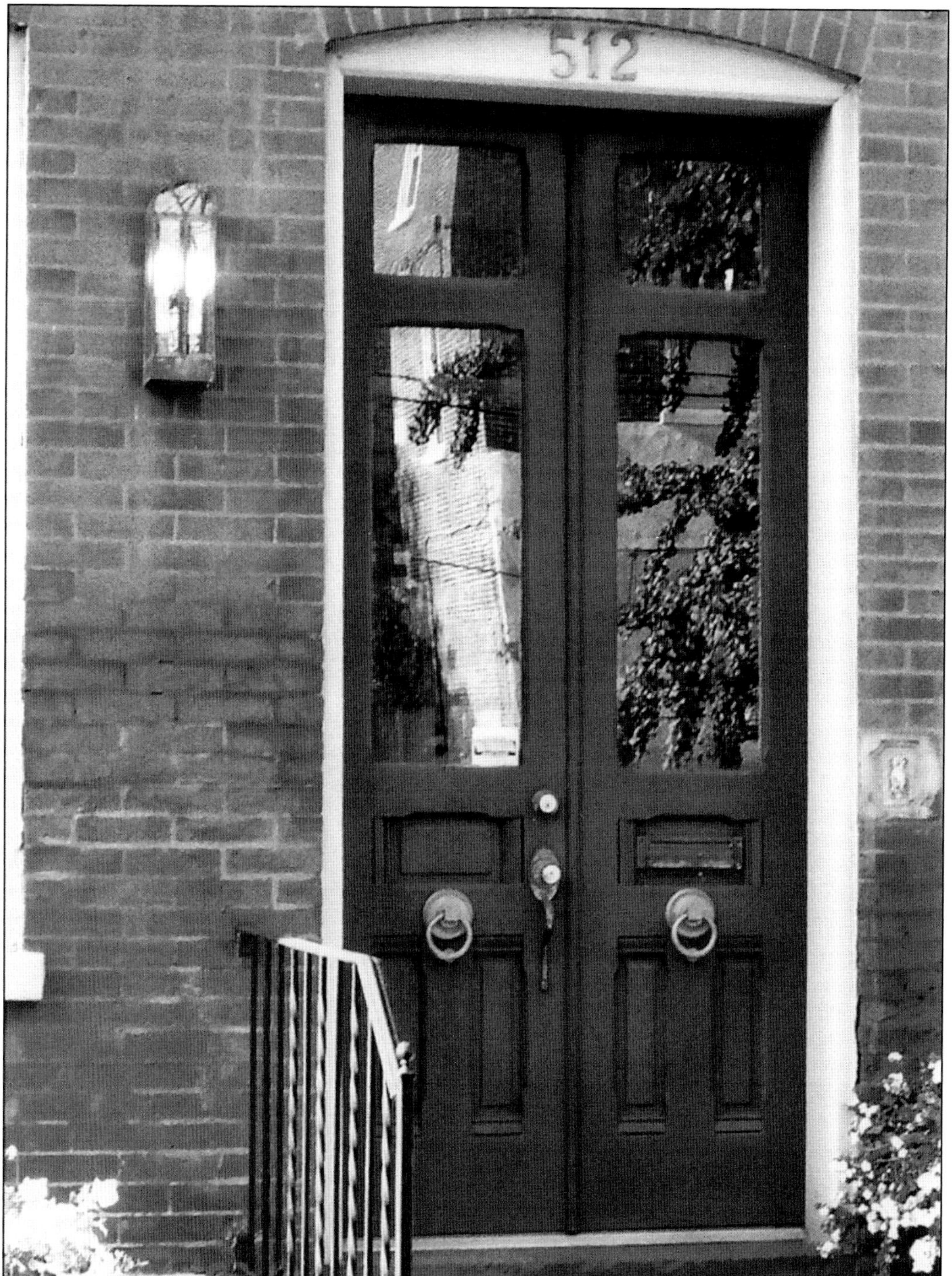

The home at 512 West Fourth Street has undergone some minor renovations and some major decorative changes, including the European-style kitchen with rosewood cabinets and Italian marble floor. (Photograph by Nicole Bright.)

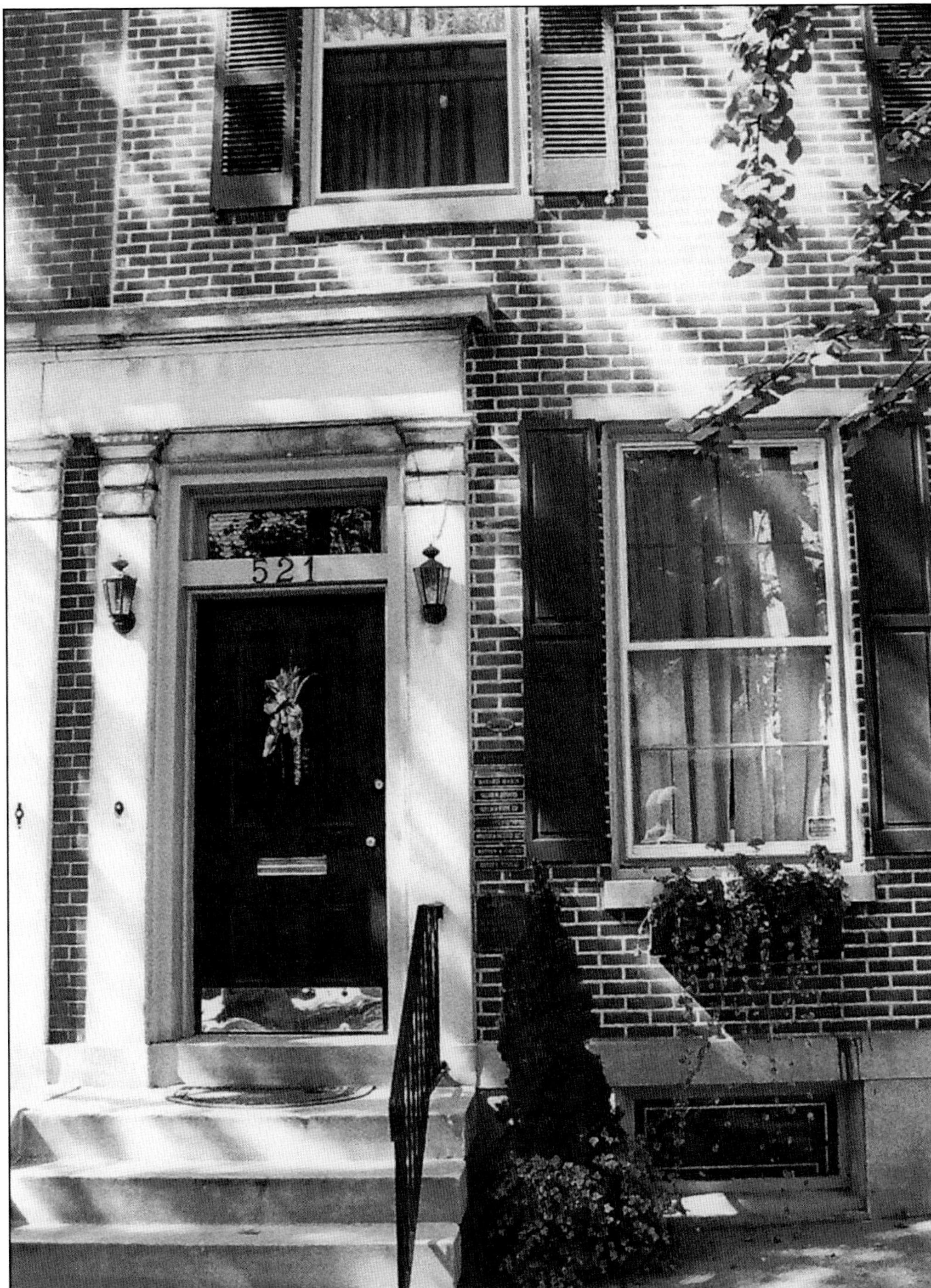

This is a picture of the Law Offices of Bayard Marin and the Quaker Hill Historic Preservation Foundation at 521 West Street, located in a building originally built by Elizabeth Grubb of Philadelphia. Its unusual features include a radial brick wall on the Sixth Street side and a second-floor verandah. (Photograph by Nicole Bright.)